D0970277

A Guide to Open Innovation and Crowdsourcing

FIRST EDITION

A Guide to Open Innovation and Crowdsourcing

Expert tips and advice

PAUL SLOANE

KoganPage

LONDON PHILADELPHIA NEW DELHI

HF 5415.153 .G87 2011

A guide to open innovation
and crowdsourcing
$26.00

Publisher's note

Every possible effort has been made to ensure that the information contained in this book is accurate at the time of going to press, and the publishers and authors cannot accept responsibility for any errors or omissions, however caused. No responsibility for loss or damage occasioned to any person acting, or refraining from action, as a result of the material in this publication can be accepted by the editor, the publisher or any of the authors.

First published in Great Britain and the United States in 2011 by Kogan Page Limited

Apart from any fair dealing for the purposes of research or private study, or criticism or review, as permitted under the Copyright, Designs and Patents Act 1988, this publication may only be reproduced, stored or transmitted, in any form or by any means, with the prior permission in writing of the publishers, or in the case of reprographic reproduction in accordance with the terms and licences issued by the CLA. Enquiries concerning reproduction outside these terms should be sent to the publishers at the undermentioned addresses:

120 Pentonville Road	1518 Walnut Street, Suite 1100	4737/23 Ansari Road
London N1 9JN	Philadelphia PA 19102	Daryaganj
United Kingdom	USA	New Delhi 110002
www.koganpage.com		India

© Paul Sloane, 2011

The right of Paul Sloane to be identified as the author of this work has been asserted by him in accordance with the Copyright, Designs and Patents Act 1988.

ISBN   978 0 7494 6307 6
E-ISBN   978 0 7494 6314 4

British Library Cataloguing-in-Publication Data

A CIP record for this book is available from the British Library.

Library of Congress Cataloging-in-Publication Data

A guide to open innovation and crowdsourcing : practical tips advice and examples from leading experts in the field / [edited by] Paul Sloane.
        p. cm.
    Includes bibliographical references and index.
    ISBN 978-0-7494-6307-6 -- ISBN 978-0-7494-6314-4   1.   New products. 2.   Diffusion of innovations. 3. Social media–Economic aspects. 4. Internet. 5. Strategic planning. 6. Organizational change. I. Sloane, Paul, 1950-
    HF5415.153.G87 2011
    658.5'038–dc22
                                                    2010048048

Typeset by Saxon Graphics Ltd, Derby
Production managed by Jellyfish
Printed and bound in Great Britain by CPI Antony Rowe

Contents

List of contributors

Henry Chesbrough is 'the father of Open Innovation', according to Wikipedia. He is the author of the award-winning book, *Open Innovation* (Harvard Business School Press, 2003), *Open Business Models* (Harvard Business School Press, 2006) and his newest book, *Open Services Innovation* (Jossey-Bass, 2011). He is the founder and executive director of the Center for Open Innovation at the Haas School of Business at UC Berkeley in California.

Paul Sloane was part of the team which launched the IBM PC in the United Kingdom. He was Marketing Director and Managing Director of database company Ashton-Tate. He was VP International for MathSoft and CEO of Monactive. He writes, speaks and facilitates workshops on innovation and lateral thinking. He is the author of 20 books including *The Innovative Leader* (Kogan Page, 2007).

Julian Keith Loren is an award-winning designer and innovator who tackles large-scale, multi-faceted design challenges. He founded the Innovation Management Institute in 2008. He promotes effective design strategy and innovation management practices as a speaker, author, trainer, and event organizer.

Renee Hopkins is founding editor of *Texas Enterprise*, an online publication highlighting business knowledge and research from the University of Texas at Austin. She is co-leader of the successful Twitter-based innovation community Innochat. Renee was a consultant in the Insights and Innovation practice at Decision Analyst, leading crowdsourced projects generating ideas for packaged goods and technology companies.

Jeffrey Phillips is VP Marketing and a lead consultant for OVO Innovation. Jeffrey has led innovation projects for Fortune 5000 firms, academic institutions and not-for-profits based on OVO Innovation's Innovate on Purpose™ methodology. The Innovate on Purpose methodology encourages organizations to consider innovation as a sustainable, repeatable business process, rather than a discrete project.

Braden Kelley is the author of *Stoking Your Innovation Bonfire* and works with clients to create innovative strategies, effective customer marketing, organizational change, and improved organizational performance. Braden served in the US Navy and traveled all around the Western Pacific. He is passionate about innovation and runs the multiple author innovation blog – BloggingInnovation.com.

David Simoes-Brown and Roland Harwood co-founded the consultancy 100%Open. David previously led the Corporate Open Innovation programme at NESTA in the United Kingdom. He has a background of helping clients to innovate and has worked with John Lewis, Peroni, Nestlé, Energizer and Epson.

Roland Harwood is co-founder and Networks Partner at 100%Open. Previously he was Director of Open Innovation at NESTA. Graduating with a PhD in Physics from Edinburgh University, he has held senior innovation roles in the Utilities and Media industries.

Steven Goers is Vice President of Open Innovation & Investment Strategy for Kraft Foods. In this role, Steve leads Open Innovation initiatives for Kraft focused on levering external innovation as an enabler to accelerate growth. He is also responsible for Knowledge Management, Intellectual Property and External Investment strategies.

Andrew Gaule is the founder of Corven's H-I Network, the leading corporate executive forum for innovation, operational excellence and corporate venturing. He is the author of *Open Innovation in Action: How to be strategic in the search for new sources of value* (from which this chapter is taken). His clients include BAE Systems, Boots, Eon, GSK and Unilever.

Matthew Heim, PhD is President of NineSigma, the world's largest open innovation firm. Matthew has over 25 years of international management and consulting experience in the areas of strategic planning, innovation, corporate turnarounds and large-scale systems change. Matthew served on the faculty of several major universities, and has written and co-authored several books, including his latest, *Breaking the Musashi Code: Transcending competition through visionary strategy*.

Hutch Carpenter is VP of Product for Spigit, a company which provides an enterprise platform for innovation management. He has worked in enterprise software, and in the lines of business for several Fortune 500 firms. He has an MBA from the University of Virginia Darden School. He writes regularly about Enterprise 2.0 and innovation.

Christopher J Rye is Senior Advisor and Project Manager, LG Electronics Collaborate & Innovate Team. He joined LG Electronics in 2007, and has been a core member of the LG Electronics' Collaborate & Innovate initiative from its inception.

Andrea Meyer studies innovative people and companies. She has written or contributed to 32 books, 450 case studies and company profiles, 73 conference reports and nine serial publications. She also develops executive education materials for MIT, Harvard, the Young President's Organization (YPO) and blogs at www.WorkingKnowledge.com/blog.

Dana Meyer, an R&D engineer, co-inventor of two patents and co-author on nine winning Small Business Innovative Research (SBIR) proposals, has performed systems design, engineering systems analysis, and developed software for data analysis for a variety of companies including Data Fusion Corporation, Vexcel Imaging and General Dynamics.

Gail Martino, PhD is Manager of Open Innovation for Hair and Skin Categories globally at Unilever. Prior to joining Unilever, she worked in R&D at The Gillette Company. Prior to her corporate career, she held academic positions at Colgate University and at the John B. Pierce Laboratory at Yale University School of Medicine.

John Bartolone, PhD is Director of Open Innovation at Unilever and is responsible for Skin and Hair Categories globally. During his tenure at Unilever he has published more than 20 patents and 25 peer reviewed papers. He holds a Master and Doctorate degree in Biophysics and Biochemistry from the University of Connecticut where he was also an Assistant Professor in residence

Frank Piller co-directs the Smart Customization Group at M.I.T. and is a Professor of Innovation Management at RWTH Aachen University, Germany.

Jan Bosch is VP at Intuit, USA, and full professor in software engineering at Groningen University, NL. He is responsible for open innovation initiatives at Intuit.

Petra M Bosch-Sijtsema is a senior researcher at Aalto University Finland. Her research is on inter-organizational innovation and global distributed work.

Klaus-Peter Speidel holds an MPhil from Sorbonne University. He gives talks and publishes on Crowdsourcing and Open Innovation. In 2008, Klaus-Peter co-founded Hypios, which now has a community of over 150,000 problem-solvers online. Hypios develops semantic web tools, strategies and customized community platforms that help identify solvers for open problem-solving. For more information see http://products.hypios.com.

Cathryn Hrudicka is CEO and Chief Imagination Officer at Creative Sage. She is an innovation program designer, consultant and trainer, and an executive/transitions coach.

Gwen Ishmael is Senior Vice President Insights & Innovation at Decision Analyst, Inc. She has led innovation activities for more than 20 years, and is responsible for helping companies around the world develop new offerings, create strategic platforms, and infuse the ideas of those outside the company into their organizations.

Boris Pluskowski was Head of Professional Services and Implementation at Imaginatik, the leading 'collaborative problem solving' software company. He now works with many of the world's largest companies to set and execute robust Innovation strategies.

Todd Boone is Director of Market Development at Psion Teklogix. His role is focused on both the development of – and ongoing execution of – Psion Teklogix' Open Source Mobility (OSM) business strategy that is inspired by the principles of Open Innovation. Prior to his current role, Todd served as Director of Corporate Communications and as a Country Manager in Asia based out of Singapore.

Denys Resnick is Director of Strategic Programs at NineSigma, the world's largest open innovation firm. She has over 25 years of experience leading strategic initiatives and new business development with global companies in the manufacturing, technology and service sectors.

Stefan Lindegaard is a speaker, network facilitator and strategic advisor who focuses on the topics of open innovation, intrapreneurship and how to identify and develop the people who drive innovation. He is the author of the Open Innovation Revolution and his blog is a leading forum on open innovation – http://www.15inno.com.

Pekka Pohjakallio is Vice President of Concepting and Innovation in Nokia's Mobile Solutions unit, responsible for creating the next wave of new products and service concepts for Nokia. With an MSc in Electrical Engineering and Industrial Management from the Helsinki University of Technology, he holds three international patents in the area of GSM packet radio.

Pia Erkinheimo is head of Crowdsourcing, Concepting & Innovation in Nokia's Mobile Solutions unit. Her career at Nokia has included roles in corporate strategy, Nokia Research Center and HR development.

Kevin McFarthing was Global Director of Strategic Alliances at Reckitt Benckiser and Global Director of R&D for Health and Personal Care. He led the development of Reckitt Benckiser's Open Innovation portal, RB-Idealink. He now runs a consultancy, Innovation Fixer.

Albert Meige is the founder and President of PRESANS, an Open Innovation intermediary, connecting business needs to scientific expertise. He has managed and carried out research in physics, computer science and innovation management in various institutions such as the Ecole Polytechnique for seven years.

Boris Golden holds a MSc in Theoretical Computer Science from the Ecole Normale Supérieure and an MSc in Management from the Ecole Polytechnique. He is currently finishing his PhD in Systems Architecture, working on new methods to design and manage innovative industrial systems and complex organizations.

Clinton Bonner is an innovation consultant, crowdsourcing specialist and digital futurist. You can connect with Clinton and enjoy his brand of informational storytelling on his site http://everything2everything.com.

Stephen M Shapiro is the former leader of Accenture's 20,000-person 'process excellence' practice, and he speaks on innovation around the world. He is an adviser to many Fortune 500 companies including Staples, GE, BP, Johnson & Johnson, and Fidelity Investments. He is also InnoCentive Inc's Chief Innovation Evangelist.

Foreword

Henry Chesbrough

Innovation has come a long way in a short period of time. Just 30 years ago, thinkers like Michael Porter of Harvard were telling innovators to invest heavily in R&D to use as a barrier against their competitors. The idea was that this investment would differentiate the company in the market, and that only those companies that made similar levels of investment could keep up. This R&D activity was organized inside the company, and shared with no one until the products that resulted from innovation went to the market.

The leading companies of the day were distinguished in part by the level of their internal R&D spending. Computer makers like IBM poured their dollars into new computer hardware and software. AT&T built its Bell Laboratories research system, perhaps the most accomplished industrial lab of its day. Auto makers like Ford, GM and Chrysler spent billions each year in rolling out new cars and trucks. Pharmaceutical giants like Merck created powerful research arms that reached back into the basic sciences of chemistry, and filled their product pipelines with compounds they discovered and developed inside their own four walls.

Today things are very different in most industries, not only in the United States but around the world. The model of industrial innovation has moved on from this inwardly focused, vertically integrated approach that I call a 'closed innovation system'. Open Innovation today prevails, as organizations make extensive use (and re-use) of external ideas and technologies in their own innovation activities, while unused or under-used ideas and technologies internally are allowed to go to the outside for others to utilize. The result is a much deeper division of innovation labour, where specialist firms contribute discoveries and innovations that connect together to form a web of innovation. Start-ups and small to medium-sized enterprises and even individuals play a far more significant role, while the large firms seek to attract and collaborate with these small, agile, skilled participants.

Data from the National Science Foundation on R&D spending in the United States over the past 30 years bears out the extent of this shift (see Figure 0.1). This chart shows that large firms with more than 25,000 employees were responsible for 70 per cent of the industrial R&D spending done in the United States in 1981. But their share of R&D spending shrunk in half to 35 per cent in 2007. In contrast, small firms with less than 1,000 employees increased their share of R&D spending from 4 to 24 per cent during that period. Note that large firms are still important in industrial R&D because their share is still very big (35 per cent). The amount of R&D spending in large firms increased from US$21.2 billion in 1981 to US$94.8 billion in 2007, a factor of 4.

FIGURE 0.1 R&D spending by size of organization

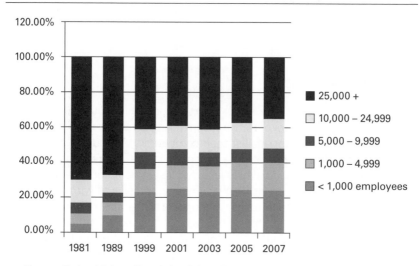

Sources: National Science Foundation, Science Resource Studies, Survey of Industrial Research Development 1999, 2001, 2003, 2006, 2008.

However, the increase in R&D expenditure of small firms is even more impressive. Firms with fewer than 1,000 employees spent US$64.7 billion on R&D in 2007 compared to US$1.3 billion in 1981 – 50 times as much! Another way to look at this is smaller-firm R&D spending overall has grown 10 times as fast as large-company spending over these 26 years. Clearly, the world of innovation has changed.

You can see this new, deeper division of innovation labour in practice, as well as in the statistics. IBM now makes more money from its services business (where it supports the hardware and software of many other companies, including its competitors) than it does from its traditional businesses. Cell phone manufacturers strive to attract applications developers to their platforms to boost the range and quality of services that customers can install on their phones. The pharmaceutical industry now licenses in most of its compounds in its product pipeline from external sources like universities and young biotech firms, rather than carrying projects from the laboratory bench all the way through to the market. The auto makers now rely primarily upon their suppliers and their suppliers' suppliers for new innovations.

Within this overall shift towards more Open Innovation, crowdsourcing is also growing in importance. The fundamental insight underlying crowdsourcing, which is shared by Open Innovation, is that useful knowledge is widely distributed around the world. No one has a monopoly on that knowledge. Once you accept that, you must face the question of how best to access the wealth of knowledge around the globe.

Crowdsourcing is an answer to that question. Done right, it taps into the knowledge, the creativity, the insight and skill of the world around you. It can help you predict next month's sales, or next season's fashions. It can improve the management of your supply chain. It can enhance your customers' experience of your products and services. It even outperforms the polls in predicting the winners of Presidential elections. And often these improved outcomes can be created with surprisingly modest investments.

You will read about many examples in this book, so I will confine myself here to one, the company Innocentive. Innocentive has built an online network of more than 200,000 people around the world who go to its website to consider challenges that companies have posted prizes to have solved. These problems are usually technical in nature, and quite difficult to solve, which is why leading companies that have not found answers internally have reached out to the Innocentive community for solutions.

One intractable problem arose from the aftermath of the Exxon Valdiz oil spill in Alaska. The crude oil spilled had settled on the ocean floor, hundreds of feet below the surface in very cold water. The combination of pressure and cold temperatures made it impossible to suck up the oil from the ocean floor. This was the challenge presented to the Innocentive community.

Happily, a solution was found. But that solution came from an unlikely place, one that suggests the value of the crowdsourcing approach. An engineer with extensive experience in the cement industry realized that vibration could make the oil on the ocean floor more viscous, allowing it to be sucked off. A test of the idea demonstrated that it actually worked. The prize was paid, and the technique recovered a great deal of oil that might otherwise have lingered for decades, continuing to damage the surrounding environment.

As you will also read in this book, crowdsourcing is not a panacea for all ills, and can lead to terrible results if it is not managed properly. If, for example, the 'crowd' of contributors are not independent of one another, the crowd can become a herd, charging off in a single direction instead of balancing the different perspectives of people to provide a reliable prediction of a future event or activity.

Crowdsourcing is thus a powerful resource for innovators. Like most powerful resources, this power can be mismanaged as well. That is why you would be well advised to read this book, drink in its insights, and then apply it to your own challenges. A world of people and organizations is available to assist you, if you have the commitment and care to engage them properly.

Introduction: The Trend to Open Innovation

PAUL SLOANE

Imagine that you are planning a big surprise party. You want it to be entertaining, spectacular, memorable and different. You could plan and project manage every element of the party yourself: the theme, venue, music, food, drink, entertainment, games, diversions, etc. Or you could involve a number of people to help you with their ideas and their skills. One person could manage all aspects of the venue, someone else could design special decorations, another person could put together a music mix and so on. If you do it all yourself then you are in complete control, you have sole responsibility and you can keep the whole thing a surprise but you have to remember to do everything and it is only as good as your ideas. If you bring in a group of friends and experts to help then you can harness their imaginations you can bounce ideas off each other. You have to delegate tasks – which involves collaboration, supervision, letting go and an element of risk. Keeping the whole thing a surprise is more difficult but can be done. The choice between doing it all yourself and doing it with a group is the choice between a closed and an open model.

There was a time not very long ago when companies primarily used closed models for all their new product development. They focused on their own resources – research, development, marketing, etc to bring new products to market. This model gave them control and seemed to work well.

In 1982 two McKinsey consultants Tom Peters and Robert Waterman published a book entitled *In Search of Excellence*. It set out to analyse the key attributes and behaviours that made highly successful companies successful. As management books go it was a sensation. In its first four years it sold 3 million copies and became the most popular library book in the United States from 1989 to 2006. It became highly influential in management thinking. One of the precepts that the book expounded was 'Stick to the knitting'. This meant focusing on what you did well and avoiding distractions. Many corporations took this motto to heart. They concentrated on and developed their core strengths. They focused on building market share in their main markets. They developed and protected their intellectual property.

Companies not only stuck to the knitting, they used only the knitting patterns that they created.

It turns out that this principle which worked well in more stable times is dangerous in today's turbulent climate. There are countless examples of companies that focused on their core strengths, improved their current offerings, listened closely to their customers and then went bust. Smith Corona made beautiful typewriters. Its customers loved its typewriters. Smith Corona focused on improving quality, efficiency and customer service. The advent of word processors and then word processing software on PCs wiped it out. Encyclopaedia Britannica produces highly accurate and dependable reference works in handsome hardback volumes. An inexpensive and often inaccurate encyclopaedia on CD, Microsoft Encarta, offered the novelty of search and spelled doom for the mighty Britannica. Indeed many of the companies that were held out as shining examples of best practice in *In Search of Excellence* have since badly underperformed or burnt out (including Atari, Data General and Wang Labs). Meanwhile we have seen the rise of companies like Virgin Group, which deliberately sets out to break the precept of sticking to the knitting. Sir Richard Branson's company leaps from one field to another – airlines, trains, banking, books, cola and music to name but a few.

Mike Carr was the Chief Science Officer at British Telecom. For many years BT had invested heavily in developing its own technologies and products. He told me that BT examined the total amount it was spending on development R&D – it ran to hundreds of millions of dollars – and compared the figure with its best estimate of the global total spend on R&D on telecoms at all its competitors' research centres and universities worldwide. The estimate showed that BT was spending around 1 per cent of the worldwide spend. This implied that it would get around 1 per cent of the best ideas and that just was not good enough. So it changed its approach to a much more open and collaborative policy where it reached out to universities and other research centres to capture and develop more of the best ideas.

Nowadays most CEOs see collaboration as key to their success with innovation. They know they cannot achieve their innovation targets using internal resources alone. So they look outside for other organizations to partner with. A good example is Mercedes and Swatch, which collaborated to produce the Smart car. When Mercedes wanted to produce an innovative town car it did not choose another automobile manufacturer – it partnered with a fashion watch maker. Each brought dissimilar skills and experiences to the team.

The next step beyond collaboration is 'Open Innovation', a concept developed by Henry Chesbrough to describe the process of harnessing external resources to work alongside your team to develop new products and services. This is something that many leading companies including Procter and Gamble, IBM, Unilever, Reckitt Benckiser, BMW, Nokia and Kimberly-Clark have focused on as a way of driving innovation. OI replaces the vertical integration of processes within one company with a network of collaborators working on innovation projects. Using outsiders can speed up processes, reduce costs, introduce more innovative ideas and reduce time to market.

Kimberly-Clark reduced the time is takes to bring out new products by 30 per cent through OI. It launched Sunsignals in just six months by collaborating with a smaller company, SunHealth Solutions. Sunsignals is a self-adhesive sensor that changes colour when the wearer is in danger of burning in the sun. Procter and Gamble aims to source 50 per cent of its innovations from outside using OI. Early results include new products such as Mr Clean Magic Eraser and Pringles Prints.

Crowdsourcing is an extrapolation of OI in which you throw out a challenge to a group of people that you may or may not know and solicit their ideas and solutions for your issue. Many web-based companies specialize in different crowdsourcing fields. So if you want a name for a new brand of product you can get many suggestions by using the crowdsourcing site Naming Force. If you have a tough programming problem you could use Topcoder.com, which will set the challenge for ace freelance programmers from around the world. Similarly if you have a difficult technical or scientific challenge you might use Innocentive or Nine Sigma.

If you are considering setting out on the road of OI or of enhancing your current efforts in this arena then this book should prove an invaluable guide. Some of the leading thinkers and practitioners in the field address important questions such as:

- What is OI and what are its risks and benefits?
- What are the different types of OI and which is best for me?
- What is crowdsourcing and when should I use it?
- What have other people done and learnt? What is best practice?
- How can I get started?
- How can I measure success?
- What kind of corporate culture and processes are needed?
- What kind of people are best for this?

There is a powerful surge towards OI and crowdsourcing for the many reasons you will find in the chapters that follow. These concepts hold the enticing promise of turbo-charging your new product development. How can you harness this trend and benefit from it? These are probably the two most important questions that this book addresses.

Chapter 1
What is Open Innovation?

JULIAN KEITH LOREN

O pen Innovation is powerful – it can expand your design capabilities, mitigate risk and grow revenue. A well-implemented OI programme can release the pent-up value of unrealized ideas. It can allow new types of thinking to permeate your company, transforming business models and enabling you to edge ahead of your competitors. OI can allow you to take more ideas to market, and to do so with greater speed and at lower cost.

OI can also be a hard sell. Despite the strategic and tactical importance of OI, it can take considerable skill to argue the case for it and to design an OI programme that optimally fits your organization. This chapter will provide a multi-faceted definition of OI and briefly describe a few ways that OI principles can be applied – practical information designed to aid you as an OI advocate, architect, or manager.

Viewed through the simplest lens, OI is the flow of ideas into and out of an organization. In Henry Chesbrough's landmark book, *Open Innovation: The new imperative for creating and profiting from technology*, he provides the following succinct definition:

> Open Innovation means that valuable ideas can come from inside or outside the company and can go to market from inside or outside the company as well. (p 43)

Closed innovation, by contrast, is 'closed' to outside-of-company involvement. Chesbrough describes the implications of a closed innovation approach:

> Companies generate their own ideas and then develop them, build them, market them, distribute them, service them, finance them, and support them on their own. (p xx)

A closed innovation approach means that ideas either have to exploit existing internal infrastructure and capabilities, or that their introduction to market will be delayed while new production, marketing, distribution, service, financing and support systems are built internally or acquired and integrated. At the same time, outside companies may have ideas that are a poor fit for

FIGURE 1.1 Closed versus Open Innovation (inspired by and extending diagrams in Chesbrough, 2003: xxii, xxv, 31 and 44)

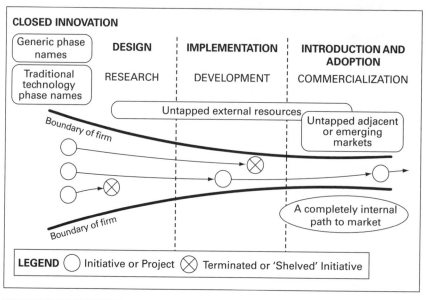

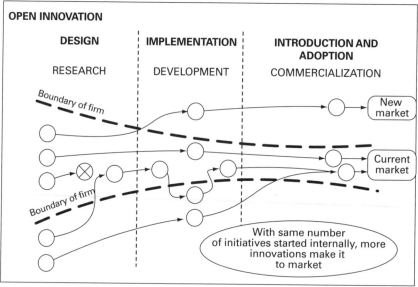

their internal aptitudes and systems but a great fit for those of your company. If the related infrastructure at your company is idle, then a closed innovation approach – by keeping the infrastructure-leveraging ideas out – results in opportunity cost. An open approach, by contrast, allows ideas to flow where complementary infrastructure, capabilities and business models already exist – the key to the speed and cost advantage of OI approaches over closed innovation approaches.

OI is not merely important for your organization. It can be important for you too. The precise implications depend on your role. The core meanings of OI for two roles are shown below – the roles of manager and innovator.

Manager's perspective

From the manager's perspective OI means access to broader design expertise and a wider range of innovation capabilities. For the manager, OI also means that return on innovation investments is more closely linked to market demand rather than being governed by the company's ability or inability to bring specific innovations to market. Better return on innovation investments increases support from upper management, may lead to improved compensation, and helps justify future budget requests.

Innovator's perspective

From the innovator's perspective OI means that there can be collaboration with a more diverse team and that designs and ideas can be enhanced by a wider array of viewpoints. The addition of external paths to market also means that the innovator can design products, services, systems, or models with a greater focus on consumer needs and less emphasis on the constraints dictated by internal paths to market – constraints imposed by previously unavoidable manufacturing and distribution limitations, for instance.

Where did Open Innovation come from?

OI has existed in certain industries and domains for a long time. Chesbrough cites the Hollywood film industry, which:

> has innovated for decades through a network of partnerships and alliances between production studios, directors, talent agencies, actors, scriptwriters, specialized subcontractors (eg, suppliers of special effects), and independent producers (2003: xxvii).

For decades and across industries, most large corporations have relied on external innovation partners in the advertising and marketing domains. However, in many other domains, OI principles have not been applied until recently. The closed innovation paradigm persists in most domains until a convincing case is made for introducing OI principles. An elegant case for OI can be found in Chesbrough's book, and it has had a vast impact on innovation practice in major corporations around the globe.

Before you can implement an OI programme in your own organization, you will probably have to make a case for it as well. OI can fly in the face of years of internal practice, disrupt deeply engrained work patterns, and cause political friction (see Chesbrough, 2003: 149–53 on the political friction caused by Lucent's New Venture Group).

External resources and ideas can make internal personnel feel threatened (in other chapters you will find helpful advice on overcoming internal resistance to OI). Companies that have prided themselves on the number of patents that they file may be more focused on stockpiling ideas than on taking them to market. These companies may have innovation practices that are geared more towards patent-winning novelty and less towards proven market demand (see Chesbrough, 2003: 158 on the prevalence of nonperforming patents).

Larger-than-expected external success of internally generated ideas can be the source of embarrassment to those who let the ideas 'escape'. These factors and others mean that you will probably need to argue the case for OI before you and your organization can reap the benefits of it. To succeed as an OI advocate it is critical that you have a multi-faceted understanding of what OI is and that you are aware of some of the compelling ways that its principles can be implemented.

Multiple facets of Open Innovation

Facet 1: Different contexts, different types of ideas

Many organizations make the mistake of looking at OI merely as a way of gleaning ideas from smart people who do not currently work for them. For organizations that already have more ideas than they can evaluate, filter, prioritize and prototype, the prospect of having a greater number of ideas is not very appealing. Rather than focusing on idea quantity, a well-crafted OI programme places emphasis on soliciting different types of ideas.

These externally generated ideas are fundamentally different because they are born from contexts that have no equivalent within your company – organizational structures, team compositions and individual profiles that cannot be found internally. If we look back at the innovation domains where large organizations have historically applied OI principles – advertising and marketing in particular – we understand this immediately. The network of agencies that large organizations have turned to for advertising and marketing innovation do not use the same evaluation methodologies for employees, do not structure teams in the same way, and typically have different organizational dynamics and structures. Professionals from different disciplines are likely to have infrequent and formal interactions within a large organization. In an advertising agency, professionals representing those same disciplines will work together within the same team, collaborating continually in an informal and creatively charged environment. The important

ways that external innovation partners may differ from your organization are
shown in Table 1.1.

TABLE 1.1 How external innovation partners may differ from your
organization

DIFFERENCE	EXAMPLE
Organizational structures	They may have less-hierarchical ('flatter') or more-matrixed structures allowing them to form multidisciplinary teams more easily.
Employee profiles	Compared to your firm, they may have employees with education and professional experience representing a wider range of disciplines or employees with fewer educational credentials and an emphasis on work experience over education or on portfolio over degrees
Divisional boundaries	They may combine divisions that are separated in your organization allowing individual employees to more readily perceive multiple facets of a given problem set
'Wearers of multiple hats'	They may have employees who perform duties that are spread across multiple divisions in your firm, providing insights into opportunities for business process improvement or business model innovation
Fiscal imperatives	They may have little access to outside capital and be focused on cash flow optimization while your firm may have great access to capital and be concerned with quarter-to-quarter growth in revenue. Fiscal imperatives allow or eliminate options early in the idea-generation cycle
Balance of power	They may have less power vested in the legal department or in human resources, meaning that their ideas are developed in a less-constrained context
Culture	They may have an underdog culture rather than the culture of an industry champion. A 'nothing to lose' collective mindset will be open to ideas that would be quickly kyboshed in a 'we have everything to lose' environment

Facet 2: It is your network. What do you need it to do?

We mentioned the challenges associated with large quantities of ideas. If an external innovation partner understands your needs well enough to be able to generate valuable ideas, they may be able to help you with these challenges as well – aiding you in filtering, prioritizing, grouping, refining and prototyping ideas that you have generated internally. If you do not have the internal capacity to select which 'warehoused' ideas could be taken to market by an external partner, they may be able to help with this evaluation as well. Rather than just placing participants in your OI programme at the 'ends' of the idea spectrum – as originators of ideas or as a last-mile delivery mechanism for ideas – you may consider using them at any point along the idea-to-innovation-to-market spectrum. By understanding this facet of OI you may be able to derive far greater value from your OI programme.

Facet 3: You are doing it already

If something has never been tried before in your organization, it is likely to be more risky and may create some anxiety. Even if you are developing an OI programme at an unprecedented scale, you will be able to implement the programme with greater ease if you can first demonstrate that OI principles are already being applied in your organization. It is likely that OI has been practised in certain divisions of your organizations for years. If you can find the individuals in your organization who have worked with external innovation partners and involve these internal 'OI veterans' in the development of your OI programme, you may be able to significantly reduce risk and allay fears. While you may quickly find these 'veterans' in marketing and information services, it is worthwhile expanding the search across the entire organization. An internal, multi-disciplinary team of OI practitioners can help you tailor an OI programme that is better suited to your company, your industry and your market. They can also be helpful in making the case for OI and remind the organization that you are expanding 'the known' rather than introducing 'the unknown.'

Open Innovation implementations

There are many ways to put OI principles into practice. You may find that certain types of OI programmes violate company policies, undermine important elements of your organization's culture, or turn out to be a 'poor fit' for other reasons. Rather than trying to force the implementation of a specific type of OI programme, it is better to carefully consider a broader array of implementation options and create a tailored programme that integrates the implementations that are best suited to your company or to specific business units.

FIGURE 1.2 Current innovation approach: the gap between perception and reality

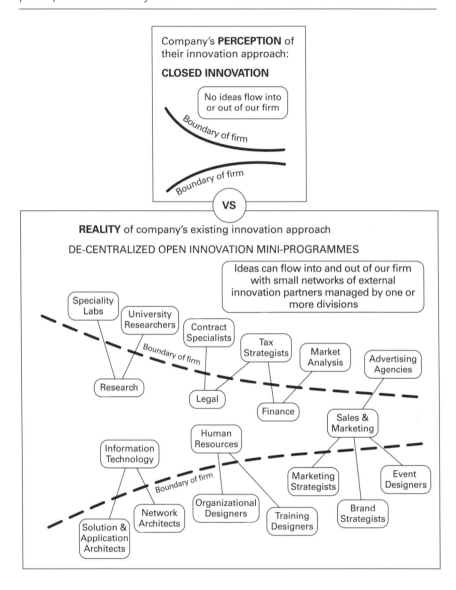

Implementation 1: Paid programme

An OI implementation that involves your organization paying external companies for the ideas that they generate and that your organization takes to market. Conversely, your organization is paid by an external company for ideas that your organization generates but the external company takes to market.

Implementation 2: Campus programme

Universities and other educational and research institutes form the external innovation network for this type of programme. Since these institutions do not typically take ideas to market, this OI implementation is focused on the in-flow of externally-generated ideas. In some cases the institutions are happy to have 'real world' challenges to present their students, and do not charge for the ideas that are generated. In other cases your organization may provide compensation to all institutions involved in the programme, or cash prizes may only be awarded to those institutions that generate the best ideas. (See Chesbrough, 2003: 188–90 for advice on harnessing university research.)

Implementation 3: Straddling programme

This implementation is neither completely internal nor completely external to your organization. Chesbrough refers to this type of programme as employing a 'hybrid model' and provides the example of an organization-owned venture capital unit that takes internally-generated ideas to market in partnership with external investors – an arrangement that is neither 'all the way in' or 'all the way out' of the organization (ibid: 136–44).

Implementation 4: Customer partner programme

If some of the previous implementations run contrary to your organization's vendor selection policies you might want to consider a customer partner programme – an OI implementation that uses a group of customers as external innovation partners. Like the campus programme, this implementation is focused on the in-flow of ideas. Rather than 'hiring' customers as external innovation partners, the customers are compensated for their contributions with free or discounted products or services, or other non-cash incentives. The customer may be an individual or another company.

Implementation 5: Supply chain partner programme

Since money is already being exchanged with other participants in your organization's supply chain, you may be able to incentivize them to become external innovation partners in exchange for discounts, bonuses, preferential handling, or other incentives that do not require new contracts. Putting contracts in place with supply chain participants to offer periods of exclusivity for manufacturing, distributing, or selling may meet with less resistance than contracts that require up-front investment. Since there is likely to be some mutual understanding of capabilities, it may be easy to use these supply chain partners at discrete points in the innovation cycle rather than doing a one-time hand-off.

Implementation 6: Pathway programme – ecosystem

A 'Pathway programme' is an OI programme that is focused on development of a capability or system. The 'ecosystem' implementation is designed as a laboratory for developing and refining product or service offerings that can be extended by a large community of external companies – an ecosystem. Initially your organization selects and actively recruits product or service extenders as OI partners. After you have worked with them to develop product or service extension mechanisms, licensing or revenue sharing arrangements and viable support systems, your company is then positioned to support a larger ecosystem of product or service extenders. A large ecosystem can allow you to deliver a range of product features or variety of service offerings that you would not be able to develop yourself, and serve markets and niches that your company is not currently reaching. For both Android smartphones and Apple iPhones the huge pools of mobile applications created by the large ecosystems of developers are used as a major selling point – representing a range of functionality that a single company, regardless of size, could not deliver alone. Many companies recognize that the development of a large ecosystem is strategic and lucrative, but few know where to start this challenging undertaking. Carefully designing an OI pathway programme is an intelligent first step.

Implementation 7: Pathway programme – internal bridges

In large organizations the flow of ideas may be impeded between business units. Because they are under the same 'corporate umbrella', business units may expect to have free access to ideas created anywhere in the company. However, if a business unit has made significant investment in an idea, the prospect of giving the idea away and watching money and political credit flow to another business unit is not very enticing. An OI programme can help business units figure out fair market prices for their surplus ideas and for ideas that they purchase or license from outside. The OI programme also provides a space where fiscal equitability and partnership sustainability are the focus, and where political factors play a lesser role. Business units can then use this knowledge and these perspectives from the 'laboratory' of an internal-external network to build a business-unit-bridging 'between' network that is effective, balanced and sustainable.

Implementation 8: Crowdsourcing programme

Crowdsourcing is tremendously powerful, but also very complex. For this reason, crowdsourcing is treated separately in this book, starting with a detailed description by Renee Hopkins (Chapter 2). In Jeffrey Phillips chapter, 'Open Innovation Typology' (Chapter 3) you will see how crowdsourcing fits within the OI continuum.

What else is Open Innovation?

OI is extremely valuable, but it can be a hard sell. A well-implemented OI programme can be a source of significant competitive advantage, but it needs to be crafted based on your organization's structure, size, culture, hiring practices and other factors. OI has a few more important characteristics:

- OI does not have to be implemented everywhere in your organization at once. It is possible to pilot an OI programme in a single division or department, establish a track record of success, and then introduce the programme in other departments or divisions.
- OI may require changes in your existing design practice. Later chapters provide additional details about OI design practices and about co-creating with customers.
- There are cultural elements that have a large impact on the success and effectiveness of OI programmes. These cultural elements are covered in detail in Chapter 17. Open-mindedness allows for different types of ideas to get fair consideration within your company and, therefore, an open-minded culture will allow for more value to be extracted from your OI programmes.

OI has one more important characteristic: OI is worth the effort. If you do the necessary work and invest the necessary care, there will be significant dividends for your company and for you personally.

Acknowledgements

Thanks to David Cordeiro, Diane Court, Bo McFarland, Alasdair Munn, Raphaëlle Loren, Boris Pluskowski and Francisco José Puentes Vargas for help with this chapter. Thanks to Henry Chesbrough for his ongoing leadership in this area and to my many co-workers and OI partners over the years who have helped me gain a broader and deeper understanding of Open Innovation.

Chapter 2
What is Crowdsourcing?

RENEE HOPKINS

Henry Chesbrough defined Open Innovation, but crowdsourcing is one type of OI he didn't foresee. The term 'crowdsourcing' was coined by *Wired* magazine writer Jeff Howe in a famous *Wired* story, 'The Rise of Crowdsourcing' (June 2006; **http://www.wired.com/wired/archive/14.06/ crowds.html**) that led to Howe's 2008 book, *Crowdsourcing: Why the power of the crowd is driving the future of business.*

It's become apparent that there are many idiosyncratic definitions of crowdsourcing, as well as some misunderstandings. It's instructive here to return to Jeff Howe's own characterization of crowdsourcing. Howe's blog (typepad.crowdsourcing.com) contains the two best and most succinct definitions of the term. The first he calls the 'white paper definition':

> Crowdsourcing is the act of taking a job traditionally performed by a designated agent (usually an employee) and outsourcing it to an undefined, generally large group of people in the form of an open call.

The second is Howe's 'sound bite' definition for crowdsourcing:

> The application of Open Source principles to fields outside of software.

Sound bite though it may be, the second definition is quite critical, because much of Howe's taxonomy for crowdsourcing and how it works relate the activity back to the principles by which the open source software movement works.

First, though, it's helpful to consider crowdsourcing in a way Jeff Howe does not do, which is to say, to consider it as a type of OI. As Julian Keith Loren noted in the previous chapter, the simplest definition of OI is 'the flow of ideas into and out of an organization'. Crowdsourcing, as well as user-driven innovation and co-creation (both of which Howe has argued are subsets of crowdsourcing) are all simply tools through which OI can happen. Crowdsourcing is not only a tool through which companies can get outside ideas and input into their technologies and products however; crowdsourcing is a tool through which companies can apply OI to their innovation efforts not only by outsourcing ideas but also by applying innovative crowdsourcing techniques to processes such as purchasing and financing that do not specifically result in the creation of an innovation. In other words, crowdsourcing can both result in innovation and can be used to innovate processes.

The history of crowds

Let's look at the history of the crowdsourcing concept and its predecessors. Even though Jeff Howe's *Wired* article and subsequent research wasn't the first discussion of customer or consumer inputs into the innovation process, it is the most thorough, and for that reason I'm basing this discussion on it. But I would be remiss if I didn't point out that, published before the *Wired* article was James Surowiecki's (2005) investigation of how the diversity and aggregation of information among crowds drives better predictions and decision making.

Also pre-dating the *Wired* article, Eric von Hippel of MIT had been writing extensively about user-driven innovation since the mid-1980s, including his influential 2005 book, *Democratization of Innovation*. And in the years before crowdsourcing there were many companies, particularly consumer goods companies whose innovation projects often originated from their marketing departments rather than from R&D, which had dabbled for years with various 'voice of the customer' and customer ideation approaches that were clear forerunners of the 'customer co-creation' aspect of crowdsourcing.

The main ingredient missing from both user innovation and early customer-co-creation efforts was the notion of the crowd itself. The ability to truly harness any group large enough to be rightly called a crowd did not become widely commonplace until the internet gained steam in the late 1990s and early 2000s. Not only did the internet offer a means of reaching a crowd, it also offered a means by which to gather crowd input of various kinds and even a platform through which the crowd could perform specific tasks. It just wasn't clear for quite a while that there was value to be gained from doing so.

Therefore, with its plethora of internet-enabled examples run by young tech entrepreneurs who had likely never read Henry Chesbrough, crowdsourcing as described in Jeff Howe's 2006 *Wired* article was initially easy for Fortune 500 companies to ignore. The original 'poster child' for crowdsourcing, mentioned in the original *Wired* article and still an oft-cited example, is the T-shirt company Threadless. The general public (the 'crowd') submits designs at Threadless.com, votes on which designs are created, and then buys them. It was hard to see exactly who Threadless was disrupting and hard to see anything truly innovative about T-shirt designs, no matter how cool they were. So it was easy for corporate innovators to dismiss crowdsourcing as irrelevant.

Crowdsourcing can disrupt

But in that very first *Wired* article was also a bone-chilling tale of classic disruption of the type Clayton Christensen wrote about in *The Innovator's Dilemma*: the story of iStockphoto, a crowdsourced stock photo site that wreaked such havoc in the stock photo industry that that industry's most established company, Getty Images, finally ended up buying it. Getty CEO Jonathan Klein told Howe, 'If someone's going to cannibalize your business, better it be one of your other businesses' (Howe, 2009: 190–91).

Before iStockphoto, agencies that sold rights to use pre-existing ('stock') photos had been operating for years in much the same fashion as they always had – providing catalogues that detailed and classified the images available, which the agencies licensed from professional photographers who were used to earning what they considered reasonable fees (perhaps US\$40) for the single use of a single photo that was in itself the leftover by-product of a photo assignment that had already been paid for. The stock photo industry reacted to the rise of the internet by migrating their existing operations there – searchable, classified catalogues with watermarked thumbnail images were available online for potential customers to choose from. The internet originally simply widened the potential audience of the typical stock photo company, and it also widened the potential customer base, as companies began putting up websites and images were needed for these sites.

As described in *Crowdsourcing*, iStockphoto began as a community of largely amateur photographers who earned credits for photos they added to the community, credits they then spent with photos they used from the community. It was not until the community grew to several thousand that its founder, Bob Livingstone, began to sell the photos, first for 25 cents each and then for US\$1 each, to cover the costs of server space and to earn a bit of profit. While the incumbent stock photo agencies, particularly Getty, dismissed the disruptor as a purveyor of very low-quality images, the numbers were on iStockphoto's side. The site had many more photographers and many more images than the standard agency site, and the best of these rose to the top. More important, no one who was trying to profit from their work could compete with iStockphoto's thousands of amateurs, who were happy enough to see their photos get used, and extremely happy to get any money at all, much less a profit that would cover their time and costs.

This may seem fairly straightforward, so why is crowdsourcing so confusing? Back to Jeff Howe again: 'Crowdsourcing isn't a single strategy. It's an umbrella term for a highly varied group of approaches that share one obvious attribute in common: they all depend on some contribution from the crowd' (2009: 280). As I said earlier, an important consideration, and one place from which much confusion arises, is that not all crowdsourcing leads to the creation of a product or service innovation. Some types of crowdsourcing are simply innovative ways to make decisions or get projects funded.

Models for crowdsourcing

How you gather the crowd, what you ask them to do, and how you ask them to do it all determine the type of crowdsourcing and what you will get out of it.

Jeff Howe has created a taxonomy of crowdsourcing that illuminates the possibilities, defining four primary categories for crowdsourcing:

1 *Collective intelligence, or crowd wisdom.* This is one of the two most common types of crowdsourcing, in which a crowd is gathered and the conditions created for that crowd to share their knowledge. Howe cites examples as simple as employee suggestion boxes and as complex as 'idea jams', worldwide internet-enabled brainstorming sessions held among employee stakeholder groups of companies such as IBM. Companies such as Starbucks and Dell have also used idea management systems to tap ideas of customer groups. Howe also cites as an example InnoCentive, the Waltham, Massachusetts-based company that harnesses a diverse group of thinkers with scientific knowledge and skills (though some are amateurs) to solve highly technical problems. Eric von Hippel's user-driven innovation methods also fall into this category. In user-driven innovation, companies harness the 'lead users' of their products and use their ideas to make the products better or to build the next generation of product.

2 *Crowd creation.* This is the second most common type of crowdsourcing. Often confused with crowd wisdom, which is simply gathering ideas from the crowd, crowd creation happens when a company turns to its users to actually create, or co-create, a product or service. Howe bases much of his thinking on crowd creation on the tenets of the open source software movement, particularly the concept that the action of creativity must be broken down into very small individual pieces that can be performed in 'spare cycles' – eg, the bits of extra time people have available. An example is Amazon's Mechanical Turk, where people can sign up to perform small bits of work. Other examples are iStockphoto, Threadless and contests held to create ads for Doritos as well as actual products for companies such as Schick.

3 *Crowd voting.* Crowd voting uses the crowd's judgements to organize vast quantities of information. Often crowd voting is seen in conjunction with crowd wisdom and crowd creation, as a means of thinning out the daunting number of submissions that often result. Crowd voting is also seen in the rise of prediction markets that have been used internally by such companies as HP to predict sales. Google's search results are based on an algorithm that itself is based on site popularity, which means that Google search results are essentially the result of crowd voting.

4 *Crowdfunding.* The internet has also given rise to a number of sites where people can participate in micro-lending: the lending of small sums to help with efforts ranging from a woman trying to start a small business in a third world country to a band trying to gather the funds to get its first CD made. Crowdfunding is a great example of a process innovation.

How to crowdsource

The 'rules' of crowdsourcing, such as they are, offer a framework of best practices for crowdsourcing.

Pick the right crowd

Only a small percentage of the crowd – approximately 1 per cent – will actually participate fully. So it's critical to start with a large enough number. Also, Howe discusses theories of why it's critical to have disparate thinking – a notion that should be familiar to devotees of OI. Too much groupthink can ruin crowd voting and collective intelligence. The latter particularly will not function correctly without the almost random inputs of widely distributed knowledge, which can only come from a diverse crowd. Clearly, however, it will be difficult to get actionable solutions to technical problems from a group that does not have enough knowledge about the problem area to even begin to problem-solve. Some research into the psychology of creativity (see, in particular, Amabile, 1996) also holds that group creativity works best in a group whose members comprise people who have high domain knowledge as well as people with less domain knowledge but high creative skills.

Offer the right incentives

Money is not always the right incentive. Howe points out that successful crowdsourcing can't happen without a vibrant, committed community, but the way to create such a community is rarely by paying its members. A mixture of financial reward as well as less tangible motivators, both extrinsic and intrinsic, is needed. Determining the mix and the specifics of the rewards is a critical challenge in crowdsourcing.

Crowdsourcing isn't going to replace your employees

For every person who feels that crowdsourcing is cheapening creative labours in many fields, from photography to logo design, there is another person or two who tried to crowdsource a magazine or a commercial and discovered that it's just as difficult and possibly more time-consuming and expensive to crowdsource as it is to simply use your employees. If the crowdsourcing can be done at least at the same price in money and time, however, it's well worth the effort. Overall you will get more creative ideas out of a large and diverse group than you will from a small core group of employees, but you will spend at least as much time and money herding the crowd, identifying the ideas that will best work for your company and developing those ideas.

Crowds require direction and guidance and someone to answer their questions

This point address both the fact that crowdsourcing is actually at least as expensive and time-consuming as using your employees, and the point regarding incentive. Being directed, guided and otherwise made to feel a valued part of the community is in some ways a part of the compensation for crowd participation, since feeling like part of the community is such a huge incentive. So you will end up offering guidance and direction as part of the effort to build the community in the first place, as well as offering guidance and direction as part of your effort to keep the crowd focused on what it is you want them to do.

Keep it simple and break it down into the smallest manageable components

This is a key tenet of the open source software movement: that the most complex tasks are broken down into small pieces and distributed. The economics of crowdsourcing also demand this kind of task granularity. The most disruptive business models to come from crowdsourcing, such as iStockphoto, are business models based on harnessing work from amateurs who don't expect to be paid what their time is 'worth'. To get participation, the task must be small and simple enough, and fun enough, that it can fit into an individual's 'spare time' they're not devoting to anything else.

Remember Sturgeon's Law

This law states that 90 per cent of everything is crap, and 10 per cent of everything is not crap. This law drives many best practices, including having a large enough community to start with, making sure the crowd has direction, and using the crowd itself to surface the best and vote it to the top.

The community's always right

This may better be stated as: 'communities are not just any other stakeholder group' – not employees, not shareholders, not customers. Any or all of these stakeholders may be part of the community, but once a community is established, you are operating under a different set of organizational behaviour guidelines than those governing a simple stakeholder group. Top-down organization and 'management' style rarely works in communities, but true grassroots anarchy doesn't either. Howe describes the appropriate style as ruling with the moral authority the community allows, rather than simply taking charge.

Ask not what the crowd can do for you, but what you can do for the crowd

According to Howe, crowdsourcing works because, for the crowd, it satisfies the uppermost tier on Abraham Maslow's hierarchy of needs. In other words, the incentive for the community is to get their needs for self-actualization met. These are needs like creativity, spontaneity, problem-solving and, to some degree, affiliation.

Conclusion

In some ways crowdsourcing is the ultimate OI – not all the smart people work for you, so if you could harness the many, many smart people who don't work for you, what a tremendous resource that would be. And crowdsourcing sounds very simple: gather a crowd, get them to do something, and reap the financial rewards of the crowd's work.

Yet nothing could be further from the reality. Crowdsourcing is difficult if done right, and 'difficult' may be an understatement. Few of the typical organizational structures and incentive systems a company is accustomed to will work well for crowdsourcing, which must be based in community in order to work. Examples abound of companies that have been burned by crowdsourcing. So why do it at all?

Because when done right, crowdsourcing offers an unparalleled benefit – a diversity of thought and experience that simply cannot be obtained any other way than through a crowd with all its diversity. When this benefit can be harnessed in a way that the community itself feels appreciated and rewards its organizers with the best it can offer – its wholehearted participation – the results can be spectacular. Using crowdsourcing to create innovation or using crowdsourcing tools to innovate processes – when wrapped in a business model that properly monetizes its value and capitalizes on its power to disrupt – crowdsourcing can be a critical building block of successful OI.

Chapter 3
Open Innovation Typology

JEFFREY PHILLIPS

O pen Innovation is a term coined by Henry Chesbrough, who wrote a book entitled *Open Innovation* in 2003. In the book Chesbrough defined OI this way:

> Open innovation is a paradigm that assumes that firms can and should use external ideas as well as internal ideas, and internal and external paths to market, as the firms look to advance their technology.

Chesbrough argues that given the wide dispersal of information, the pace of change and the global nature of competition, innovation must incorporate ideas from external organizations – customers, prospects and business partners. Any firm that uses a 'go it alone' approach and ignores ideas from its external constituents risks missing good ideas that can accelerate growth and differentiation.

Loosely defined, OI supposes that a firm will request and receive ideas from third parties. In addition to the submission of ideas, third parties may also be involved in ranking or prioritizing ideas, evaluating ideas, and even prototyping ideas. OI techniques can span much of the innovation process, and like any innovation method or process 'open innovation' is a generic phrase, with many different implementations depending on the nature and structure of the innovation approach. OI merely defines an innovation process that embraces and encourages third-party participation, but the term 'open innovation' does not specify how the third parties are involved, what roles they play or how they are invited to participate. These factors can help us create a 'typology' of OI, examining at least four different OI methods.

This typology will help distinguish different types of OI and determine when and how to apply each type. The two defining attributes in this typology are: 1) *Participative or invitational:* should the sponsors invite specific people to submit ideas or should the innovation effort be open to all interested partners? 2) *Suggestive or directed:* should the ideas be influenced or directed by topics or needs specified by the sponsor, or should the participants be allowed to submit ideas with no asserted boundaries or conditions?

Interestingly, these two factors are also important for closed innovation programmes. Who you select from among your staff to generate ideas dictates the scope and depth of ideas. How you choose to frame the challenges and topics that the team use to submit ideas indicates what is strategic for your company. These factors take on added significance when 'open' innovation is deployed. Let's take a deeper look at both factors, and then use these two factors to create a typology for OI.

Who submits ideas

When considering who to invite to an idea generation session, the sponsor has a wide array of options, from 'everyone' to a small, handpicked team. This is true whether the brainstorm is conducted within an organization or the ideas are generated through 'open' innovation. At one end of the spectrum, the sponsor can handpick a small, talented group of individuals, chosen for their knowledge and experience. This approach is often best for:

- challenges or issues that require deep experience or knowledge;
- challenges that may generate useful intellectual property;
- challenges that require secrecy; or
- challenges that address a very disruptive goal.

Often a smaller team is more successful at radical or disruptive innovation, since it is easier to communicate a radical goal to a small team and confirm that the idea generation team are all 'on board' with the goal. At the other end of the spectrum is 'crowdsourcing' which means allowing anyone with an interest in the topic to submit ideas. The conventional wisdom is that many diverse perspectives will result in:

- more ideas;
- better ideas; and
- ideas with greater diversity.

Evidence has shown, however, that larger groups are less effective at generating disruptive ideas, since disruptive ideas seem uncertain and the 'crowd' tends to favour ideas they can understand. Secrecy and intellectual property concerns arise as more people are involved as well.

There are, of course, intermediate points on this spectrum – for example a firm can select some internal and external experts to ensure an audience with broader perspectives without opening the idea generation session to the entire web. We'll look at some examples of idea generation using each of these approaches in the paragraphs that follow. In the following pages we'll use the term 'invitational' to denote innovation programmes where the sponsor has selected individuals to participate and 'participative' to denote innovation programmes that are open to all comers.

The instructions provided

The second factor in idea generation that will help form our typology is the selection of topics for innovation. Again there is a strong dichotomy between the two options, even more so than in the previous example. A sponsor of an innovation effort can assert a topic of interest and request that the participants respond to the stated need, issue or challenge. We call this 'directed' innovation, since the sponsor directs the participants to submit ideas in line with his or her need. Alternatively, an idea sponsor can open an innovation effort without suggesting topics, seeking any and all ideas that the participants have, regardless of the alignment of the ideas to corporate needs or strategies.

For most innovation efforts, we focus on 'directed' innovation. Directed innovation has the benefit of training the participants' attention on challenges that are important and relevant for the sponsor in the hope that good ideas will result that will address the challenge or opportunity. These ideas are solving a real problem or addressing a real opportunity that the sponsor believes is important. These directed ideation sessions are more likely to result in ideas that meet the needs of the sponsor, are aligned with corporate or business line strategy and can be implemented. Directed sessions result in the generation of fewer ideas than a completely suggestive session, but the ideas are more relevant and easier to evaluate. Suggestive idea generation is useful to gain a sense of what the 'crowd' believes is important. Since there are few limits to the ideas that can be submitted, many more people can participate and the breadth of ideas is much larger. This means more ideas are generated but they often have few linkages and must be considered separately. So while more ideas are generated, they address many more topics, some of which are important for the corporation and some of which have no bearing on strategic issues.

With these two criteria in mind, we can now develop a 'typology' for OI. Why is a typology important? 'Open innovation' is just a label – your firm won't implement OI; it will implement a version or versions of OI informed by the invitees and the kinds of problems or challenges you seek to solve. The typology is especially useful when considering how to deploy OI in your business. The decisions you make about who to invite to an innovation effort and how to direct those teams will determine the kinds of ideas you receive, how the ideas are evaluated and selected, the relevance of the ideas and, to a great extent, the ownership of the ideas.

Figure 3.1 expresses the 'types' of OI possible using our two factors: suggestive and directed for the topics of innovation, and participative and invitational for the invitees. Using this matrix we'll explore the different kinds of OI and the results you can expect.

FIGURE 3.1 The 'types' of open innovation possible

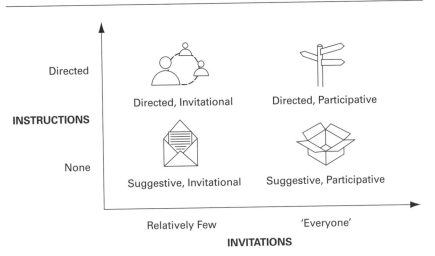

Suggestive/Participative

Probably the most familiar 'open' innovation approach is a suggestive innovation programme open to anyone who cares to participate. A suggestive, participative innovation programme encourages anyone with an idea to submit it and review and rank the ideas from others.

Dell's IdeaStorm site is probably one of the best known OI sites on the web and a good example of the suggestive, participative model. IdeaStorm is a website that allows virtually anyone with an internet connection the opportunity to submit ideas to Dell about its products, services, business model or anything else the participant cares to submit. When Dell originally unveiled the system, IdeaStorm provided no directions as to topics, so individuals were free to submit requests for changes to existing equipment, suggest new products or services or even recommend new business models. Dell receives hundreds of ideas every day on its public IdeaStorm site, and over time has received almost 15,000 ideas. Of the submissions Dell has received, over 400 have been implemented.

Note that in IdeaStorm anyone can submit an idea – Dell does not invite specific individuals or companies to submit ideas and does not weed out or preclude individuals. Anyone – customers, partners, even competitors – can submit ideas. Additionally, Dell doesn't require that the ideas that are submitted address a specific topic or concern that Dell management or product developers prefer. Over time, Dell has introduced the concept of directed ideation on its website, which Dell calls 'Smart Storms', but IdeaStorm still provides the means for individuals to submit ideas on topics that they prefer rather than submit ideas based on topics defined by Dell.

FIGURE 3.2 Suggestive/Participative

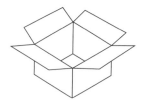

There are a number of factors to consider when evaluating the expectations, goals and outcomes associated with a suggestive, participative OI model:

1 The breadth of ideas submitted will be vast. When submitters define the topics of interest, every idea can be unique, and the ideas will span a broad spectrum of focus areas. To address this breadth, it's important for your OI system to support idea tagging and categorization to aggregate similar ideas.

2 Evaluation and selection are much more difficult than other OI types. Since submitters choose the topics and ideas they submit, it is much more difficult to establish a 'fixed' set of criteria to evaluate the ideas. Therefore, while many more ideas are submitted under this approach than others, it is possible that far fewer will be implemented than under a directed system. You can address this concern by creating a baseline set of criteria that the idea must address, or have the submitter propose how the idea should be evaluated. Selecting the ideas can be left in the hands of the participants, who can vote on or rank ideas, or selection can be placed in the hands of internal staff. Participants may 'bid up' an idea that is less interesting or valuable to the sponsor, so a firm must take care to spell out how the selections will be accomplished.

3 The number of ideas submitted can be staggering. In the IdeaStorm case, almost 15,000 ideas were submitted in just a few years. That represents close to 5,000 ideas a year or close to 15 ideas a day. If each idea took only 30 minutes to review and evaluate for further action, a team could spend over a person-year on evaluation and selection, and new ideas continue to come in all the time.

4 Secrecy is difficult and protection of intellectual property is almost impossible. A suggestive, participative OI programme happens 'out in the open' so good ideas can be viewed by all participants. Since the individuals aren't pre-selected and don't have extensive intellectual property training, it's hard to determine which ideas are valuable and should be protected, and even more difficult to determine which ideas are original or may be protected by another firm already. Most sites

include a stipulation that the participant agrees to waive ownership rights over any idea submitted to the company sponsoring the event.

5 Open, suggestive innovation is, for all intents and purposes, an example of social media and is subject to the same expectations that an individual might have about a social media platform like Facebook for example. You can expect participants to invite other participants, comment on the ideas they like (and dislike) and participate on the site or forum as if they were working on a social media site like Facebook. There's little distinction between the two and the 'rules' of social media apply.

6 Ideas submitted are likely to be incremental, especially the ideas that are ranked through the 'wisdom of crowds'. It is likely that the participants will submit a broad range of ideas, from very incremental to very disruptive, but the prevailing sentiment in a large forum will be to revert to safer, more familiar ideas. Large groups will reject ideas that they believe are too 'radical', even if your organization might find the ideas valuable.

7 Open, suggestive models are 'continuous engagement' applications. That is, the software or sites have to be continuously available to be discovered by a large number of people, and the ideas will be constantly evolving. You may be able to convert the site to a 'campaign' model over time once your participants reach a critical mass, but until that time the site needs to be available and interactive on a continuous basis.

For obvious reasons, this type of OI has garnered the most attention, since the websites are readily available to anyone who is interested. The investment to start a suggestive, participative OI programme is relatively low, but will require a software solution to capture ideas and support distributed users. Virtually any website that supports idea submission and collaboration on ideas will suffice. Spigit, Bright Idea, Intuit, Imaginatik and other software vendors support this model of OI. Dell's IdeaStorm application is supported by SalesForce.com.

There is another important consideration, however. In a robust participative, suggestive model, your innovation site tends to become one aspect of your social media strategy. This being said, once a site is available, the engagement from your team cannot flag. Participants don't merely expect to submit ideas – they expect to receive comments and suggestions about their ideas from other participants and from the sponsoring organization. Further, they expect the ideas to be evaluated, selected and implemented. Campbell's Soup discovered the hard way that failing to interact with idea submitters and neglecting communication and follow-up actions once the ideas are submitted will lead to atrophy and eventual abandonment of the site by the participants. This means your team must understand the staffing necessary to interact with the participants and sustain that level of engagement as long as the site provides relevant information to your firm. Otherwise, as noted above, the 'rules' of social media apply and your firm will quickly become a pariah online. Staffing, not just for the short term but over the longer term, must be taken seriously. As ideas enter the system, you'll need resources to respond to the ideas, reply to submitters and acknowledge their ideas, and team members to rank, prioritize and evaluate ideas, as well as the means to select and implement some of the best ideas, and provide feedback on the eventual outcome of the ideas.

Suggestive/Invitational

Another fairly common OI model is the one we term 'suggestive/invitational'. In this instance the sponsor of the innovation initiative invites specific individuals, teams or organizations to submit ideas of their choosing. There are few if any specific topics or requirements.

One of the best examples of the suggestive, invitational model is IBM's Idea Jam. Periodically IBM will invite a wide range of people to submit ideas in a number of topic areas. Other than broad topic areas such as environmental impact, green issues and sustainability there are no restrictions on the kind of idea that can be submitted. In one Idea Jam in 2006 thousands of individuals invited from sites around the world submitted over 30,000 ideas. As is the case with the suggestive, participative model, the number and distribution of the participants require that a software system supports the OI effort.

Clearly the significant difference between this model and the participative model is the concept of selecting and inviting specific participants. In this case the sponsoring organization is seeking specific perspectives or insights, or believes that carefully selected individuals or teams will provide better insights and ideas. While this can mean that the teams generate fewer ideas that are more aligned to the needs of the firm, it can also introduce 'groupthink' or limit perspectives unless there is reasonable diversity across the invited individuals.

There are a number of factors to consider when evaluating the expectations, goals and outcomes associated with a suggestive, invitational OI model:

1 The breadth of ideas submitted will be large but not as large as in the suggestive, participative model. When submitters define the topics of interest, every idea can be unique, and the ideas can span a broad spectrum of focus areas. However, the mere selection of the participants limits the range of ideas submission as the participants typically have some knowledge about what the sponsor values or where its key strategies and focus areas lie.

2 Evaluation and selection are simpler than in a suggestive model. Since submitters choose the topics and ideas they submit, it is much more difficult to establish a 'fixed' set of criteria to evaluate the ideas. Invitees typically are a bit more circumspect in the kinds and breadth of

FIGURE 3.3 Suggestive/Invitational

ideas they submit, which reduces the load for the evaluators. Typically, individuals who are invited to participate have more insight and understanding about the innovation process, so their ideas have greater alignment and are better documented, reducing the evaluation effort.

3 The number of ideas submitted can still be large. In the IBM Idea Jam example, thousands of ideas were submitted in fairly little time.

4 As the participants are invited, it becomes much easier to protect ideas and define intellectual property, especially if the individuals invited have greater sensitivity to what constitutes intellectual property or work under negotiated agreements with the sponsoring firms. Intellectual property definition and protection still remain issues as the number of participants grows.

5 A suggestive, invitational OI model is less susceptible to issues that traditional 'social media' sites bear. Individuals who are invited can be requested to keep ideas, comments and topics in quarantine. Since the site does not have to be public, it is easier to reduce the availability of ideas and topics to third parties.

6 Ideas submitted as part of a suggestive, invitational OI model are likely to span the gamut from incremental to disruptive, but as a whole they are also more likely to be relevant to strategic goals and needs and applicable to near-term needs. Evaluations of the ideas are still likely to favour incremental ideas over more radical or disruptive ideas, since a large group of people are likely to reject ideas they don't believe the firm will countenance.

7 Suggestive, invitational models are typically 'campaign' or event-driven applications. That is, the invitation is limited to a specific period of time. The invitation to participate not only invites the participant but communicates a specific period of time that the OI effort will be active. This method ensures that the sponsor can invite an ever-changing set of participants.

For all the potential benefits, this type of OI has achieved the least amount of use and awareness, most likely due to the up-front investment required to build a list of participants. Much care needs to be given to the experiences and perspectives of the people who are invited to participate, and once those lists are built, they must be maintained over time. There are also legal and financial implications when building the list. Many executives will seek to cleanse the list of any real or potential competitors, which can greatly limit the number of participants. Additionally, since this model is typically event-driven, new and existing innovators must be invited to new sessions as they occur, which presents more work and more effort to the sponsor. Spigit, Bright Idea, Intuit, Imaginatik and other software vendors support this model of OI.

Once a good list of participants is built, however, the vast majority of the work involved in this model is accomplished. Since most of the innovation programmes are event-driven and time-bound, and the number of invitees is far fewer than in a completely 'open' innovation model, fewer ideas are generated, and they tend to be more focused and of higher quality, which reduces the efforts in categorization, aggregation and evaluation. Additionally, since the participants are invited and engage on the initiative for only a short time, there is far less expectation for feedback and follow-up on the ideas that were submitted. This approach has some 'social media' aspects but those attributes are much less emphasized than in the continuously available suggestive model.

Directed/Invitational

The type of OI that offers the most promise to larger organizations is the concept of directed ideation with invited partners. In this case a firm can build a web of pre-identified and pre-screened partners to participate in idea generation on topics of special interest or strategic importance. The sponsoring organization controls both the list of invited participants and the topics for ideation.

There are several examples of these directed, invitational OI programmes. Probably the best known is P&G's Connect + Develop programme, which allows firms to partner with P&G to participate in innovation activities. Like P&G, many firms are creating 'proprietary networks' consisting of selected partners, customers and prospects who participate in innovation activities. These partnerships require much deeper development and address many of the legal and intellectual property issues that can arise in traditional OI models.

A second example of a directed, invitational OI model is Innocentive. In the case of Innocentive, the sponsoring firm produces a specific problem or specification, which Innocentive posts as an anonymous RFP on its site. Any registered third party can respond to the specification, submitting ideas to Innocentive for review. Anyone who has been accepted as an Innocentive solution provider can see the specification but doesn't necessarily know which firm has posted the issue or challenge. Also, within the Innocentive model the submitters don't see the ideas that are

FIGURE 3.4 Directed/Invitational

submitted by other parties, so while this is 'open' innovation the amount of collaboration on ideas is far lower.

In these directed, invitational models firms seek to build trusted partnerships for idea generation. While there is a risk of 'groupthink' since the number of firms or participants is far lower, the level of trust and depth of relationship with the participants is much higher, and the quality and value of the concepts that are generated can be very high. A significant amount of business development and market assessment work must be completed to build these proprietary networks, but once in place they can generate ideas that are rapidly vetted through the entire value chain of an industry. These directed, invitational models can be thought of as the natural evolution of OI from a corporate perspective. John Seely Brown, of Xerox fame, recently said:

> For OI to realize its full potential, it will have to navigate from a narrow focus on transactions to provide much richer support with long-term, trust-based relationships around joint initiatives to address real problems or opportunities.

When considering a directed, invitational innovation model, the main factors are:

1 The breadth of ideas submitted will be limited by the defined need or challenge, but the depth of the ideas is much greater than in other forms. Having built a network of trusted firms, the needs and challenges behind an innovation request are well understood. The participants in this format will offer fewer ideas, but those ideas will have great alignment to the needs of the firm and a much greater viability than in other forms of idea generation using partners.

2 There is a risk that the firms within the trusted partnership and the participants in the OI programme 'know too much' and don't stretch their thinking far enough. If there are too many 'experts' in the trusted network, their thinking may be constrained and governed by 'what they know' rather than what's possible. Evaluations may become too easy and the evaluation criteria may need to be relaxed for these efforts.

3 The number of ideas submitted is likely to be far smaller than in other OI formats but, as noted above, the viability of the ideas is much greater.

4 Since your firm is working within trusted networks, many of the intellectual property issues and other confidentiality concerns have been addressed as the partnership developed. As you gather your network to address a specific topic or issue, most of the legal issues have already been addressed.

5 Directed, invitational innovation while 'open' is open only to those partners who have been vetted and achieved certain status. This format is the only kind of OI that isn't really 'public' and available for a large swath of the population, so your communication can be constrained and the visibility of the event is limited.

6 Ideas submitted within this framework are governed by your instructions rather than by the 'crowd'. While participants are likely to be more comfortable submitting incremental ideas you have the chance through your instructions to encourage them to be as incremental, or as disruptive, as you care to be.

7 While the relationships and trusted networks have longevity, this level of engagement is by definition periodic or episodic based on specific needs or market events. These programmes should be thought of as 'campaigns' or events, not as an ongoing idea generation programme. However, the relationships within the network and communication to sustain and refresh the trusted network must be sustained regardless of the current innovation activity or lack thereof.

A directed, invitational OI approach is different from the other types in that there's far less need for a software solution in a trusted relationship. That's because far fewer people will be involved, and far fewer ideas will be discussed. When creating an OI platform of this type, you can use some of the same tools we've documented above, but there's far less need for idea management systems in this approach.

As noted above, we believe that many firms will evolve their 'open' innovation programmes to focus primarily on this kind of OI. A directed, invitational OI programme has a number of advantages. First, your firm works with known, trusted partners, customers and prospects who understand your business and may participate in the same value chain. That means they understand your markets, your customers and your operating environment. They probably understand your revenue streams and business models. Second, due to the nature of the arrangement, there are far fewer concerns with intellectual property and confidentiality. While these are significant concerns in other OI models, they are greatly reduced through the use of trusted partners. Third, the ideas you receive within this model will be valuable, applicable, timely and in line with your business strategies.

For all the benefits associated with the directed, invitational programme, there are several significant challenges. First, these relationships require a significant amount of work to develop. That investment is why Innocentive, with its distinctive offerings, has become popular. Second, there is a risk within the trusted network of relying too heavily on partners who may have a similar perspective and worldview, failing to incorporate individuals or firms with different perspectives. This can mean your ideas are more incremental than is helpful, missing market windows and customer opportunities. Third, while you may include some customers in your trusted network, the 'voice of the customer' isn't heard as distinctly or as broadly in this model. You will need to incorporate other means to gain insights into what customers want and need and not rely solely on this model for that insight.

Directed/Participative

The final type of OI model we'll review is the directed, participative model. In this model, a sponsor 'directs' a group of people to address a specific problem or opportunity. Anyone who cares to participate based on the topic can participate. In this regard the directed, participative model is fairly similar to the suggestive, participative models like IdeaStorm, except that the topics are defined by the sponsor. Many OI models follow this progression from suggestive, participative to directed, participative because the value of the ideas remains relative high while the number of ideas is greatly reduced. Additionally, the directed nature of the programme or event allows the sponsor to direct the teams to pursue opportunities that are of interest to the company, rather than simply submit any idea they prefer.

Examples of the directed, participative model include the 'Storm Sessions' on the IdeaStorm site, where Dell managers provide specific topics or challenges that any prospect or customer can respond to. Other directed, participative models include idea contests. As this chapter was written the Deep Water Horizon oil disaster unfolded. BP and the US Federal Government created a site to allow interested individuals and companies to submit ideas about capping the well or recovering the oil in the waters of the Gulf of Mexico. A number of firms and organizations sponsor idea contests to attract the best ideas or solutions to stated problems or challenges. These idea contests allow anyone to respond to a specific issue or challenge; thus they are participative and directed.

As should be apparent through these examples, directed, participative innovation attracts people with similar interests and goals, or similar passions. Many interest groups, birds of a feather groups and LinkedIn groups use this approach to obtain ideas from a relatively homogeneous but distributed group of people. Typically the people who are engaged in these OI efforts have a deep interest in the topic or issue, and are willing to work within the guidelines or confines asserted by the sponsor. The fact that the topic is dictated and rules of engagement are created weed out a lot of people who would have otherwise participated.

When considering a directed, participative innovation model, the main factors are:

FIGURE 3.5 Directed/Participative

1 The breadth of ideas submitted will be limited by the defined need or challenge, but the depth of the ideas is much greater than in other forms. In this model we are tapping into people with a great interest in or passion about the topic, who have sought out the opportunity to participate and want their voice to be heard.

2 Evaluation and selection are simplified because the topic or challenge is usually well defined, but evaluation and selection can be complicated by the fact that people participating in this kind of innovation model have a strong personal or emotional attachment to their ideas or to the topic. They may be less inclined to support an analytical assessment of the ideas and may engage in more heated discussion in online forums and comments about the ideas.

3 Depending on the topic and the breadth of interest and engagement, you may find that this model attracts as many participants and generates as many ideas as a suggestive, participative model. Generally topics that engender a significant amount of emotion or passion – cleaning up the Gulf, for instance – will encourage individuals to submit many ideas.

4 As these ideas are often available on a public forum, the issues of intellectual property, secrecy and confidentiality arise. These concerns are somewhat overcome by the fact that many of these programmes using this model are intended to cure an ill or address a problem like the oil disaster where people care more about fixing the problem than gaining compensation.

5 Directed, participative innovation, like suggestive innovation is a social media exercise and is subject to many of the same challenges and issues. A community will form around key topics and the participants in that community are often passionate. They will invite others and will have strong opinions about the ideas that are submitted. Your team may need to provide a moderator to track the ideas and the communication within the community.

6 Ideas submitted as part of a directed, participative OI model are likely to span the gamut from incremental to disruptive. Since the topic has been suggested by a sponsor, he or she can indicate the type of ideas

that are more favoured and indicate a preference for incremental or disruptive ideas.

7   Directed, participative models are typically 'campaign' or event-driven applications. That is, the topic or challenge is focused on a problem that needs to be solved or is bounded by a time period. Clearly, given the nature of the challenge or problem these campaigns can exist for quite a long period of time. However, this model is best viewed as supporting events or campaigns.

A directed, participative model of OI is easily supported by software, which will be necessary since many participants are likely to submit ideas, and those participants are likely to be highly distributed. Any of the software applications mentioned previously will support a directed, participative OI model.

This approach and its success will depend significantly on the definition of the challenges or opportunities the sponsor creates. For 'cause' oriented topics that allow people to submit ideas to solve problems in line with their passions or worldviews, a significant number of ideas will be generated. For more technical or arcane topics or those that seem to have relevance to the business, you may find that this approach has less value because it requires the participants to seek out the idea generation opportunity and have some affinity to the problem or challenge.

Conclusion

Within this chapter it has been our goal to introduce an OI 'typology' based on two factors: how the topic or challenge of the innovation programme is conveyed and how the participants are invited. From the four descriptions given you can see that the term 'open innovation' actually represents a loose confederation of very different innovation techniques and styles, and can result in very different outcomes.

OI should be part of any firm's innovation toolkit, and choosing the best implementation of an OI model for your firm involves some choices on appropriate structure the OI effort. Some critical questions to ask your innovation sponsors are:

- Do you prefer to engage a lot of people generally or a few people specifically?
- Do you have specific topics or opportunities to address or are you more interested in the ideas of the 'crowd'?
- Do you seek incremental ideas or more disruptive ideas?
- Do you have a deep bench of talent that can actively engage a large audience or do you prefer to interact with a smaller, more selective team?
- Are you seeking to conduct OI to attract public attention and extend a

social media strategy, or do you prefer to conduct efforts more discretely?

- Do you have specific partners that you trust to provide insights and ideas? Can you build trusted relationships with them on innovation topics?

Asking and answering these questions may take time, but that time will be well spent if it prevents your organization from kicking off a public, suggestive model when in reality the goals were for quiet, disruptive innovation. Not all OI is alike, and as should be apparent through this short typology, the different styles require different investments and will result in very different outcomes. Make sure your OI structure achieves your OI expectations and goals.

Chapter 4
The Importance of a Strategic Approach to Open Innovation

BRADEN KELLEY

Beyond your four walls

There is a lot of buzz around the topic of Open Innovation, and too often people talk about OI as a way to cut costs by somehow off-loading or out-sourcing the innovation efforts of a company. But, even in these challenging economic times, you still can't get something for nothing.

While theoretically you can engage an army of people outside the walls of your organization to help you with your innovation efforts, there is still a lot of work that must go on inside the organization to prepare it to receive innovation ideas from outside. Organizations choosing to engage in OI must approach it in a holistic and strategic manner.

Should Open Innovation live in R&D or marketing?

When it comes to OI, too many organizations treat it like an extension of Research & Development (R&D) when it should be seen as an extension of marketing. Not viewing OI as a marketing activity presents great risks to the organization's brand equity while in some cases there may be a great opportunity to increase the organization's connections with other stakeholders (customers, partners, researchers, suppliers, etc).

OI should be the domain of marketing for two main reasons: 1) marketing specializes in bringing new solution offerings to market; and 2) marketing specializes in crafting and optimizing external communications. So, please involve your marketing department in your OI efforts, or even better, let them lead the communications and presentation (with product groups and R&D

providing guidance on the strategy and content). That way you'll hopefully avoid OI approaches like MyStarbucksIdea that result in huge amounts of duplication, clutter and little competitive advantage. And, on the other end of the spectrum, by having the innovation folks talking to the marketing folks you'll hopefully avoid empty promises like Nissan's 'Innovation for All' tagline, where the 'All' really aren't involved in the innovation.

Innovation is social

Don't forget that innovation is social. I said this in *Stoking Your Innovation Bonfire* (2010) but it's worth repeating:

> While many people give Thomas Edison, Alexander Graham Bell, and the modern-day equivalent, Dean Kamen, credit for being lone inventors, the fact is that the lone inventor myth is just that – a myth. All these gentlemen had labs full of people who shared their passion for creative pursuits. Innovation requires collaboration, either publicly or privately, and is realized as an outcome of three social activities.

1. Social inputs

From the very beginning when an organization is seeking to identify key insights to base an innovation strategy or project on, it often uses ethnographic research, focus groups, or other very social methods to get at the insights. Great innovators also make connections to other industries and other disciplines to help create the great insights that inspire great solutions.

2. Social evolution

We usually have innovation teams in organizations, not sole inventors, and so the activity of transforming the seeds of useful invention into a solution valued above every existing alternative is very social. It takes a village of passionate villagers to transform an idea into an innovation in the marketplace. Great innovators make connections inside the organization to the people who can ask the right questions, uncover the most important weaknesses, help solve the most difficult challenges, and help break down internal barriers within the organization – all in support of creating a better solution.

3. Social execution

The same customer group that you may have spent time with, seeking to understand, now requires education to show them that they really need the solution that all of their actions and behaviours indicated they needed at the beginning of the process. This social execution includes social outputs like trials, beta programs, trade show booths and more. Great innovators have the patience to allow a new market space to mature, and they know how to grow the demand while also identifying the key shortcomings with customers who are holding the solution back from mass acceptance.

While I wrote these words in relation to insight and to innovation in general, they apply to OI as well. You must also remember that these three phases are not completely discrete. New insights and innovation ideas do not just emerge in the social inputs phase, but can also expose themselves in other phases – if you're paying attention. Flickr changed its business model and strategy during the social execution phase from online gaming to online photo sharing when it recognized the most used feature was one that allowed people to share photos, and that people were using it to share photos that had nothing to do with the game. You can see the opportunities that can be harvested or wasted depending on whether you take a haphazard approach to OI or a holistic and strategic one.

A strategic approach to Open Innovation

If you choose to jump into OI and throw up an electronic suggestion box that is open to the world without laying any strategy and process groundwork (ideally by running an internal innovation effort with employees first), then you are likely to fail. Also, if you choose to keep things small and throw out an innovation challenge through an innovation intermediary (Innocentive, Idea Connection, Hypios, Nine Sigma, etc) either without making the challenge selection based on a clear innovation vision, strategy and goals, or without first preparing the organization to take on board a successful challenge solution, you are also likely to fail.

What this means is that you must instead take a measured, strategic approach to OI, including matching up your OI effort to a pre-existing innovation vision, strategy and goals. This can be done by asking yourself a series of questions that I like to classify into a simple why/when/what/who/where/how framework. Some of these include:

- Why
  - Why are we pursuing OI?
  - Why is OI a key part of our overall innovation strategy?
  - Why should people want to give us their ideas?
- When
  - When will we be ready to pursue OI?
  - When will we have our idea gathering tools in place?
  - When will we have our idea selection policies in place?
  - When will we have our idea development processes in place?

     – When will we have our marketing and communications strategy and infrastructure in place?
- What
  - What kind of innovation is the focus of our OI effort?
  - What do we hope to gain from OI?
  - What value will we provide to make people want to participate?
- Who
  - Who do we want to participate in our OI effort?
  - Who will be selecting the ideas to pursue?
  - Who will be developing the ideas selected?
- Where
  - Where will we find our targeted participants?
  - Where should we invest our communication efforts (which channels)?
- How
  - How will we know when we have been successful?
  - How will we encourage our targeted participants to participate?

A holistic approach to Open Innovation

To take a holistic approach to OI, you must involve a number of different organizational departments from the very beginning, including:

- Public Relations: Broadcast your efforts through appropriate news sources and online channels.
- Marketing: Target and communicate with your intended audience (e-mail, advertising, social media, etc), evaluate market opportunities for ideas, etc.
- R&D: Establish teams to evaluate technical feasibility, combine and complete partial solutions, evolve proposed solutions, etc.
- Finance: Assist with market projections, financials, budgets, capital, metrics, etc.
- Operations: Evaluate ability to manufacture proposed product solution or to scale proposed service solution, assist with production cost estimates, etc.
- Human Resources: Ensure that resource flexibility exists to staff chosen innovation development projects, up to and possibly including the hiring of idea submitters, etc.
- Legal: Create appropriately flexible but secure partnership agreements, verify intellectual property (IP) ownership, etc.

Much as diversity of thought is one of the keys to successful innovation, involving a diverse set of functions in crafting your strategic approach to OI means you'll increase the likelihood that your OI effort will be a success.

Mobilizing for success

To start a conversation about success – whether business success, marketing success, innovation success, or personal success – I have to jump back to my two guiding principles that are most likely to create success: *increase value* and *reduce friction*. Because we are talking about OI, let's examine each principle in turn as they relate to OI.

Increase value

No matter how hard we try to get around it, people always want to know what's in it for them. This doesn't mean that you have to pay people to get good ideas in an OI effort. There are many types of value that people can receive from participating in an OI effort, including:

- recognition from the organization;
- recognition from their peers;
- monetary rewards;
- a chance to do good;
- competitive drive;
- a chance to belong;
- an opportunity to use latent skills or passions;
- an opportunity to collaborate;
- an opportunity to bring something new to the world.

As you can imagine, it is very difficult to help the targeted participants manifest all of these different types of value, so you have to design your OI effort to focus on just a few of them. Smartly designed, you can actually focus on more than one, so I won't say you can only focus on one type of perceived value.

OI is a social media activity. Because of this, organizing your community and considering your audience are your keys to success. If you do a good job of creating value for the targeted participants, you will then be able to activate your community and pull in the ideas and solutions that you seek to your organization.

Reduce friction

Every interaction between individuals, or between individuals and organizations, has a certain level of inherent friction. This is because individuals have different goals and extract value from the exchange in different ways. The actions of an organization can either work to increase the friction of the OI effort with the targeted participants (and make it seem like too much trouble), or to reduce the friction (and make it easier to participate). You must always remember that your targeted participants have lots of ways of using their attention, their time and their mental effort. Your goal is to make it as easy to participate as possible.

One way to reduce friction is to focus on telling the story of your OI quest in a clear and compelling way that will resonate with your targeted participants (given the sources of value that you choose to focus on). Another way to reduce friction is to clearly state the rules of engagement up-front, so that the expectations of your targeted participants are set accurately. The legal department can be instrumental in either increasing or reducing the friction of an OI effort. Careful attention must be paid to appropriately balancing the risks, probabilities and impacts of the potential IP questions.

Bringing it all together

So, please lay the groundwork for your successful OI effort through a strategic and holistic approach that has the marketing and R&D folks working together with lots of the other functions to craft an OI vision, strategy and goals that tie into the organization's innovation vision, strategy and goals. And never forget that innovation is social and so you should focus on your audience, and to have success you must aim to increase value and reduce friction. Do all of this together through a compelling story told through consistent communications to your targeted participants, and you will have a much higher chance of OI success. May your innovation collaborations outside your four walls be fruitful and multiply!

Chapter 5
Start at the End

DAVID SIMOES-BROWN AND ROLAND HARWOOD

We tend to think of innovation as starting at the beginning, with an invention or a eureka moment. To make Open Innovation a success it is critical that we think in reverse and start at the end.

In common with good product design practice, all innovation has to fulfil an unmet need. For example, diabetics used to have to go to a doctor every day to be injected with insulin. This was so inconvenient to one 'lead user' that he trained to become a doctor for seven years so that he could inject himself. Hence, self-injection of insulin was born. This is an extreme example but it illustrates that we must start with the demand rather than the supply of ideas. OI adds another twist to starting at the end: the unmet needs of the partners in the collaboration must also be fulfilled.

This chapter unpacks two themes within the 'starting at the end' approach to OI. First, it means that we need to clearly understand the end goals for our partners and become adept at setting and working towards clear and measurable shared rewards. Second, we need to fully appreciate the motivations of such partners in order to build the effective collaborations upon which OI depends. We call this 'business empathy'; it is built on a solid foundation of mutual understanding and is what generates the necessary level of trust for successful OI.

Measuring shared rewards

Many organizations are beginning to embrace more open and collaborative approaches to innovation. Inspired by the success of open source products such as the Apache web server and the Firefox browser, many multinational companies such as P&G, Orange and IBM have made 'open innovation' – the sharing of the risks and rewards of the product development process with partners – a top priority. Yet such a sharing of risks and rewards often throws up difficulties as a business partnership develops. 'How can we compare your risk with mine?' 'Are my rewards in the same form as yours?' 'How can I be sure that my costs won't rise?' In fact when companies are forced to evaluate these questions with external partners they are often forced to realize that their own internal innovation metrics are poor and incomplete.

Firms spend billions on innovation – between 7 and 8 per cent of turnover in traditional industries and 12 and 15 per cent in high-tech sectors. But is this seen as an investment or a cost? A sobering fact from a 2007 BCG survey shows that only 37 per cent of company execs are satisfied with the way they measure innovation. Those measures that do exist rely overly on keeping tabs on spending. Compared to capital investment, overheads or even marketing communications, innovation can seem more like an act of faith than a business process. In the frontier of OI we have an opportunity to start afresh. A true appreciation of the new benefits and costs of innovating with others will help these collaborations make the transition from marginal to mainstream.

The whole subject of metrics might seem like one for the inno-nerds. In fact, it is key for the survival of every business. The more sophisticated your process for measuring innovation, the more you can control the apparently uncontrollable. Setting goals and measuring progress towards them enables you to flex your tactics before mistakes become expensive or great ideas are buried – all within the comforting context of an overall plan. The 100 per cent Open Innovation Challenge project for P&G is an example of such a strategy. The goal for return-on-investment was clearly defined as US$100 million new products from the wellness and laundry sectors. Together with P&G we also set expectations for the number of entries, the short list and the sorts of partnership models we were aiming for. As another measure of efficiency, P&G remarked that it would have cost four times as much to source ideas of such quality using its usual methods.

Of course, one of the most exciting things about innovation is its unpredictability and many will argue that too much measurement stifles it. So can metrics tell you which innovations will go on to be successful? Accurately picking winners is largely impossible, but setting a strategy will at least help you control the 'I' of ROI and maximize the 'R', giving better value. And as innovation is a cyclical process you will also be arming yourself with benchmarks for future Rs – and also establishing whether you are getting better at innovating.

The most widespread measure of innovation is total funds invested in growth projects (71 per cent of firms; BCG, 2007). If a marketing director relied on the simple cost of advertising campaigns to justify the expenditure, he or she would not have a budget for long. Those firms that measure more than cost do indeed look at a variety of metrics, such as profit, idea generation, selection and time to market. However, it's not sophisticated – most companies have fewer than five such measures. No wonder that in constrained times innovation is one of the first activities to be cut. Perhaps if firms looked at innovation with more rigour and higher expectations it would be the last.

There are a few shining examples of a more developed approached. The Real Options methodology for evaluating potential treats innovations like a financial option contract. 3M has used an independent outside team to predict the probability of success for new R&D projects and prioritize the projects in which to invest. Some companies such as Apple search for 'key value commodities' to create products that meet unspoken need such as 'coolness', a commodity that Steve Jobs has been able to mass market.

TABLE 5.1 Innovation value

Innovation Benefits	Innovation Costs
Percentage of sales and profit from new products	Total funds invested
Sustainability of revenue	Ideation, R&D
Diversity of innovation	Incentives
Strategic alignment	Time to market
Product quality and reliability	Production
Idea generation and selection	Distribution and marketing
Stock value	Opportunity costs
Increase in knowledge	Potential loss of share
Intellectual property	
Customer satisfaction and loyalty	
New customers, new segments	
Reputation and brand image	
Ease of recruitment	
Product distribution	
Price elasticity	

Table 5.1 contains a checklist of the sorts of direct and indirect measures that firms can use to capture all the value that innovation brings. The list of benefits and costs also holds true for OI. You will want to profit from collaborations and there will still be the usual associated costs. Given the motivations to collaborate (better innovations delivered cheaper and faster) you would expect the benefits to be larger and the costs smaller with OI. Interestingly, firms we've worked with such as Virgin Atlantic and Orange concur, reporting that they get more discontinuous innovations, cheaper and often faster.

However, measuring OI is a new field and consequently even less developed. There are three sets of factors unique to OI. First, aligning the metrics of both parties is important, so the partners continue to get what they need out of the relationship and remain keen. Second, measuring the health and strength of the relationships is vitally important because this is the glue that holds collaborations together. Third, we must learn to value networks and factor in the anticipation of future rewards from them. So Table 5.2 contains a list additional to the usual measures that helps OI to be more accountable.

Given that OI involves innovating with others, the key observation is that you need to measure each factor from two (or more) points of view. There are two sets of profit metrics, two sets of costs and two markedly different levels of risk. So the first decision to make is how transparent each partner wants to be about sharing these. In fact this is an entirely healthy, albeit rare, conversation as it ensures that objectives and processes are aligned in some detail, avoiding uncomfortable 'moments of truth' halfway through the relationship. These conversations should encompass the envisaged business model and IP strategy, as well as who shoulders which costs and risks at what points in the relationship. Our corporate collaboration project with McLaren and NATS, via the HI Network, exemplified this. The two organizations worked closely together in a mutual and flexible business partnership in order to repurpose Formula One race control software to power air traffic control.

How do we measure the relationship itself? The metrics of closed innovation have parallels in open systems. For example, customer satisfaction is broadened to include the satisfaction levels of your partners or network; brand reputation is augmented by a firm's reputation as a trustworthy partner. In practical terms, enhanced trustworthiness may well increase your chance of seeing new opportunities before your competitors. By leading the charge in OI, P&G is seeking to be the partner of choice in key business sectors. On the cost side of the equation, the time to market and ease of decision making need to be viewed in the context of partnerships – both can take longer. We found this in our Open Alchemy project in which Oracle, the NHS, Pfizer and BT joined forces to create the national wellness scheme, Wellbe. This successful outcome would not have been achieved without careful attention paid to the roles of each company, their expectations and the practicalities of running a consortium.

How can we value our OI networks? Entrepreneurs and inventors tend to innovate serially. As in the examples set by Hasbro and GSK, it can pay dividends to cultivate long-lasting relationships with such a network. This being the case, measures of the size, connectedness, diversity and quality of OI networks make sense. In our Open Ventures Challenge with Cancer Research UK, we created a 600-strong network that was tasked to crowdsource new ventures. Along the way to the successful birth of five of these, we measured and benchmarked community growth, rate of ideation, comments, member reputations and the level of buzz. These same observations about measuring external networks also hold true inside large firms. But how many identify and cultivate their 'intrapreneurs' or appreciate, measure and grow the innovation mindsets of their employees? Valuing our networks will also give the added benefits of easier and more regular filling of the innovation pipeline with better ideas, many of which may be submitted unprompted.

TABLE 5.2 Open Innovation value

Benefits	Costs
Two sets of profit	A shared set of costs
Partner satisfaction	Two perspectives on risk
Network engagement	Costs of crowdsourcing
Trustworthiness	Networks and scouting
Seeing new opportunities first	Venturing
Time to market	Partnering
Ease of decision making	IP and legal
Employees focused on core	Managing relationships
Network size and connectedness	
Network diversity and quality	
Employee innovative capacity	
Better ideas submitted	
Scientific value	

In conclusion on metrics, it is time for innovation to become a true part of a firm's core growth strategy rather than a kind of corporate hobby. NESTA's work on a national innovation index has started defining scores that can compare the innovation fitness of different firms and sectors. Perhaps having to make the case for OI in a more rigorous way will also rub off on traditional innovation.

More effective collaborations

We have seen that we need to start at the end by clearly understanding and measuring the business goals for our partners. The other half of successful OI is on a more human level: the need to fully appreciate the motivations of our partners, a business empathy that leads to effective collaborations.

The last few years has seen the rise of numerous OI and crowdsourcing initiatives such as Ideastorm and TopCoder. These have undoubtedly been successful in part due to their novelty of approach, but if OI is to deliver sustainable business advantage then we need a better understanding of what motivates contributors to these initiatives. If we don't, there is a risk of a backlash against them if it is perceived that big brands are getting 'something for nothing'. Our experience has shown us that the following steps should be observed when embarking upon an OI programme.

First, start new conversations. Most large organizations are extremely difficult to talk to. The official communication channels are rigid and restrictive and it often feels to the outsider that they are trying to prevent communication rather than encourage it. What would happen if the customer service strategy and the innovation strategy were more closely integrated? For instance, Frank Eliason of Comcast has been described in *Business Week* as the most famous customer service manager in the world. His strategic use of Twitter to search for people talking about its products, often negatively, engages his company proactively in trying to solve its problems or deliver a better service. Furthermore, it needs to be easy to contribute to OI invitations. One indisputable trait of innovative people and organizations is that they have lots of ideas, many of which are mediocre, but a few that – with a whole lot of iteration, socialization and combination - can have real impact. Therefore it is crucial in any OI project or process to encourage quantity of ideas before quality. If incentives are aligned around quality first, this will inhibit contributions. Therefore we need to make sure that it is easy to engage and that all contributions are at least recognized and preferably rewarded. The consumer-focused Mystarbucksidea platform does at least recognize contributions even if many of the ideas do appear to be about Frappacinos!

Second, we need to ask more engaging questions. It's never hard to get people to help you out if you ask them a really great question that forces them to tap into their knowledge and creativity. However, most OI programmes start with a vague question (ie, bring me your good ideas) or too specialist a question. The art to writing a good brief is to find the sweet spot between the two. For example, Karim Lakhani and Robert Wolf conducted a web-based survey of 684 software developers to seek to understand what motivates contributions to open source projects. They found that the only significant determinants of hours per week dedicated to projects were, in order of magnitude of impact: a) enjoyment, b) meaningful rewards (such as payments or prizes) and c) a sense of community.

Third, shift your focus from 'what' to 'who'. The cost associated with finding new knowledge is falling fast, to a point where in the not too distant future we can reasonably assume that all knowledge will be in principle accessible – quite possibly violating various intellectual property rights and other constraints, but nonetheless available. In this scenario our knowledge will no longer differentiate us as individuals or organizations. Rather it will be our network, and our reputation within it, which will be the key to innovation.

Open innovators therefore must ask more 'who' questions instead of just 'what' questions. In other words, focusing as much on whom we should innovate with, as what specific innovation needs or opportunities we have. For example, our Virgin Atlantic project was to develop new social media applications by first engaging frequent fliers and actively seeking to buy services and ideas from them in addition to selling to them as customers. This is a significant shift from the traditional idea-led approach to innovation and resulted in eight new innovations being developed quickly and at a fraction of the cost of a traditional in-house innovation process. IDEO, the legendary design company, is famous for recruiting 'T-shaped' people, namely those who can demonstrate both depth of expertise and breadth of interests/ networks. Ultimately, all organizations will have to become more 'T-shaped' than they are in recognition of the fact that their next big innovation opportunity, or new competition, will increasingly come from outside of their core domain of expertise.

Fourth, we need to focus less on ownership and more on access. Traditional economics of supply and demand operate when the dominant mode of consumption is through ownership of scarce products and services. However, in a world where the core asset is our knowledge and ideas, there is no such scarcity. Here, the most efficient mode of consumption is through access to products and services where the revenue streams come usually from a combination of usage, donation and advertising.

For example, Streetcar offers a pay-as-you-go car service in urban areas, as a more cost-effective alternative to car ownership. Similarly, the music industry, a reluctant trailblazer in reinventing business models due to the web, has seen the rise of access-based business models such as Spotify (the music streaming service) and artists such as Prince and Radiohead who give away their music for free, and derive their income by other means such as concerts. Really valuable ideas such as oral rehydration therapy, essentially just water and glucose, saves millions of lives and their value lies precisely in the fact that they aren't protected.

It is perhaps surprising that the public sector is arguably leading the way with opening up access to public data through initiatives such as the Open Data movement. Most organizations still default to secrecy and only ever open up when they are required to. Legislation such as the Freedom of Information Act is slowly forcing public bodies to default to a more transparent mode of operation where access to certain information is only restricted (at least in theory) in exceptional cases.

In the private sector we are seeing many examples of the value in partnerships deriving from the co-delivery of a product or service, rather than the outright ownership of intellectual property. Our OSCR project for Orange and our Open Ventures Challenge for Cancer Research UK were more than a search for ideas from the crowd. They set out to find solid, mutually rewarding business partnerships in which attaining intellectual property was not the main goal.

In summary, to make OI a success it is critical that we think in reverse and start at the end. We need to clearly understand the needs of consumers and the end goals of our partners, and set out clear and measurable shared rewards. We then need to develop business empathy to establish the effective collaborations upon which OI depends.

Chapter 6
Institutionalizing Open Innovation

STEVEN GOERS PHD

S uccess in Open Innovation requires significant cultural and behavioural changes across your organization. Developing the best tools, processes and operating models alone is not a guarantee of success. Addressing people's early and often internal behavioural 'derailers' and building a culture that focuses on what innovation is versus where it was developed is vital to leveraging the potential of OI. The principles and approaches of OI are best viewed as complementary enablers to the internal innovation capability of your organization. Harnessing the power of your organization's internal innovation networks complemented with tapping into vast external networks is the recipe for success and competitive advantage.

Embedding OI into how everyone innovates is the vision of the OI team at Kraft Foods. Getting there is hard and Kraft Foods is still early in its journey. About four years ago, Kraft Foods R&D made the strategic decision to put more focus, rigor and discipline into our OI efforts. The intent of this chapter is to share some of our approaches and what we learnt about institutionalizing OI into our innovation process.

Making the case

Kraft Foods is building a global snacks powerhouse and an unrivalled portfolio of brands. With approximately US$48 billion in revenue, we're the world's second largest food company and the largest in North America. We're the largest in global confectionery and biscuits with sales in approximately 170 countries. We have a long history of developing innovative products, with more than 3,000 scientists and engineers based in 15 R&D research centres around the globe. Kraft Foods holds the third largest global patent estate in food/beverage with the Number1 position in North America.

In summary, Kraft Foods is a large, global company with iconic and powerful brands and a strong innovative R&D organization. So, what's the issue? Our corporate strategy is to deliver 5 per cent+ organic growth rate. For Kraft

Foods, that translates into generating approximately US$2.5billion in new revenue every year – that's the equivalent of creating a new Fortune 1000 company year after year. To deliver this level of new revenue, there is no question that Kraft Foods must effectively harness the innovation horsepower of our R&D organization. But, will this be sufficient? The rapid pace of innovation, rising costs of innovation, the 'need for speed' and the downward pressure on R&D budgets all make a compelling case for OI. To be successful, we must complement our internal mastery in core areas with the vast array of external innovation that exists.

How vast is that external innovation? The chart in Figure 6.1 has been the single most powerful vehicle to communicate our case: it clearly identifies our call to action. To be successful, we must tap into the vast streams of intellectual property and innovation that exist outside our company. OI is the way forward.

Defining Open Innovation

OI is first and foremost a mindset and an approach to how you innovate. It's based on the premise that there exists, outside of our company, a solution (or partial solution) to our challenges and strategic needs. OI is about making connections and collaborating to realize a win-win outcome. One of the most powerful messages we communicated to the R&D organization was when we changed our positioning statement from 'OI will ...,' to 'The principles and approaches of OI will ...'. This may seem to be a subtle change, but it sent a strong message to our organization that OI is not a standalone function/group approach to how everyone needs to be innovating. Ultimately, our success lies in embedding the principles of OI with everyone's innovation toolkit (more on this later).

It is also helpful to the organization to explain what OI is not. OI is not new. Kraft Foods has a long history of forging external partnerships to drive growth – we just didn't call it OI at the time. In our coffee business, we've had a long standing partnership with Starbucks where Kraft Foods markets and distributes Starbucks packaged coffee into retail grocery stores – and it's a profitable win-win for both companies. To develop and launch Tassimo, a revolutionary single-cup hot beverage system, Kraft Foods partnered with a brewing manufacturer and distributor to introduce Tassimo products across Europe and North America. It's another terrific example of OI before the term was even being used. So, while we have some history in developing these relationships, they have primarily been opportunistic. Going forward, we need to consider OI as a strategic business imperative.

OI is not about out-sourcing or marginalizing R&D. It is critically important to reinforce within the organization that OI is about elevating R&D to increase the scientist's or developer's value by expanding their capability and capacity to innovate. The new paradigm for R&D employees needs to be that their value is determined not only by what they know but also who they know.

FIGURE 6.1 External vs internal innovation

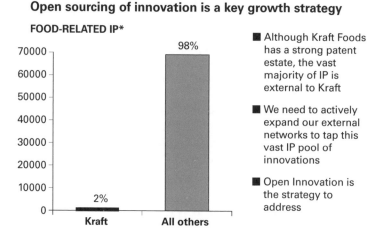

Open sourcing of innovation is a key growth strategy

FOOD-RELATED IP*

- Although Kraft Foods has a strong patent estate, the vast majority of IP is external to Kraft

- We need to actively expand our external networks to tap this vast IP pool of innovations

- Open Innovation is the strategy to address

* From 1990–2007. Food Related means patents coded with International Patent Classficiation A21/A22/A23 or US Classification 426. US, Europe and PCT.

So, OI is about doing more with existing relationships, external networking and building new capabilities. It's about complementing and extending our internal innovation horsepower. And, it's a mindset, belief and approach to how we innovate.

Start small, get focused, build capability, get some wins and then expand

While our vision is to have the principles of OI fully embedded with how everyone innovates at Kraft Foods, we recognize that this is a journey and will take time to institutionalize. On this journey, we began by starting small and establishing a tight group of dedicated people who would champion and drive the principles and approaches of OI. Finding experienced, passionate people who are comfortable working in new and ambiguous environments is essential. However, it is important to channel their passion and drive towards opportunities that 'really matter'. We learnt this lesson the hard way, and we're still learning! Early on, we scouted external networks and found many innovative and potentially disruptive technologies we could apply across our food and beverage categories. But translating that enthusiasm from our OI team to our internal business partners often proved quite difficult. That is, if an opportunity didn't clearly align with an existing priority, it meant a low probability of success in getting internal engagement and resource commitment to pursue it. We certainly don't want to dismiss opportunistic finds, but it's critically important to focus our primary efforts on proactive prospecting to answer defined needs (that is, what really matters).

With this in mind, we refocused our efforts on strengthening the alignment of our OI priorities against the defined business needs (a pull vs push strategy). In doing so, we've found success, particularly with our suppliers. Much of our early success in OI has come from working more collaboratively and innovatively with our suppliers. We've learnt that our suppliers have terrific innovation capability. And we're moving beyond the more typical transactional relationships to more innovation and collaboration relationships. By sharing more of our strategy, being less prescriptive in our needs and working together, we've been able to expand our capacity to develop new products, gain access to new technology enablers and increase our speed to market.

A great example of the power of supplier-based innovation is our 'Supplier challenge' process. The process is outlined in Figure 6.2.

In a supplier challenge, a brief is developed that describes a specific product/package need, consumer insight and boundaries for success. Importantly, the ownership for the brief lies in our marketing group – which is critical for ensuring ownership of the outcomes. Suppliers are asked to develop solutions against the brief. Suppliers present their solutions at a showcase event day for senior business management. And to put skin in the game and encourage suppliers to provide their best innovations, Kraft Foods commits to a 30-day go/no-go decision. If we decide not to proceed, the supplier is free to look elsewhere with its innovation. Knowing that Kraft Foods will commit to a decision within 30 days really helps with supplier engagement. So far, we've conducted more than 100 challenges globally, and we've launched many new products with more in the pipeline.

So while we've demonstrated success by tightening our OI and business linkages, we've discovered an important watch-out. The closer we get to aligning our OI efforts to specific business needs, the more incremental and smaller the opportunities tend to become. In hindsight, we should have anticipated this scenario given that the time horizons of our business innovation needs are relatively short. Our ongoing challenge is to seek the right balance between direct support for specific business needs and prospecting for bigger, more game-changing innovations that OI can deliver. To this end, our OI team also partners with strategic, longer-term enabling technology groups to identify external sourcing solutions. Regardless of the internal partner, matching the specific need and level of OI 'maturity' to the type of prospecting approach is important for achieving alignment and engagement. Figure 6.3 demonstrates the value creation that OI can provide and is a useful guide for aligning on the most appropriate approach to take to solve the need.

To build capability in leveraging OI, we needed to address three fundamental pillars of innovation:

1 *Tools* – developing and extending our internal and external networks to mine what we know, what others know and how to connect and

FIGURE 6.2 The 'Supplier challenge' process

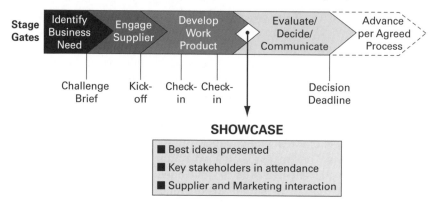

Supplier Challenge

Disciplined approach ensures engagement and internal urgency

Stage Gates

| Identify Business Need | Engage Supplier | Develop Work Product | Evaluate/ Decide/ Communicate | Advance per Agreed Process |

Challenge Brief | Kick-off | Check-in | Check-in | Decision Deadline

SHOWCASE

- Best ideas presented
- Key stakeholders in attendance
- Supplier and Marketing interaction

FIGURE 6.3 The value creation that OI can provide

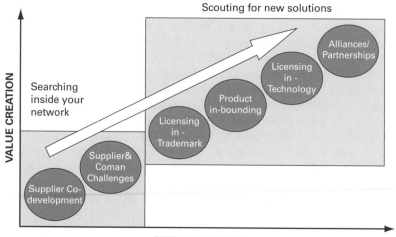

Open Innovation Driving Value Creation

Scouting for new solutions

VALUE CREATION

Searching inside your network

- Alliances/ Partnerships
- Licensing in - Technology
- Product in-bounding
- Licensing in - Trademark
- Supplier & Coman Challenges
- Supplier Co-development

DIFFICULTY & TIME

collaborate. To this end, we developed a suite of enabling tools by first matching a vendor with a receptive internal partner and then, where successful, expanding the use of the tool/capability across the organization.

2 *Processes* – supportive and collaborative business frameworks to enable OI. Rather than create new processes, we've found it to be more effective to integrate OI into existing business processes.

3 *Culture* – encouraging 'proudly found elsewhere', recognizing and rewarding desired behaviours, focusing on the 'what' vs the 'where', embracing the principle of needing to give to receive, storytelling successes, and communicating … communicating … communicating.

Developing the desired OI behaviours in the organization is by far the most important criterion of success, and by far the most difficult to achieve. Deep-rooted norms and expectations in how innovation and technology/ product development are conducted need to be changed. As many others facing this challenge will attest, the corporate 'antibodies' resisting change can be quite strong and pervasive. But addressing these derailers is critical to leading culture change. Figure 6.4 shows some common derailers we've found and how we've tried to address them. In speaking to the organization, I use these examples to show how we need to think and act differently.

Institutionalizing Open Innovation

Expanding the adoption and use of OI beyond a core group of advocates is essential to achieving our vision and realizing widespread business value. If the premise of OI as a mindset and approach to how you innovate is correct, then everyone in the organization needs to think and act that way and fully embed the principles of OI into their project work. In benchmarking other leading OI-enabled organizations, we have found that the 'hub and spoke' organizational model is a best practice. The hub functions as the central core team developing the strategy, goals and governance for the organization. The hub builds the capabilities the organization will need and drives the desired culture change. The spokes are OI scouts who are embedded, and line-managed, in the individual business units or COEs (Centres of Excellence – R&D organizations focused on global category technology platform development). The spokes play the critical role of being the local champion and advocate for their business. Spokes are responsible for scouting and prospecting against specific needs of their business. They're also responsible for fast-adapting and transferring best practices, tools and learning from the hub and the other spokes. The hub and spoke functions collectively as a community of practice – meeting regularly to share and transfer learning and align on our organization's needs. For Kraft Foods, where we have geographically dispersed business units that are independently led with full P&L accountability, the hub and spoke model has proven invaluable to advancing the OI strategies and engaging more OI champions to help facilitate adoption and use. The hub and spoke structure in place at Kraft Foods is shown in Figure 6.5.

FIGURE 6.4 Addressing common derailers

Addressing the culture...

'I was hired to create'

What you create is equally important as what you **find** and who you know

'Didn't find internal solution – lets now look external'

Build OI strategies into business plans

'We need to own the IP'

You need **rights to use** of IP

'OI is what they (that group) do'

OI needs to be embedded into how **everyone** innovates

The hub and spoke model has been a key enabler in facilitating the use of OI across our R&D organization. However, to fully embrace the principles of OI across the global R&D enterprise, we needed to find a way to embed it into everyone's job description. The way forward came from directly linking OI to the organization's mission, vision and strategy. Kraft Foods' higher purpose is: 'Make Today Delicious'. R&D's mission is: 'We Invent Delicious.' Our vision statement speaks to the importance of 'leveraging our collective know-how to seek the best solutions, whether internal or external'. We named the approach we developed to link OI to our higher purpose the 'Inventing Delicious Framework'.

FIGURE 6.5 Kraft Foods' 'Hub and spoke' structure

Get organized and drive adoption:
Internal 'Hub & Spoke' Network design

- **HUB**
Tools, Process, Culture
- Builds organizational capabilities and networks
- Scouts for game changers and new business partnerships
- Governance and metrics
- Lead OI Community of Practice

- **SPOKE**
Scout, Content, Collaborate
- Identifies key business unit priorities
- Scouts for opportunities (suppliers, innovation brokers, licensing, game-changers)
- OI champion/change agent

Inventing Delicious Framework

The Inventing Delicious Framework was developed as the 'how to' guide to achieve our mission: We Invent Delicious. OI is one of three core competencies that are mission-critical for the R&D organization:

1 Knowledge management (the documentation and reuse of information and intelligence).

2 Open innovation (the consideration and integration of external solutions and capabilities).

3 Intellectual property management (the development of IP strategy and assessment of freedom to operate).

The purpose of the Framework is to strengthen how we innovate by integrating the competencies and best practices of knowledge management (KM), open innovation (OI) and intellectual property (IP) into the technology development process. The Framework shows the organization that OI is a key competency and, importantly, an integral element of the discovery/development process. The Framework's key elements are shown in Figure 6.6.

To bring the Framework to life and empower our organization, we created in-depth workshops with every business unit, R&D Centre of Excellence and functional group. The three higher level questions – What do we know? What

FIGURE 6.6 The Inventing Delicious Framework's key elements

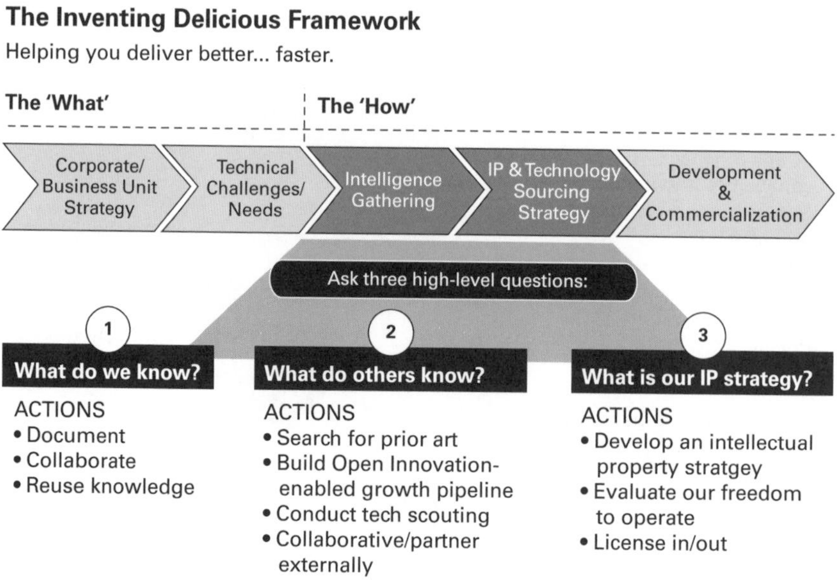

The Inventing Delicious Framework
Helping you deliver better... faster.

The 'What'		The 'How'		
Corporate/ Business Unit Strategy	Technical Challenges/ Needs	Intelligence Gathering	IP & Technology Sourcing Strategy	Development & Commercialization

Ask three high-level questions:

1 What do we know?

ACTIONS
- Document
- Collaborate
- Reuse knowledge

2 What do others know?

ACTIONS
- Search for prior art
- Build Open Innovation-enabled growth pipeline
- Conduct tech scouting
- Collaborative/partner externally

3 What is our IP strategy?

ACTIONS
- Develop an intellectual property stratgey
- Evaluate our freedom to operate
- License in/out

do others know? What is our IP strategy? – are further broken down into more specific questions. These questions prompt the developer to ensure that his or her project is being addressed in the most efficient and effective manner and that they're using the full arsenal of innovation-enablers. To aid the scientist or engineer, we developed an 'answer' toolkit – an internal website that provides links to relevant information, subject matter experts, external vendors, and more. The Framework is not only for the developer – it's also for the manager, because manager support and reinforcement of the Framework are critical to widespread adoption and use. We expect managers to reinforce the Framework's principles, create accountability and proactively communicate and embed it in their organizations.

Where are we?

The Inventing Delicious Framework is our key strategic initiative to help institutionalize OI across Kraft Foods. As mentioned earlier, we're on a journey and we're still early on the path to achieving our vision. We've made good progress, but we still have a way to go to achieve our desired culture change and demonstrate sustained, game-changing innovations realized from OI. Figure 6.7 summarizes our progress.

The ultimate measure of success will be demonstrating sustained business value creation via OI. To get there, we will need to stay the course and build on the foundations in place.

FIGURE 6.7 Progress made in institutionalizing OI

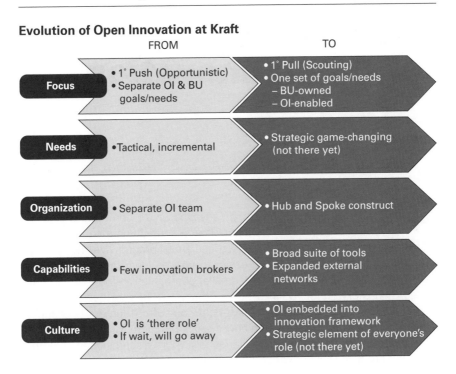

Evolution of Open Innovation at Kraft

FROM — TO

Focus
- 1° Push (Opportunistic)
- Separate OI & BU goals/needs

- 1° Pull (Scouting)
- One set of goals/needs
  - BU-owned
  - OI-enabled

Needs
- Tactical, incremental

- Strategic game-changing (not there yet)

Organization
- Separate OI team

- Hub and Spoke construct

Capabilities
- Few innovation brokers

- Broad suite of tools
- Expanded external networks

Culture
- OI is 'there role'
- If wait, will go away

- OI embedded into innovation framework
- Strategic element of everyone's role (not there yet)

Chapter 7
The Strategic Context for Open Innovation

ANDREW GAULE

H ugely increased computing power, advances in telecommunications and networking technology, offshoring, lean manufacturing, smart logistics, trade liberalization and harmonization – these are all progressive changes that now make it cheaper, quicker and easier to take an idea from conception to the point of sale. As a consequence, smaller companies are now often better placed than their bigger rivals to pursue market niches, or even to disrupt whole sectors. At the same time, the behaviour of consumers is changing radically. The deluge of information now available to them, via the internet and other means, has made them, simultaneously, more discriminating and more promiscuous. If you fail to diversify your product or service portfolio adequately, they will readily go elsewhere.

You might think a sensible response to these trends would be to invest more in research and development, and thereby generate more and better ideas. This is certainly a strategy that many large companies have adopted in recent years. However, it is not enough now to guarantee sustainable growth (at least, not without a broader strategy for generating value from the innovation process), for three main reasons:

1 Generating more and better ideas does not guarantee demand for those ideas, especially given today's surplus of products and services in so many industries.

2 It is no longer the case that vertically integrated organizations can claim to be more efficient than their rivals in every stage of research, development and commercialization. Those that try to keep everything in-house risk wasting money and passing on that waste to end consumers in the form of higher prices.

3 It is now beyond the capabilities of any single organization to monopolize the knowledge in its industry.

OI is being implemented by a growing number of leading organizations and could be the antidote to many of these problems. In essence, it holds that ideas should be allowed to flow to where they can be most efficiently researched, developed and commercialized, regardless of where they originated, thereby generating maximum value for all the organizations involved.

However, research and experience working with leading organizations has shown that the basic OI theory, as defined by Professor Henry Chesbrough of the University of California, Berkeley (2003), needs to be extended to address several issues vital to a sustainable innovation process.

Scouting for technology but we need effective communication

In my view, the ideal OI system resembles a beehive. A queen bee depends on worker bees and scouts to develop an accurate picture of the external environment, while overseeing construction of the hive. Similarly, a chief executive may have no time to grasp the many external factors influencing the future of his or her organization. 'Technology scouts' and 'corporate venture capital' are a key part of the OI efforts of many leading companies. A queen bee may face questions such as: 'Where is the best source of nectar under the present circumstances?' or, 'If one plant is going out of season, should I shift my search for new food sources to another species?' Similarly, a chief executive must continually ask him- or herself the question: 'Are my markets changing to the point where I should shift resources into new lines of business?' There may even come a time when the entire hive has to be moved to ensure the survival of the swarm, analogous to the emergence of 'disruptive technology' that renders traditional core markets obsolete.

The key to success under all these circumstances is communication. When bees find a new source of nectar they communicate the discovery to their queen, and to other bees, via a complex series of movements known as the 'waggle dance'. Methods of communication that can be carried out in an organizational context need to be implemented so that senior executives are alerted to new sources of value and have all the information necessary to put the pursuit of that value in a strategic context.

How to focus your innovation efforts

What the incumbent best practice models of corporate innovation lack is a sense of market perspective. This is one of the strongest findings to emerge from research and contact with innovators at major companies. To use OI effectively, your company must concentrate not only on where new technologies are emerging but also on where new markets are possible. The old image of innovation coming through a funnel to a point that could be your usual market and business model is now too narrow. If you can improve your knowledge at both ends of the 'bow-tie' – from technology to new markets – you can become more effective at identifying value-creation opportunities throughout the process (see Figure 7.1). Thus, if a market need can be predicted far enough in advance, the need for a particular innovation can be identified. Better still, a technology already in development can be steered so that its market appeal is redirected or broadened. In this context, the essential role of any large company becomes to create links between innovation and markets, no matter where that company extracts its value.

For example, Tate & Lyle realized it needed to shift its focus from commodities to added-value products and services if it wanted to sustain its growth and competitive advantage. So, it invested more in end-consumer research. It then responded to trends in the needs of end-consumers by concentrating its innovation resources on a handful of key areas, such as nutraceuticals, and launched services to help clients incorporate ingredients in their products. However, the change was not just one of budgetary reallocation. It required major organizational restructuring – its sales people, for example, had to adapt from selling bulk commodities to selling specialized ingredients, based on a deeper understanding of end-consumers. Added-value and food ingredient business in the 2009–10 annual results account for over two-thirds of Tate & Lyle's profits; even though they account for a much smaller proportion of its sales. In 2010 Tate & Lyle announced the disposal of the sugar refining business, which is what many people associate with Tate & Lyle. To support the new technology scouting it has financed Tate & Lyle Ventures LLP with around US$40 million to look for promising new horizon technologies and businesses for corporate VC finance.

When innovations get stuck, it is often because their contribution to the overall strategic vision is not recognized or understood. Frequently, the leaders of innovation projects say: 'We don't understand where we fit.' They don't get the attention of the top people, they don't get enough 'airtime' throughout the company and, ultimately, they don't get adequate resources. It is possible, of course, that the innovations in question are worthless, or that they have the wrong people working on them. A strong idea is unlikely to succeed unless it has a 'champion' fully invested in it. However, imagining you will 'learn by doing' is a sure-fire way to waste resources. Progressing an innovation will always be an iterative process and there are always failures along the way to success, but you are unlikely to find a strategic reason for commercializing an idea in retrospect. Starting to innovate from a clearly defined area of strategic interest is far more efficient, and ensuring you have an effective structure of communication, eg between the CVC fund managers and key corporate executives is critical.

Rather than thinking about innovations in terms of 'widgets', think of them as value-delivery methods. An idea doesn't become a true innovation until it has demonstrated its ability to generate value (that is, more value than existing alternatives, or value from an entirely new source). We prefer to use the term 'thinkers' to describe those who generate ideas, and the term 'innovators' to describe those who distinguish the benefits of ideas and determine ways to realize them.

FIGURE 7.1 Creating links between innovation and markets

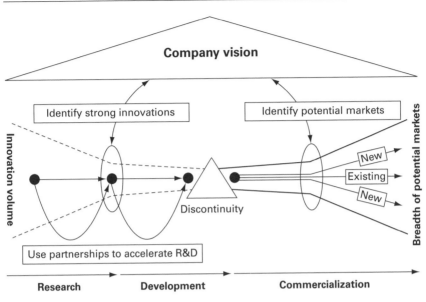

Source: Gaule, 2006

Innovation is an exercise in entrepreneurship and the 'extrapreneur'® is a necessary component for any organization wishing to become an innovation leader. An extrapreneur is someone with all the characteristics of an entrepreneur in an organization plus a set of extra skills and capabilities. He or she has strong networking, influencing, negotiating and inspiration skills; keeps an eye on markets, technologies, socioeconomic trends and best practices; provides political support and cover for innovations that require a business model or management structure different from that of the parent organization; facilitates the building of external partnerships; and maintains a clear vision of where ventures should be headed, in the medium- to long-term, as well as outlining exit strategies.

Key to building the innovation approach is building and maintaining an innovation strategy fully aligned to an overall business strategy through the '5 Ps' (see Figure 7.2):

1 *Purpose.* Why do you want your organization to be more innovative? What are your ultimate objectives for any innovation programme? What type of innovation do you need to practise?

2 *Process.* Are you observing best practice in the way you research, develop and commercialize products and services? Which additional processes may be especially suited to your industry? Could other ancillary processes be helpful?

FIGURE 7.2 Building and maintaining an innovation strategy: the 5 Ps

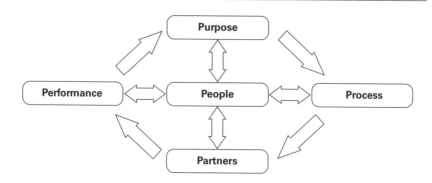

3 *People.* Do you have the human resources available to ensure innovations are supported in the right way at the right time? The people aspect is central and usually connected to each of the other key areas.

4 *Partners.* Could an external partner help you to, a) accelerate the development of certain innovations, b) unlock their value more easily, or c) provide a destination for licensing deals and divestitures?

5 *Performance.* On what performance criteria will you judge the successfulness of individual innovations? How will you judge the success of your innovation programme as a whole?

Developing the 5 Ps structure for innovation and corporate venturing approaches that an organization is implementing will provide a strategic framework and give you the 'waggle dance' to discuss with your queen bee.

Chapter 8
Leadership Issues and Challenges in the OI World

MATTHEW HEIM

Many factors in recent history have led to the need for companies to become more innovative. As markets stagnate and competition for new business continues to intensify, business leaders are now forced to identify and develop the next best thing that will attract new customers while sustaining and growing existing accounts. Open Innovation may offer an alternative to help accelerate traditional innovation pipelines. However, given the novelty of OI as a formal discipline, managers today often struggle to identify best practices that they can apply as they mobilize their organizations to go to the outside for new ideas, concepts and intellectual property.

Until the early 20th century large companies relied primarily on external research organizations to provide them with new ideas and technologies. This began to change as management theory evolved, giving way to such disciplines as division of labour and the five-year strategic plan. With division of labour came the development of core competencies, which eventually brought research and development departments into large companies. With the introduction of internal R&D, along with the five-year strategic plan, companies became ever more secretive about their new innovation pipelines and competition as we know it today was born, leading to a closed innovation paradigm that lasted well into the new millennium.

As competition levels continued to rise, product development lifecycles were accelerated to bring new products onto the market earlier, creating first-to-market advantages as well as barriers to entry for the competition. This necessitated an increase in R&D productivity within shorter development cycles, thus dramatically raising the demand and cost of R&D to the point where companies had to begin looking to the outside once again to maintain their competitive edge. OI, if executed properly, can provide new sources of ideas and technologies as well as new market channels, allowing companies to maintain their edge. But OI itself comes with its own unique set of issues and challenges. Business leaders must eventually depart from those processes, reward systems and cultural attributes that were once viewed as desirable but, in reality, work against the very idea of OI.

In this chapter we will discuss the challenges that leaders most frequently face with the rollout and management of a new OI programme, and what early adopters are doing to achieve excellence with these new initiatives. Then we will take a look at how OI is unfolding as a new management discipline, and what new hurdles may lie ahead for leaders in this space.

The new OI leaders of today are faced with high expectations of achieving breakthrough innovations within a fraction of the time that it would normally take with traditional product development processes. However, when they try to launch their new OI programmes, many are confronted with a myriad of unanticipated challenges which, unfortunately, create barriers to success. Most of these challenges can be overcome or avoided simply by being aware that they exist and then establishing measures to mitigate the risks that they present (see the latter part of this chapter for some suggestions). The most common of these challenges are described below.

Common challenges

Executive sponsorship

New OI programmes are introduced to companies in a variety of different ways. Occasionally, senior management will see the need for their company to become more innovative and mandate OI across the organization in order to accelerate innovation throughout the value chain. While this is an ideal situation for the launch of any new programme, OI is more likely to be launched at the department level by some daring manager who is willing to take the risk of trying something new. In these situations, those fearless individuals encounter countless problems and challenges that have to be solved at a grass-roots level. Without the right level of executive sponsorship in place to remove roadblocks and mandate participation, these intrepreneurs may end up spending more time trying to overcome barriers than enhancing innovation productivity. Eventually, they will either be asked to stop what they are doing or simply run out of steam.

Company-wide buy-in

When introducing OI to the company, leaders should encourage buy-in across the entire organization. However, resistance is likely to be strong from a variety of key stakeholders. For example, most R&D departments have gone through some degree of job trimming in the past few years, and those who have survived often fear that they may be next. OI is designed to help a company to extend beyond its core competencies, but if the new programme is not introduced properly, employees may be likely to perceive it as a means of replacing jobs.

Once a new programme is instituted, many R&D managers are challenged to get their innovation counterparts to look to the outside for new ideas and technologies. Most employee development systems and bonuses in these departments are aligned with first-to-patent objectives, which make OI a threat to their measured success. Finally, business leaders outside of R&D who are not educated in the benefits and methods of OI will often view it as a potential risk through which corporate plans and strategies can be leaked to the public. These scenarios are examples of the fears and concerns that have stalled the success of many well-intended OI programmes.

Finding the right people

New OI programmes most often have their origins somewhere within the R&D department. An R&D manager or director is typically chosen to scout out best practices, to begin developing both internal and external networks, and to rally people across the organization to participate. The criteria for choosing someone to spearhead such an initiative are too often based on the person's history of success with the company. However, success attributes for the R&D practitioner are not always the best for choosing an effective OI champion. For example, successful R&D practitioners are handed problems or challenges, and then expected to come up with new ways to solve them. They often work alone, or in small teams, and spend a significant portion of their time developing and testing new technologies and solutions. While scientific and technological aptitude and comprehension are important attributes for OI champions, most of their success will be dependent upon their ability to educate people in different areas of the business with different backgrounds, and to sell them on the benefits of OI. They must also interface with many different people on a daily basis to build relationships and networks that will ultimately become new sources of inspiration and solutions for the company's innovation process. People all along the innovation chain must be led (and motivated) to realize that they no longer have to be the smartest, or the one who single-handedly came up with the solution.

Developing an effective organization and processes

OI leaders must be able to develop and manage an organization and processes to support their new objectives. However, such efforts often end up in a cycle of trial-and-error when these newly minted professionals fail to find any established management theory, best practices or metrics upon which they can build their new programmes. Decisions on roles and responsibilities, whether to centralize or decentralize operations, and how to establish management reports are left to the best judgement of the initiator. OI leaders frequently build their processes around their own organization, and only recognize the value of input from other departments when they are facing unanticipated delays during technical evaluations, legal reviews and acquisition of new intellectual property. If the initial rollout is done on a company-wide scale, the mistakes resulting from such a trial-and-error-based learning curve can become very costly, and can lead to the eventual abandonment of the programme.

Finding the right tools for the right need

For years, OI has been synonymous with external R&D sourcing. More recently, new concepts and tools have been developed, such as crowdsourcing and technology intelligence that utilize OI principles to meet needs that manifest both upstream and downstream from the more common external technology search. New OI methods are beginning to replace traditional marketing tools to identify new consumer and technology trends, and to identify potential market channels. It is being used to find leaner and greener processes and technologies for manufacturing, and it is being used to find new supply sources and market-ready products to acquire. OI leaders must strive to keep up with the rapidly evolving tools that will be needed to support the increasing demands across all areas of the business.

Anticipating costs

When new OI organizations are established, cost budgeting typically includes labour and expenses associated with the management of the new process. However, departments struggle, and often battle to decide who will actually pay to acquire a newly identified technology. If OI budgeting is done in a closed loop, these types of delays are inevitable. Finger pointing begins between R&D and the business units – each insisting that the other should bear the cost of development. It is rarely a question of whether or not the company has the funds to acquire the new technology, but rather one of whose cost centre will be impacted. In the meantime, while the various departments are slugging it out, the solution provider loses interest in the deal because of the delayed decision making. Solution providers are often smaller organizations that depend on the monetization of their intellectual property, and when a deal takes too long, they are likely to withdraw and seek new and faster ways to make money.

Demonstrating success

With the recent buzz around OI, many lofty promises are being made through the media and other sources that highlight isolated success stories about a breakthrough innovation caused by OI. While this sort of Holy Grail success does occur on occasion, the majority of OI successes occur at the component level, resulting in incremental improvements. For example, a company that is working on a new product will often need a new sub-component or technology that it does not have access to, and will look to the outside to find it, rather than make it. When the company does find the solution externally, it may end up saving the company many months or even years of valuable time, as well as money. However, most leaders have a hard time measuring the overall benefit of OI in such instances, because of the complexity and sheer number of moving parts that need to come together for the final product. Measuring success at the component level can be extremely challenging. When times get tough departments are forced to demonstrate their worth and, with recent trends in downsizing, many new OI programmes were unnecessarily scrapped, merely because they were unable to adequately articulate their success.

These and other challenges that tend to surface within OI programmes can appear to be daunting to the new practitioner. But with the proper knowledge and resources, such challenges can be significantly minimized. New knowledge pertaining to OI is increasing at a rapid pace. Many new conferences and workshops oriented towards sharing best practices and case studies are offered on a regular basis. Some universities are now offering courses, and even programmes dedicated to turning out new OI professionals. It is merely a matter of time before some measured degree of normalization begins to occur within this discipline. Following are some key considerations and best practices that OI leaders can take into account now to significantly enhance the likelihood of their success.

Key considerations and best practices to enhance success

Establish OI leadership and sponsorship at all levels

OI leadership does not stop at the director or vice-president level. It must be instilled at the highest levels of the organization to ensure enterprise-wide success. Executive-level sponsorship begins with education. Executives must not only understand but also buy into the value proposition before they will commit to sponsoring the programme. With full buy-in by CEOs, CTOs, CMOs and business unit leaders, the OI champion can rely on them to remove obstacles that would otherwise block success. As their strategic objectives shift, they are likely to be more proactive in providing their business objectives and feeding new projects to the OI team. When the OI team can operate at a strategic level, success is more likely to be realized.

Create an integrated OI organization and processes

For OI to work, a company's absorptive capacity must often be increased to allow new knowledge to permeate the organization. To achieve this, the OI leader must consistently strive to ensure that bridges are built and maintained between the various functions and departments of the company. The OI leader must operate at the strategic level, gathering new business goals and objectives, and translating them into next steps in the OI process. He or she must effectively discern which initiatives are best suited for internal development and which will most likely find success through OI. The leader must ensure that inclusive processes are established to incorporate decision criteria and inputs from all parties involved in the technical and legal review, and the selection and purchase of new outside knowledge. These processes should support a service model that spans the entire value chain beginning with ideation, and expanding into market and technology research, partner search, engineering and manufacturing. Funding pools must be set aside either within the OI function or within the business units to ensure that both anticipated and unanticipated acquisitions can be made in a timely manner, without disrupting the process. OI intermediaries can be used to augment these processes, expanding to a broader, global innovation community. Intermediaries can also be used to post requests for proposal (RFPs) and challenges for highly sensitive needs, where the company does not wish to reveal its identity or discuss the product that it is developing because of potential competitive threats.

Establish appropriate metrics and reporting

There are two predominant schools of thought on how to measure OI success in an organization. The most common approach is to track individual successes (ie, actual external acquisitions) within the various stage gates of the innovation process. These successes are then compared in cost and time against an estimate of what it would have taken to develop the new capability internally. This approach requires tracking and reporting at many different levels and within the departments where OI is practised. The complexity of this micro-level approach can be overwhelming and confusing, and often leads to mixed results.

The other approach, which was first introduced by Procter & Gamble in its 'Connect & Develop' programme, is much bolder, yet less common. This approach requires an enterprise-wide mandate to seek a significant percentage of new product ideas and non-core development solutions through OI channels rather than developing them internally. With this macro-level approach, the percentage of R&D spend against revenue is benchmarked before implementing OI, and then tracked annually after the OI programme is launched. This more strategic approach is only tracked at the highest levels in the company, but in order for it to work, OI adoption must be assured across all business units of the company.

Select the right people for the job

Depending on the size and scope of the OI programme, its complexity can range from a single champion to a decentralized or multi-layered organization of senior and mid-level management, technology scouts and knowledge management experts. Regardless of the team structure and size, selecting the right people for the job can be challenging if the proper skill sets are not identified in advance. OI managers and practitioners should possess at least the following attributes:

- *Entrepreneurial mindset* – self-starter, with the ability to work in a start-up situation with limited resources.
- *Change agent* – the ability, passion and determination to drive change throughout the organization.
- *Team player* – ability and desire to enable and facilitate collaboration across various business functions and departments.
- *Process-oriented* – the ability and discipline to develop and manage enterprise-wide OI processes.
- *Listening skills* – a good listener who can comprehend and take action on complex technical requirements.
- *Articulation skills* – the ability to articulate complex technical requirements in simple terms.
- *Systems thinking* – the ability to see the patterns and trends emerging across various business units and processes.
- *Networking and communication skills* – the ability to develop and maintain internal and external networks and to join together various entities to optimize innovation.
- *Intellectual curiosity* – a natural desire to learn new concepts and technologies, and to determine how they can fit together to meet or support strategic goals and objectives.

Cultural and behavioural considerations

Despite many past attempts, corporate cultures cannot be changed in a totally controlled and predictable manner. However, individual and group behaviours can be guided in a desired direction if the proper reward systems are established. Influencing positive behaviours in support of OI can be challenging in most R&D organizations today, as their traditional rewards often work against those necessary for successful OI. For example, the key behaviour that drives success in both the business unit and the OI programme is speed – speed to acquire new knowledge, speed to develop new innovations and, ultimately, speed to market. If innovation is to be aligned with the objectives of the business, then why are so many R&D managers and practitioners still motivated based on first-to-patent or first-to-invent objectives? This first-to-market vs first-to-patent dilemma creates an obvious conflict that must be resolved for OI to work. Reward systems for the R&D professional must reflect this new direction, basing their rewards on first-to-obtain objectives, which no longer puts the onus on the R&D professional to come up with the solution in isolation, thus opening the door for collaboration with the OI team and external collaborators.

Change management and communication

The institution of any organization-wide change requires a rigorous change management programme. Because of the fears, uncertainties and doubt that new OI programmes often face, effective change management and communication must begin well in advance of launching the new initiative. Company-wide communication and training programmes can be initiated to create awareness of the new programme and to eliminate the common drivers of fear. Communication campaigns can be used to generate anticipation and excitement about the new programme across all business units and functions, as well as within the company's ecosystem of suppliers, universities and innovation partners. Well-executed guidelines on how to participate will save much time in the end, often eliminating much of the need to recruit new participants. Finally, a more detailed level of training will help users of the new process to navigate through the tools necessary to manage and track innovation projects. The end goal should be a strong sense of organizational and ecosystem readiness, buy-in and excitement about the new programme.

Utilize the right mix of OI tools and solution providers

Having the right set of tools to support the variety of innovation needs across the company is vital to obtaining and sustaining buy-in and success. Many new service providers have emerged over the past 10 years, providing software tools and intermediary services that help source external knowledge without having to invest in developing the same functions internally. Many companies use these services to either temporarily or permanently augment their OI function, thus providing more flexibility and choice. Table 8.1 provides an overview of the business departments and functions most frequently associated with the innovation cycle, their most common innovation needs, and the tools and techniques that leverage OI resources to support those needs.

Talk to others who have done it

There are now many companies that have dabbled with some sort of OI endeavour. Some of them are well on their way to creating formal organizations, processes and rollout strategies based on experiences gained from previous pilot programmes from somewhere within their organizations. These pioneers are often willing to talk about their experiences, pitfalls and best practices with others. More and more conferences are introduced each year that focus primarily on OI. These conferences are a great place to hear from the seasoned professionals, and to hear about the latest tools and techniques they are using

TABLE 8.1 Open Innovation departments, needs, tools and techniques

Department or Function	Innovation Need	Supporting Tools and Techniques
Marketing	Sourcing ideas and concepts for new innovations	• Corporate innovation websites • Crowdsourcing • Traditional consumer insights assessments • Include industrial design experts early in the conceptual phase
Marketing, R&D	Assessing the global technology landscape associated with a new product idea or direction	• Technology Intelligence landscape assessments
R&D	Seeking new knowledge, technologies or experts to support innovation	• Technology/expert search (via a 'request for proposal' (RFP) process) • Corporate innovation websites • Prize-based challenges • Ecosystem engagement
Manufacturing, Engineering	New manufacturing technologies and processes to enhance productivity, quality and sustainability	• Technology/expert search via RFP • Prize-based challenges • Ecosystem engagement

TABLE 8.1 continued

Department or Function	Innovation Need	Supporting Tools and Techniques
Supply Chain	Identify new and unique sources of supply	• Component search via RFP • Ecosystem engagement
Business Unit, Marketing	Identify new market-ready products to purchase	• New product search via RFP • Ecosystem engagement
Business Unit, Marketing	Identify new market channels for existing technologies or competencies	• Technology intelligence (assess technical compatibilities in new and adjacent markets)

to increase their innovation capacity. Whether you are just starting a new programme, or you are now considered a veteran, these conferences serve as a great venue to network with other OI practitioners and leaders to reduce the learning curve, and to remain on a path of continuous OI improvement.

Conclusion

With these initial considerations, OI leaders can jump start a new programme, avoiding many of the pitfalls that earlier adopters have encountered. Existing OI programmes can also adopt these considerations after the fact to optimize productivity and yield. There are, however, many more challenges and opportunities that will surely lie ahead as this new discipline continues to evolve. Universities, professional associations, corporations and OI service providers, as well as regional and national governments, are working diligently to aggregate, validate and disseminate best practices. The OI leader will have to keep up with these changes, as well as the growing demands for OI within their organizations.

OI leaders will have to instil a discipline of continuous improvement in their organizations to ensure that they are keeping abreast of all new capabilities so that they can introduce them proactively wherever there is a good and justifiable fit. They must avoid adopting new capabilities too early or too late, ensuring that the right tool is introduced to address the right need at the right time. Although they may have to start their new initiatives as a pilot programme, OI leaders will have to continue gathering success stories from across and outside the organization to create buy-in and motivate others to participate.

As the field of OI expands, many more companies, organizations and governments will engage in OI by posting their technology and marketing needs on their websites. New regional and national exchanges have already begun to emerge, providing new venues to communicate their government and non-profit needs, while at the same time stimulating economic growth within a targeted geography. With an increasing number of innovation portals, it will become challenging for external solution providers to effectively scan and monitor each site for new sources of opportunity. OI leaders will have to continue seeking new and efficient ways to disseminate their needs to the global innovation community.

While the issues and challenges of OI leadership are likely to persist, the potential rewards are very promising. The recent boom in OI has offered private industry, non-profit organizations, research institutions and government agencies many new opportunities for growth and development. Unobvious, cross-industry connections are being made every day through OI, narrowing the gaps that exist between the various sectors. Achieving this requires a flexible management style that can deal with ambiguity, complexity and a certain degree of risk, while bringing together people who would have normally never considered working together in the past. OI is no longer just a buzzword or a fleeting trend. It is here to stay. Those professional who are able to introduce and optimize these processes within their organizations will stand among the early adopters who have already realized the many benefits of OI success.

Chapter 9
Motivating the Crowd to Participate in Your Innovation Initiative

HUTCH CARPENTER

T he value in crowdsourcing derives from the diverse viewpoints brought to a community. Key here is the 'crowd' part of the term. There needs to be a healthy level of participation to generate sufficient input. But it's not enough to set up a community site and assume participation will take off on its own accord; there are several keys to tapping the motivations of people.

In any crowdsourcing initiative, there are two fundamental questions that must be addressed: What is the goal of the initiative? What's in it for participants? Answers to the two questions are actually intertwined, but they are distinct components. The success of any crowdsourcing initiative hinges on how they are answered.

The goal of the initiative

The end of a crowdsourcing initiative is its start. Here's what I mean. Organizations must identify what outcomes they want from the crowdsourcing initiative. What are the actions that can be taken from the initiative? Obviously, understanding the business case for the OI effort is vital to a company that must allocate finite resources.

But it's just as critical for potential participants. The first step of motivating people is to give them a clear understanding of why they should participate. What difference will it make? People won't make the effort if they see a crowdsourcing initiative as little more than a glorified discussion forum.

Here are three examples of companies and the goals (or lack thereof) they set:

1 Cisco runs an OI event called the I-Prize. This is a crowdsourcing initiative where Cisco is seeking ideas that can lead to US$1 billion businesses. Winners of the I-Prize earn a US$250,000 reward. The rules for selection are spelled out clearly. The efforts have led to nearly 2,000 ideas, and two separate initiatives that are in development at Cisco.

2 Starbucks runs My Starbucks Idea. The site asks for customers' ideas, big or small, and tells the community, 'We're ready to make ideas happen.' The site is an ongoing OI community, with over 92,000 ideas as of August 2010. Around 90 of those ideas have been implemented, reinforcing the rationale for customers to participate.

3 Fleishman Hillard ran an event called 'Innovation & Creativity Week' in April 2010. What was asked of participants was clear through five questions, including ideas for driving more innovation across the globe and for managing and protecting companies' brands. What was missing was an actionable outcome; after the week was over there were no next steps. As a result, participation was low, with only 23 ideas (many from staffers) and 37 site members. For the public at large, it was hard to see what difference their participation would have made.

A good crowdsourcing goal has two essential qualities: a clear request of the community, and clearly identified actionable outcome(s) for the best submissions.

After establishing a good, actionable goal, the next question to be considered is: What's in it for me? If I can't see how your initiative benefits me, I won't bother.

Motivations

In the preceding section, did you notice the ratios of ideas that were implemented to those that were submitted for Cisco and Starbucks? Approximately 0.1 per cent. Other OI initiatives will have higher idea acceptance rates, but will still be a low percentage. With these odds of individual success, what makes people continue to participate?

The answer is multi-faceted. Human motivation is a complex characteristic. What energizes you has no impact on me. You may have one, two or three separate motivation sources. Danish researcher Mia Reinholt (2006) talks of a motivation continuum, and identifies 10 separate motivation types. She admits there are likely more.

These variations in motivation are actually quite valuable, as they create a rich environment of different personality types, actions and cognitive diversity. They are the impetus for a range of submissions, discussions and feedback. The key in a crowdsourcing initiative is to enable different motivations to flourish. For purposes of discussing motivation, the focus is on external, non-employee communities here. This eliminates some sources of motivation such as, 'My manager said this is important.'

These are the motivations that mobilize the innovation energy of a target community:

● cause;
● achievement;

- social; and
- efficacy and learning.

Not all of these apply to every crowdsourcing initiative. They're very much aligned with the goal set for the effort and the crowdsourcing model itself (eg ongoing home for submission of new ideas, or a time-boxed contest with a single winner).

Cause

The term 'cause' is often associated with an altruistic orientation towards helping improve some part of society, and that certainly applies here. But I use 'cause' in a broader context:

Cause is the motivation of an individual to see improvement in something of personal interest. In this sense, a person's cause can include improving a product sold by a commercial enterprise. Cause here is not about the societal good of a crowdsourcing goal; it's about the intrinsic desire the initiative taps inside a person.

When it applies

Cause is a natural for crowdsourcing and OI. People decide to participate to scratch an itch they have. This is the best form of crowdsourcing: tapping people's innate desire to see something improved, something that is important to them.

The most readily apparent situation where cause applies is for customers of a company's products. Customers who are using an organization's products have a deep understanding of what the product does and how well it fits the job they need done. They want to satisfy their own needs.

Cause extends to what you'd expect as well: government improvements and addressing societal issues. In the government realm, citizens' motivation travels an already familiar path of motivation: voting. We vote because we want policies consistent with what we believe is needed. That mentality expands to new government initiatives emerging in the public sector.

We see similar motivations sparking innovation for societal issues. People have issues that are personal to them; they embrace the opportunity to make an impact via crowdsourcing,

Examples

Starbucks crowdsourcing site, My Starbucks Idea, is an example of a product-based cause motivation. Customers submit and vote on ideas for improving the coffee, food, merchandise and experience of the stores.

In the government realm, the city of Manor, Texas, is blazing a path for crowdsourcing citizens' ideas to improve their communities. Its Manor Labs site accepts ideas for the police department, utility billing, information technology and other areas.

Pepsi eschewed advertising in the 2010 Superbowl to launch its Pepsi Refresh crowdsourcing initiative. People around the world post ideas to help societal needs, and the community votes for its favourites. Pepsi then funds the top accepted ideas.

Watchouts

The primary watchout for the cause motivation is a failure to engage the community. People have volunteered their creativity, knowledge and experience for something about which they have some passion. Woe to the organization that fails to match that motivation and engage participants on their submissions.

Engagement doesn't necessarily mean commenting on every idea, although that is terrific for community-building. At a minimum, weigh in on the ideas getting the most buzz. It also is important to find the good ideas, implement them, and let everyone know you've done so.

Achievement

Achievement is a powerful form of motivation. Outside OI and crowdsourcing, it is a primary motivator for many activities. In the context of a crowdsourcing initiative, here is a definition of this motivation:

> Competing – against benchmarks, against others – to accomplish a goal of personal interest.

You can't separate achievement from competition. Competition, in this case, can be more than what we typically think of it as: 'I win, you lose.' Competition encompasses multiple winners, as well as competing against benchmarks. Achievement is a wide area of motivation. Many different goals can be tied to achievement. Here's a survey of several ways to tap people's achievement motivation.

Cash prizes reward one or multiple participants for submitting the top idea(s). The larger the cash prize, the bigger the impact and more diverse the crowd that is attracted. The awarding of prizes has been around for centuries. But the change in recent years has been from awarding prizes for prior achievements to offering prizes as inducements for new ideas (McKinsey & Company, 2009).

Non-cash prizes reward with products, services and special opportunities. They can reflect an organization's own merchandise, or products that work well with the crowdsourcing challenge itself.

Status is a method of highlighting top participants along various metrics. A common method of conferring status is through leader boards. Shining a spotlight on individual participants and contributions is another basis of awarding status.

Badges, levels, ratings and earned privileges are forms of game mechanics, and are emerging as a basis of achievement uniquely accessible and scalable via digital platforms. They combine status with personal benchmarking.

Publicity is a reward unique to large companies, or organizations with a leading presence in a market. Top ideas earn their contributors special mention in press releases, blogs and articles. This publicity can have valuable business or career purposes.

Opportunities to contract with the organization are a powerful reward in OI. Top participants engage in deeper, contractual relationships with the sponsoring organization.

When it applies

The achievement motivation is appropriate in nearly all circumstances of crowdsourcing. The more critical consideration is which of the various forms of achievement to apply to an initiative. For instance, deeply technical challenges are often better served by cash prizes rather than status. Ongoing innovation communities are great candidates for the effective application of game mechanics. Co-creation with other companies is well served with opportunities for contractually working together.

Examples

The second Cisco I-Prize niftily combined different aspects of the achievement motivation. The most obvious motivation is the US$250,000 prize for the top selected idea. In addition, participants bought and sold ideas on the site, resulting in a clear indication of where the market valued each idea. And participants earned reputation scores based on their various contributions, presenting a clear status element to the community.

TopCoder is a site where companies post requests for software development, and individuals compete to provide the best solution. Motivation for participants is highly achievement-oriented. Winners of posted requests earn bounties, while a monthly pool of money is divvied out based on general performance, irrespective of wins. The site also maintains a number of lists of top-ranked contributors in different areas, invoking the status achievement motivation.

The X PRIZE Foundation combines high-value prizes with challenges that are well beyond current technologies. The two aspects dial very directly into both extrinsic and intrinsic achievement motivations of individuals. The Oil Cleanup X CHALLENGE, for instance, offers a US$1 million prize for the top-performing new solution to clean up surface oil from a spill.

Watchouts

When money, potential contracts or some kind of non-cash prize is involved, it is critical to spell out exactly how winners will be selected. Participants need a clear, unambiguous understanding of how their contributions will be evaluated and how they can help their own efforts.

Gaming of rewards is likely to be done by a small minority in a large community. People are clever, and some will apply their ingenuity to understanding the dynamics of any reward. Be vigilant, moderate contributions and adjust as necessary during the course of a crowdsourcing initiative. These tactics generally won't be initiative-busters, more an annoyance to be addressed.

Social

The social motivation consists of two parts, which are interrelated. One part of the social motivation is interacting with others with similar interests. The second is the crowdsourcing effort's fit with a person's social identity. As reported by Badri Munir Sukoco and Wann-Yih Wu (2010), theorist H Tajfel proposes that social identity is achieved through self-awareness of membership in a group, and the emotional and evaluative significance of this membership (Jones *et al*, 2010). Thus the social motivation can be described as:

> Desire to find and interact with others sharing an interest, and the fit of the community and its goals with one's social identity.

With a sponsoring organization and a clearly defined goal, crowdsourcing provides the basis for attracting participants sharing a common interest. Key though is not to let the community become stale. One dynamic of longer-term communities is that they require refreshing of membership on a regular basis (Nielsen, 2006). The social motivations benefit from new perspectives, and new personalities are introduced. Norms of the community are enforced upon new members through the social engagement and observations of participants.

When it applies

Because the social motivation applies in many circumstances, it's easier to describe the case when it won't be a factor: highly competitive, high-value prize crowdsourcing initiatives. The strong achievement orientation crowds out the social motivation.

Longer-term OI communities are great candidates for tapping the social motivation. Initially, connections are made via interactions over ideas. Later, participants return for the relationships they form. Shorter-term, contest-oriented initiatives can also tap the social motivation, with interactions being the extent of the connections.

Organizations with strong brands are good candidates for tapping the social motivation. Customers will feel a kinship based on the brand attributes they value. It helps if the community has a longer-term profile, as that lets people get to know one another and build bonds. Shorter-term initiatives can work, with interactions rather than relationships as the basis of the social motivation.

Examples

SAP maintains the SAP Community Network (SCN). SCN is a community where SAP's employees, customers and partners engage with one another. SCN covers a spectrum of activities, including project collaboration, documentation, solution marketplace and innovation. The community is vibrant and growing, and provides an excellent look at tapping the social motivation among participants.

Mountain Dew ran Dewmocracy, a crowdsourcing effort where the global community helped select the next flavour in the soft drink maker's line. Along with having the crowds select the ad agency and packaging, Mountain Dew has created an image associated with extreme sports and fun. In Dewmocracy, Mountain Dew tapped that association to drive a social identity motivation. Fans wanted to be part of the effort and share it with others.

Watchouts

With social motivation, inevitably some of the less attractive behaviours of people will surface. A common issue can be 'flame wars'. Participants, through passionate differences of opinion or clashes of personalities, occasionally may hurl brickbats at each other. This won't be common, but it is an issue that needs to be managed strongly to avoid a deterioration of the social motivation.

The other watchout is one of expectations. A well-known community heuristic is the 1-9-90 rule of participation: 5.1 per cent of people will be active contributors, 9 per cent will contribute sometimes and 90 per cent of visitors will generally read without contributing. A vote-oriented crowdsourcing initiative is likely to see higher participation rates for that second level. But organizations need realistic expectations of how many site visitors will be contributors in some fashion. Not everyone will be social.

Efficacy and learning

My six-year old son made this observation to me regarding Lego: 'It's more fun to build them than to play with them after you finish.' Even for adults, there is a certain joy and playfulness in the process versus the end result. This is the efficacy and learning motivation:

> Opportunity to exercise one's existing skills toward a goal, learn new ones, and receive feedback for improvement.

Efficacy and learning are deeply intrinsic motivations, tapping a wellspring of internal energy. Efficacy relates to 1) matching one's ability to solving a request; and 2) having the ability to make an impact (Ahonen, 2007). As Frank Pajares of Emory University writes:

> The higher the sense of efficacy, the greater the effort, persistence, and resilience. People with a strong sense of personal competence approach difficult tasks as challenges to be mastered rather than as threats to be

avoided. They have greater intrinsic interest and deep engrossment in activities, set themselves challenging goals and maintain strong commitment to them, and heighten and sustain their efforts in the face of failure. (Pajares, 2002)

Efficacy differs from achievement in that the focus is more on the process, not the outcome. The outcome informs how well someone's skills and abilities perform. And learning is both the feedback received, and the application of new insights towards improvement.

When it applies

Crowdsourcing initiatives built on people's creative or problem-solving submissions are ideal for tapping the efficacy and learning motivation. People need a good challenge that requires them to utilize their creative and even analytical skills. Contrast this with simpler idea-posting efforts: the barrier to submission is lower, but the efficacy and learning motivation remains dormant.

Examples

Netflix ran an excellent example of the efficacy and learning motivation with its Netflix Prize: US$1 million in prize money was offered for anyone who could improve Netflix's existing recommendation algorithms by 10 per cent. While the prize money was certainly the draw, the challenge itself became a key driver of efforts. It was fun to apply statistics creatively and see how one performed.

crowdSPRING runs a site where businesses solicit submissions for various digital and physical designs. A typical project generates over 110 entries. With those odds, an obvious question is, why enter? Because the act of working on a design tests one's abilities, hones existing skills and becomes a basis for adding new skills. This is a great example of the efficacy and learning motivation.

Watchouts

Take care with intellectual property rights here. Given that people are applying their talents, they need to know up-front what rights a sponsoring organization has to their submissions. Releasing rights to unselected submissions can be a smart strategy.

The other watchout is that some crowdsourcing initiatives based on participants' creative work are seen as versions of 'spec work', that is, producing something that the company gets for low cost or for free. Obviously, people will self-select whether they want to participate, but there may be some criticism from the creative quarters.

Conclusion

Any or all four types of motivation outlined here will be present in a crowdsourcing initiative. It's really a matter of degree, and which motivations are the focus of the effort. As mentioned at the start, focus on creating a clear objective with actionable outcomes. Then determine the best approach to motivate your community.

Chapter 10
How LG Electronics Is Transforming Itself into an Innovation Company

CHRISTOPHER J RYU

T he consumer electronics market is fiercely competitive. Many new players have entered and disrupted the market with their innovative products, technologies and business models. As the competition intensifies, the lifecycles of consumer electronics products get shorter. For example, a mobile phone's product lifecycle used to be six months, but you are now seeing new phones every month. Also, because the R&D cost is increasing rapidly and you cannot possibly own all the intellectual property in your industry, you cannot rely on your own internal R&D any more.

Vision

LG Electronics' top executives recognize the importance of innovation. Our company's new vision, 'World best at enriching lives through Innovation', has led to our focus to transform ourselves into an innovation company. Strong commitment from the top management has been the main force of our recent ongoing transformation. There are currently many innovation activities in our company and Open Innovation has been one of our key initiatives. I would like to share some experiences and lessons learnt from implementing OI process in LG Electronics' innovation strategy.

Approach

There are many different OI approaches. There is no one-size-fits-all approach and different companies should take different approaches. For example, IBM is embracing its open source initiatives, Intel has 'lablets' near key universities, and Philips is known for its High Tech Campus in Eindhoven. If you blindly try to imitate their approaches without giving too much thought to it, you risk wasting your time and deciding that OI does not work for your organization.

It was critical for us to find out which OI strategy actually fits LG Electronics. We spent a significant amount of time and resources to find the right strategy. Studying cases from OI pioneers is a good way to start, but always keep in mind that you constantly have to think about what these success cases mean and how to implement them for your company. You should consider which OI approach fits with your company's strategy, culture, business areas, business models, structure and resources. I suggest that you run small pilot projects to see which one works for you, and implement it at a larger scale if you see some promising results.

After carefully studying these factors, we set our focus on building and executing the OI process for effectively acquiring innovative technologies from outside through technology scouting. Even though we had done similar activities in the past, most of the previous technology scouting was ad hoc and did not treat external organizations as equal partners. OI was a paradigm shift for us.

Brand

Our next step was to develop our own OI brand. One of the key aspects of OI is to portray you as the best partner to outsiders. Why would anyone propose their technologies to a company that is known for stealing other people's intellectual property or taking a long time to respond? Having your own OI brand can be a powerful way to communicate with external companies. Creating your own OI brand is an effective way to communicate with your internal members as well. We developed our own OI brand, 'Collaborate & Innovate', defined as 'The practice of collaborating with partners and innovating together towards a common goal.'

Organizational structure

There are various ways to set up a dedicated organization for OI initiatives. Just assigning roles and responsibilities to existing organizations does not work, because they are still trapped in their old roles and responsibilities and closed mentality. I strongly encourage you to assign this role to a new organization unless your company has already been embracing a very open culture. LG Electronics set up a new organization, the Collaborate & Innovate team, which can lead the corporate-wide initiatives. The Collaborate & Innovate team is placed under the CTO division and acts as a hub to work closely with business units. If you work for a big organization you probably have experienced frustration and difficulties while trying to work with other business units. Setting up an organization that acts as a hub can help break down these organizational silos. Having a corporate-wide coordinated approach is a key success factor for our OI initiatives.

Tools

The right tools for OI can significantly boost your technology scouting activities. How easy is it to submit any idea or technologies to your company? Do you have any public channels for external organizations to submit their ideas and technologies? How do you share external organizations and technology information within your organization? Because people are so busy with their daily tasks, much valuable information stays inside personal computers and is not shared across business units. To tackle this problem and to encourage cross-functional collaboration, we developed an internal IT system that allows us to share external company business and technical data including product needs and proposals from outside. This internal website is closely linked with our external OI portal, The Collaborate & Innovate portal (**www.collaborateandinnovate.com**). This website is open to everyone. Even our competitors can come to the website and download any of our RFP (request for proposal) documents. You can browse and submit your proposals to our specific R&D needs and interesting technologies that fit our broad R&D themes. We believe that opportunities to find innovative solutions for our needs are worth more than the risk of letting our competitors know what we are looking for.

Process

Once you set up your OI focus, then you need to develop processes. We defined our OI process into three stages: define needs, technology scouting and technology incubation.

Define your needs

If your needs are not accurately defined in the first place, you are going to spend a huge amount of resources to fix your problems. Make sure to spend some time clearly defining your needs that align with the business and technology strategy. The Collaborate & Innovate team spends a significant amount of time defining what we are looking for. There are two approaches that we take to define our needs: specific needs and broad themes.

Specific needs consist of our R&D labs' R&D needs for solutions. Many of these needs are usually narrowed down to a level that enables people from different industries to submit proposals without understanding the whole project concept. The Collaborate & Innovate team provides the guidelines and templates to engineers when they write the RFP documents. After drafting many RFPs, we have learnt that you cannot just rely on engineers to write them. Most of the R&D engineers are hired to do R&D, not to write reports. It is difficult for them to express R&D needs in a way that external organizations from different industries can easily understand. We found that many of our engineers used LG's own technical terminologies and acronyms when we asked them to write the RFPs.

Another way to define our needs is broad themes. We define our broad themes as generically as possible in order to receive interesting technologies that we were unaware of. When you define your needs and open them to the outside, you are going to face confidentiality issues. You need to consider these issues in articulating your needs and carefully assess the risk and the opportunities involved.

Technology scouting

Once you define your needs, the obvious next step is to look for the solutions. We take many different approaches to look for technologies: worldwide technology trips, web searching, using intermediaries, the Collaborate & Innovate website, and many more. From my experience, the best way to find what you are looking for is to actually visit the places. However, in reality, it is not easy to travel to different countries all the time, so we set up dedicated technology scouts in each region. These technology scouts are locally based and act as a point of contact for organizations in their region. The key regions that we identified are North America, Europe, Japan, Israel, Russia, India and Korea. Each region has its own strength. Russia is strong in basic science research and India in software, Israel in telecommunication technologies, and so on. Using intermediaries can be an alternative to your own technology scouting activities. However, keep in mind that using intermediaries can be costly. Many intermediary firms do not guarantee their outcome and their broker fee is very high, sometimes US$10,000 to US$30,000 for one search request. You can also utilize intermediaries that provide free services, such as embassies or inventors' associations in your country. Whether you decide to use paid or free services, it is important to build a long-term relationship. You have to understand their business models and goals in order to produce meaningful results.

Once we find potential candidates, we conduct a quick initial screening before introducing them to internal organizations. This initial screening process is very simple and quick. We only use two simple criteria: business impact and technology fit. There is no scorecard or complicated framework to evaluate technologies. We believe that using your gut feelings and insight is more effective during this stage, Technology scouts use their own judgement to decide go or no-go. If your initial screening criteria are too strict, most of the technologies that you find would not move to the next stage and you would lose opportunities to find any breakthrough technologies. However, if you do not have any initial screening process, and forward every single technology that you find to your internal organizations, they would not be able to handle this, and technology scouts would lose their credibility as well.

It is important to manage your expectations for technology scouting activities, because the chances that you will find something breakthrough and truly disruptive through technology scouting are very low. Setting up the right Key Performance Indicators and managing them are also critical parts of technology scouting activities.

Technology incubation

So you find what you are looking for. Now what? Promoting external technologies and assigning internal owners are the most difficult yet important parts of our Collaborate & Innovate initiatives. We call this the 'technology incubation' process.

It is very unlikely that external companies have technologies that perfectly fits your needs when you first find them. The Collaborate & Innovate team takes ownership of external technologies until the ownership is assigned by internal organizations. Often many internal organizations are busy with their own internal projects and are suffering from 'not invented here syndrome'. You are going to struggle to make meaningful progress by sending e-mails with just technical information of external technologies to our internal labs. Whoever introduces external technologies to internal organizations has to act as if he or she were the sales person of the external organization. You need to constantly promote the benefits and the opportunities that come with the external technologies that you are incubating. Presenting in-depth technology analysis and business cases always helps your internal organizations to realize their true value.

If your company is big and has many different departments, do not just introduce external technologies to the ones that you think might be interested. Unless you are absolutely sure that a certain internal organization is not related to a technology, introduce the technology and start a dialogue with them. We cannot count how many times we were surprised to see the business unit's interest in the technology. Also, if one business unit or lab does not show any interest, get some help from other support functions such as investment, product planning, technology strategy planning, the intellectual property team, chief innovation officer, chief strategy officer, and so on. It is important for the members that are in charge of the technology incubation process to be creative and to be able to identify the right contact person in the organization.

Here is an example of how technology incubation can help with in-sourcing external technologies. Many of the external technologies that we evaluate are not at the stage of development we want. Since we are a manufacturing company that sells consumer products to customers, we often want to see working prototypes. However, sometimes an external company's technology only has a proof of concept and requires us to provide project funds to develop a working prototype. This is a potential problem. Internal labs said that they cannot properly evaluate this technology because we need to see a working prototype first, and external companies probably say that they cannot invest any more of their resources in something without any commitment from us. When a situation like this happens, the Collaborate & Innovate team contacts various internal groups to support the technology incubation. If the external company we are dealing with is a venture company and looks for investment, then contacting the investment group to invest in the company definitely helps the external company to work on prototypes. Also, the Collaborate & Innovate team can suggest to internal labs that we provide a small fund to an external company to build a prototype that meets certain criteria. The chances are very slim that external organizations already have the exact technology that you want. You have to work with external organizations to get to that stage.

Once we assign the internal owners for a technology that we find, the Collaborate & Innovate team manages the interface between the internal and external organizations. Do not ever underestimate how different languages, cultures, communication and confidentiality can affect your collaboration with external companies. It is important to have a team that can help bridge this gap between internal and external organizations.

Long journey

Shifting corporate culture from closed to open innovation is a long journey. I strongly encourage you to focus on finding a quick success and promoting it across all business units early on. I hope the LG Electronics story has helped you with your OI journey.

Chapter 11
Bridging Open Innovation Gaps

ANDREA MEYER AND DANA MEYER

Open Innovation requires interactions between external innovators, internal innovators and other internal partners to make an innovation operational. These interactions occur across six kinds of natural gaps. On the external-internal frontier, OI faces two types of gaps: 1) the gap between the investor/buyer of an innovation and the inventor/seller of an innovation; 2) the gap between potentially 'dirty' external intellectual property (IP) and internal IP. Inside the firm, four more types of gaps can occur between: 3) risk-taking vs risk-avoiding groups, 4) diverse business units, 5) functional silos, and 6) ideas and action. Although these gaps may be wholly natural outcomes of the pressures on different groups in OI, the gaps create obstacles to innovation. Practices used by Cisco, Clorox, Invention Machine, Johnson & Johnson, Manitowoc, NASA, P&G, Roche, Unilever and Whirlpool show how to bridge these gaps.

External and valuation gaps

The first pair of gaps occurs in the interactions between external innovators and the company's internal systems. The first big gap is the expectations gap between the investor/buyer of the innovation and the inventor/seller of that innovation. Whereas inventors often see their precious invention in terms of the millions in revenues it might reap, the investor or buyer of the innovation sees the potential of millions in costs that the innovation will almost certainly incur. Not only does the situation create a valuation gap, but inventors may feel a parental instinct towards their invention and expect the buyer to not modify the invention. This gap can create ill-will or break negotiations, or stall an OI implementation.

IP Gaps

The second major type of external-internal gap arises from the risks of contaminating internal IP with external secrets and knowledge of third-party IP. The growing use of OI raises the issue of IP hygiene: ensuring that the company does not incur excessive risks from the intermingling of external and internal IP. IP hygiene becomes especially challenging with 'dirty' environments such as online innovation contests and crowdsourced OI, like Cisco's I-Prize and Clorox's CloroxConnects community. Companies want to avoid contamination of pre-existing internal IP, disputes over IP ownership and the potential for misunderstandings between the company and diverse OI participants.

Bridging external gaps with communication

Good communication skills drive OI and collaboration by bridging the gap between external and internal parties. In fact, all of the gaps discussed in this chapter can be ameliorated by communication. A think tank panel at World Research Group's 2010 Open Innovation Summit and other presenters at that conference concurred about the crucial role of communication in innovation. The think tank group emphasized the importance of leaders using a deliberate communication strategy with holistic internal and external communication. For example, Dr Gail Martino, Principal Scientist in the Open Innovation Group at Unilever, described seven soft skills communicators need to persuade, inspire and garner support for OI efforts. Communication involves being a good listener, she said, to build trust and feel empathy for others' situations. At Unilever, top-notch communication skills include a balance of being convincing and being an advocate for the innovation partner.

Cisco, Roche and Whirlpool all advocated having clear and simple terms for IP ownership or licensing in OI efforts. Community-based innovation efforts have the added issue of the ownership of collaboratively created IP. If someone submits an idea and someone else adds a comment with a new idea, how does the company track whose idea is whose? Clorox's Dr Andrew G Gilicinski, Director of R&D-Innovation Networks, said that Clorox separates the idea submission process from the idea discussion process. Specifically, community members are told not to inject new ideas into existing discussions but to submit them separately instead. Defining an IP etiquette and IP ownership terms for the community helps prevent misunderstandings. Nona Minnifield Cheeks, Chief of Innovative Partnerships Program Office, NASA Goddard Space Flight Center, noted that consistent messages and behaviour (ie, walking the talk) improve trust and outcomes.

Companies can forestall IP hygiene problems by modulating the degree of confidentiality during discussions with new OI partners. For example, Roche Diagnostics uses a phased approach to communication. At the start, Roche holds 'open meetings' in which the parties provide only public information about the innovation, business applications, strategies, etc. That way, neither party could be accused of misappropriating the other's IP. If the initial 'kick-the-tyres' meetings go well and the relationship moves forward, Roche uses non-disclosure agreements (NDAs) for more confidential disclosures. One of the recommendations from the conference's roundtable discussion was that companies should use limited-term disclosure agreements to reflect the fact that no new innovation can remain unknown forever. Good OI leaders have the confidence to share what they know but also to maintain proper disclosure limits with OI partners.

Addressing IP gaps with due diligence

Due diligence plays a major role in handling both the expectations gap and the hygiene gap. To deal with this expectations gap, crane-and-food-service company Manitowoc looks at the technical and business experience of the inventor when deciding whether and how to craft a deal (eg, patent assignment, acquisition, or joint venture) with the inventor. The company evaluates potential OIs on five dimensions:

1 the current level of development of the idea;

2 the status of IP;

3 the potential for competitor workarounds of the idea;

4 the degree of technical competitiveness offered by the innovation; and

5 the expected business impact.

Public OI contests bring significantly more hygiene challenges due to less control of who submits ideas and a greater diversity of ideas. Whereas more targeted 'solution-research' OI projects can rely on pre-qualified external partners, publicly open idea-submission platforms attract submitters with a much broader range of IP of uncertain provenance. Both Cisco and P&G perform due diligence on incoming IP from OI efforts. In the context of open contests, Cisco vets the winning ideas for ownership issues. Although submitters to Cisco's contests must affirm that they own the idea, Cisco doesn't want to take any chances and it independently assesses potential winning ideas for ownership issues. Similarly at P&G, due diligence efforts focus on delineating foreground vs background IP. P&G has noticed that OI participants are often smaller companies or independent inventors who have neither the resources nor the intention of doing IP-related research. P&G performs this work to ensure that it knows what it's getting and to minimize the chance of infringement of patents that are not cited.

Public idea-submission sites also run the risk of overlap with a company's secret skunk-works project. Given that so many people live in the same global environment with the same global business opportunities and information sources, it's no wonder that two or more inventors or businesses converge on nearly identical innovations. A company's leading opportunities for innovation are seldom secret. Clorox noted that any competent competitor would expect Clorox to be working on low-emission charcoal or natural food preservatives. To mitigate this type of issue, Cisco culled candidates of its I-Prize contest that were too close to unrevealed projects in the existing Cisco pipeline.

Finally, companies can use outside evaluators to help with due diligence and maintain a clean IP environment. Cisco enlisted outside counsel on internal IP issues because such a large number of its I-Prize contest submissions came from foreign and multinational teams. Clorox goes a step farther and partners with a third-party evaluator for vetting ideas received through the company's CloroxConnects community site. The third-party evaluator, Evergreen Innovation Partners, creates a literal firewall between incoming ideas and Clorox's own internal IP. To ensure that Evergreen doesn't become an entirely risk-averse obstacle to the flow of good ideas, Clorox shares the gains from launched new ideas with Evergreen.

Internal gaps

Even if an organization's OI initiative can handle the external-internal gaps of valuation and IP, innovation still faces at least four key gaps inside the organization. These gaps occur due to the diversity of people and pressures inside large-scale organizations. A few companies have found ways to navigate these gaps.

Innovation vs operations

Johnson & Johnson illustrates how to cross the first gap, which occurs between groups involved in long-term innovation versus those responsible for short-term operations. On one hand, the near-term viability of a firm depends on minimizing risk and costs while consistently delivering value to the customer. On the other hand, the long-term viability of the firm depends on spending money to find new, more competitive and more productive ways of delivering value to the customer. Whereas failure might be essential to innovation, failure can be fatal to operations.

To handle this very natural and necessary gap, J&J created COSAT (Corporate Office of Science and Technology) to provide a sanctuary or 'sandbox' for new innovations (including external ideas). This sanctuary protects the innovation from the rightfully risk-averse operations side of the organization; it also protects operations from the rightfully risk-taking innovation side. In addition, COSAT provides low levels of funding (about US$50,000 to US$250,000 of angel-style capital) to help develop projects to the point the organization is ready for them.

Divisional gaps

A second kind of gap occurs in large, diversified companies. For example, J&J has more than 250 divisions that make everything from over-the-counter painkillers to in-the-body artificial hips. The diversity of regulations (consumer products, pharmaceuticals and medical devices), markets (consumers, retailers, doctors and surgeons), and technologies (consumer products, drug chemistry, high-tech materials and electronics) means that innovations in one part of the organization – even innovations that failed – might be useful in a different part of the organization.

To address this second gap, J&J's COSAT helps ferry ideas from their source (from both inside and outside the company) to potential applications at the different divisions of J&J. This ferrying process includes:

- aggregating good ideas from across the J&J portfolio of companies and outside sources;
- validating ideas with key opinion leaders inside J&J;
- providing low levels of funding to keep good ideas alive;
- brokering ideas to different divisions.

Functional silos

Appliance-maker Whirlpool described a third kind of gap, one that's caused by functional silos. Each functional department (engineering, manufacturing, marketing, HR, IT, legal, etc) has its own metrics, goals and performance pressures that drive that department's tactics. But these finely-tuned local optimizations can cause different departments to operate at cross-purposes to each other. The result is problems such as local protectionist tendencies within silos, barriers to coordination between silos, and money-wasting misalignment in the organization.

Whirlpool's solution is to bridge the gap between silos through aligned strategy and common processes, in combination with communication and training that engage the organization. Whirlpool uses strategy reviews to help the silos see the bigger, shared picture of the organization's future and the role of innovation in that future. Whirlpool cascades its overarching goals down to local goals so that the silos support rather than hinder the overarching goal. A combination of common processes and flexible teams helps create broad organizational engagement. Communication and web-based training called 'Whirlpool Foundations' help everyone in all departments understand the key role of innovation. Whirlpool developed training programmes for all levels of employees, including a mandatory half-hour web course that taught all employees about Whirlpool's innovation strategy. The training created a common language for innovation at Whirlpool and helped transcend silos.

Ideas-to-action gaps

Finally, Jeff Boehm, Chief Marketing Officer of Invention Machine, noted the challenges of driving adoption of innovation initiatives. Boehm explained why and how marketing or internal communication supports the use of a good innovation platform, process and execution of top-management mandates. Boehm suggested that three key elements are necessary – but not individually sufficient – for creating successful, ongoing innovation programmes. First, offering a powerful platform for innovation helps but doesn't guarantee that innovation occurs. A 'build it and they will come' approach doesn't work because too many people are too busy to take the time to find and participate in even the most exciting innovation initiative.

Second, top-down mandates may be necessary for engaging busy people, but mandates alone aren't sufficient to ensure innovation participation, either. Employees typically assume that daily operational pressures trump innovation mandates, so it's easy for them to short-change innovation or allow it to slip out of awareness over time. That implies using a third element – marketing or internal communications – to reach users, communicate the value of the programme, remind them of mandates, and convey the excitement and accomplishments of the effort. For example, putting an innovation icon onto employee badges creates a natural reminder and talking point about the effort.

Boehm, who has extensive experience leading these communication efforts, listed the following four actions as the critical steps for internal communications to drive participation in innovation initiatives:

1 *Make innovation relevant.* Ask different users (executives, peers, functional silos, external partners, etc) about their struggles and challenges and show how the innovation initiative can help them.

2 *Promote innovation.* Create a road-mapped stream of communication that spans time and multiple channels (eg, lunchroom posters, e-mails, podcasts, newsletters, tent cards, tchotchkes, badges) to reach, inform and encourage people to participate.

3 *Provide easy calls to action for innovation.* Avoid obstacles such as convoluted registrations, approvals processes and delays.

4 *Sustain the momentum of innovation with ongoing communication.* Continuously relay successes, platform improvements, ongoing activities, training and new information to avoid attenuation of attention to innovation.

Other companies also rely on internal marketing to create interest and energy for OI. Cisco's Sharon Wong recommended that OI platform operators communicate simply and often to maintain excitement and interest in the OI effort. NASA's Nona Minnifield Cheeks said it's vital to establish a clear sense of why the organization is doing OI, set the context, and create a sense of urgency. Balanced communication also includes conveying both the rewards and risks of innovation, not just mindless cheerleading.

Conclusion

Overall, these six gaps reflect the world's natural diversities in a complex business and technical environment. Different people in different divisions, departments and roles really are different. External innovators, especially those recruited by a public crowdsourcing platform, add even more diversity. Rather than homogenize everyone, many companies have found ways to evaluate (Cisco, Clorox, Manitowoc and P&G), communicate (Cisco, Roche, Unilever and Whirlpool), protect (J&J), bridge (Whirlpool), ferry (J&J), and market (Cisco, Invention Machine and NASA) innovations within a gap-filled context. The following gap-handling tactics increase the effectiveness of innovation processes:

- Modulate confidentiality with OI partners and segregate prime IP (ie new ideas) from secondary content (eg, comments, votes and minor refinements of core ideas).

- Evaluate OI IP for ownership, background/foreground IP issues, and conflicts with ongoing but unrevealed internal development projects.

- Determine if the innovation is ready to cross the gap (and worth bringing across the gap).

- Use a sanctuary to protect the innovation from hostile forces on the other side of the gap (and to protect the people on the other side of the gap from disruption by the innovation).

- Use communication to bridge the gaps: explain to both sides the respective benefits of bridging the gap (eg, why the operational side needs the innovation, and why the innovation needs to be operationalized).

- Create a ferrying process or group to help develop, broker and transition innovations across the gap.

Chapter 12
Soft Skills for Open Innovation Success

GAIL MARTINO AND JOHN BARTOLONE

Introduction

This chapter focuses on the soft skills that underlie success in Open Innovation – those skills that are hard to quantify and even more difficult to find. These thoughts are based on our collective experience working as OI practitioners at Unilever. During this time, we helped build OI capability and put in place a process called Want-Find-Get-Manage (Slowinski, 2005) now adopted Unilever-wide. On the journey of establishing the OI capability, we had to learn quickly what skills matter and how to find people who embody them. As such, our comments are geared towards three likely audiences: leaders interested in building an OI capability, managers building an OI department or human resource professionals interested in identifying or interviewing high potential OI candidates.

The OI professional

The role of the OI professional is to deliver technology and business opportunities through partnership, thereby creating value for both partners. The OI professional is a rare breed – part entrepreneur, part deal maker, alliance manager and part project manager. Success in this role requires a true balance of talent and skills to drive growth from new sources and business models. Practitioners must both be technically proficient and demonstrate a high degree of business and social acumen – skills that are sometimes found in different places within an organization.

We do not deny that some of the skills we describe here overlap – they probably do. But like a diamond, each has various facets that work together to create a brilliant whole.

OI soft vs hard skills

Some skills are easier than others to teach someone interested in becoming an OI practitioner. Ironically, these are typically referred to as the 'hard skills'. Hard OI skills are specific to the tasks or activities the OI professional does. These include, for example, developing a project brief, scouting for technology, evaluating technology, performing diligence, developing and negotiating deal structures, and overall project management. Given that they are easier to teach, they tend also to be easier to measure, strengthen and reward.

OI soft skills, by contrast, are more broadly applied across OI tasks and activities. They are a combination of personal traits, habits, attitudes and interpersonal abilities that can enhance or detract from an individual's ability to build and manage OI relationships, develop win-win deals and deliver project goals. To the extent that these soft skills are a product of individual traits and habits, they are difficult to teach, although some may be strengthened through experience, mentoring or by balancing the overall skill set across an organization.

Why it matters

One of the biggest mistakes a manager can make is to downplay the importance of soft skills in the ultimate success of the OI organization. This is because the OI job is ultimately about people, relationships and trust. We have seen high potential projects fail and lower potential projects succeed in part because these three elements were (or were not) in place. With the right soft skills in place, partners feel energized and connected even through the difficult moments of negotiation. Both sides work hard to build the opportunity and they look forward to working together in the future. Without them, each side feels depleted, exhausted or worse – headed for litigation.

We believe that soft skills are so important that they need to be part of an individual's ongoing OI performance evaluation; specifically, evaluating individuals not just on what they get done, but also how they get it done. If individuals were to appear productive but leave a trail of burnt bridges in their wake, their performance should suffer as it would if they were not productive. How will you attract and partner with people with the best ideas if they don't want to work with you?

Soft skills

Intrapreneurial orientation

We believe that one of the most valuable traits that underlie success in OI is the tendency to be intrapreneurial. The term 'intrapreneur' was coined by Pinchot (2000) to describe employees of large corporations hired to think and act as entrepreneurs. An intrapreneur is someone who focuses on innovation and can transform an opportunity (concept, technology, strategic partnership) into a profitable venture within an organizational environment. Intrapreneurs offer an organization a new way of thinking, making companies more productive and profitable in the process.

Intrapreneurs and entrepreneurs embody similar characteristics, by definition. These characteristics might include being proactive or demonstrating conviction and drive, for example. More critically, there is a visionary quality about them – they see opportunities and drive them forward with and within an organization, sometimes before the organization realizes it needs them.

There are, however, differences between intrapreneurs and entrepreneurs. One such difference may be how they define personal success. For the entrepreneur, taking the opportunity to the marketplace or to a buyer may be the ultimate reward. For the intrapreneur, however, success may involve moving an opportunity from an initial organizational 'push' to an organizational 'pull'. Indeed, for the OI professional to be truly successful, he or she needs the organization to adopt his or her idea so it can take it though to its logical conclusion – a marketplace event, for example. Organizational adoption requires the OI practitioner to relinquish control over the project. Although that may not always be easy for the entrepreneurial-minded, it is critical to allow the dream to become a reality within a corporate environment.

The six remaining skills described below are likely part or parcel of an intrapreneurial orientation. Yet they are important in their own right, as it is difficult if not impossible to bring an opportunity to life without them.

Strategic influencing

To take an idea forward successfully within an organization and to be an effective alliance manager, intrapreneurial conviction and drive is not enough. It requires a high degree of organizational awareness and political savvy – aspects of strategic influencing. Strategic influencing is the 'act of employing carefully planned approaches to persuade or convince others. Strategic influencing is about being able to move things forward … without pushing, forcing or telling others what to do' (Larcen, website).

Strategic influencing begins with an understanding of what each party wants from the partnership or, if these needs are incompatible, realizing it quickly and parting amicably. Along the way, the OI practitioner must 'speak multiple languages', often coordinating efforts across organizational boundaries from R&D to marketing, finance or legal for example.

Critical to effective strategic influencing and alliance management is the ability to be a good listener. It requires listening to each party to fully understand objectives, needs and points of view. It is only in this way that you can put together 'win-win' goals to serve each party's long-term interests.

In the course of deal making and alliance management, strategic influencing becomes indispensable. Consider the situation when the OI practitioner finds him- or herself in debate about the partnership opportunity or the deal terms with his or her own company. In this case, the OI professional must serve as a bridge, bringing the sides together, keeping the size of the opportunity versus the cost of failure foremost in mind.

Communication skills

Demonstrating top-notch communication skills supports strategic influencing. Communication skill is the ability to communicate ideas to the right people (team or sub-team), at the right time, in the right way (presentation, e-mail, text, etc), in the right amount (detailed discussions vs quick updates) to garner the support of others. This typically involves knowing stakeholder's 'currencies' or triggers that motivate them to action. Without this support from the organization or a 'champion', forward momentum will slow or cease.

Talent for relationship building and maintenance

The most successful OI professionals tend to be well-networked both within and outside the organization. More than just the number of acquaintances, individuals with a talent for relationship building and maintenance develop quality relationships by building rapport, trust and personal credibility. They effectively manage key stakeholders and people like working with them.

In the context of a project, those with this skill demonstrate the ability to build and maintain alignment, spot and resolve conflict, demonstrate empathy, establish effective ways of working, see situations from multiple angles, and maintain strong relationships while negotiating 'win-win' deals.

Quick study

Even for an organization the size of Unilever, there may not be a technical expert within the organization to help evaluate every technical opportunity. This is particularly true when the technology is emerging or disruptive, an area in which we specialize. As such, the OI professional must be able to get up to speed sufficiently quickly to be able to communicate the opportunity in a clear, transparent but motivating manner to the organization. This includes both the rewards and possible risks. The faster the individual can come up to speed, the easier he or she can spot potential issues that could derail the project, thereby helping mitigate risks.

We find that successful OI practitioners and intrapreneurs are energized by learning new technical subjects and demonstrate a mental flexibility that allows them to apply knowledge from one area to another in new ways. The OI practitioner who discovers and leads an opportunity may remain a core team member or may assume a project leader role.

Tolerance for uncertainty

Like most innovation projects, OI projects require a high tolerance for uncertainty due to technology, market, business-related or other reasons. OI professionals must feel comfortable making decisions based on what they know 'now' despite not having perfect information, understanding that they will revise plans once more information is known. An insistence on precision or an individual who succumbs to 'analysis paralysis' is not a good match for this role.

Passion and optimism

Finally, there are two emotional traits that are important for OI professionals – passion and optimism. Perhaps it is best captured by a quote widely attributed to Steve Jobs who said, 'My experience has been that to create a compelling new technology is so much harder than you think it will be, that you are almost dead when you reach the other shore.' To make it to the other shore, it is vital to stay above the fray, keep moving forward and stay positive. OI professionals must believe in the opportunity as their passion becomes their best ally to see it through to success.

Where are these people?

With the soft skills identified, the next task is to find individuals who demonstrate them. If, as mentioned above, they are a rare breed, how can you identify them?

One way to find them is to take stock of individuals inside your company. Look for the people who routinely drive new ideas forward and manage to get them resourced. This last part is critical as it is much easier to come up with ideas than it is to get an organization to devote resources to them.

When looking inside your organization, it is important to look wide and far. If you are in R&D, make sure your search includes marketing, finance and legal, for example. If you are unfamiliar with these departments, ask colleagues who they consider to be the intrapreneurial types.

This method has its fallibilities, however, as not all departments may encourage and support intrapreneurial thinking and behaviour. In this case, holding an internal business plan competition may be another option (Lindegaard, 2010). A competition can help individuals upgrade their intrapreneurial skills as well as identify new potential ideas.

In a typical competition, participants prepare a business plan for an idea that they feel passionately about, which is evaluated by a steering committee. The steering committee evaluates the proposals using a set of predetermined evaluation criteria and identifies and rewards winners. In our experience with these contests, working with an external coach is instructive. He or she helps participants refine their ideas and the communication of them, and requires sequestering fewer internal resources.

A further tweak on the business plan competition idea is to allow internal participants to work with strategic suppliers or partners to bring new business plans forward. In this way it would be possible to identify good ideas and the internal and external teams that could bring them to life.

If your plan to identify OI candidates includes an interview, Table 12.1 may assist you in tailoring your approach.

TABLE 12.1 Interviewing candidates for soft skills

	Interview Questions	Reflection Questions
Intrepreneurial Orientation	Describe a time when you brought an idea forward and the organization adopted it.	• Does this person have good ideas? • Can he or she follow through on them and get them resourced?
Strategic Influencing and Communication	Describe your hardest 'sell'. How did the idea or opportunity finally become accepted?	• Does this person demonstrate a high degree of political savvy and communication skills? • Can he or she apply these skills appropriately to get new ideas adopted by an organization? • Is this person a good listener?

TABLE 12.1 continued

	Interview Questions	Reflection Questions
Relationship Building and Maintenance	• Describe how you developed relationships with external partners. • How would you convince an external partner to trust you or your company? • Give me an example of a situation in which you managed or led a team and were able to create a high-morale, high-productivity work group.	• Is this person well-networked both inside and outside the organization? • Does this person inspire trust? • Do people like working with him/her?
Quick Study	Describe a time when you had to learn a topic or skill far outside your area of expertise – how long did it take and how comfortable did you feel fielding questions?	How does this person feel about getting up to speed on topics that are outside his or her comfort zone?
Tolerance for Uncertainty	Describe a time when you had to make a project decision when the outcome was uncertain. How did you feel? How did you mitigate the risk?	• Does this person feel comfortable making decisions under uncertainty? • Or conversely, does this person seem to 'shoot from the hip' too much, not putting structures in place to plan adequately for success?

TABLE 12.1 continued

	Interview Questions	Reflection Questions
Passion and Optimism	Describe a time when you worked on a team that didn't work well together. How were you able to create forward progress?	• Does this person drive things forward or drop the idea if it is not immediately supported? • Can this person stay above the fray or is he/she reactive or cynical or does he/she blame others?

Finally, at Unilever, there are other ways one can get experience working with externals and experiencing the 'culture of entrepreneurship' other than working within the OI department. This is by taking a secondment at one of our associated venture firms. In this programme, visiting scientist-secondees learn about a sector of mutual interest from an investment point of view. We find that many of the individuals who participate in this programme return with an interest in the OI organization and secure positions there. Although secondments with venture funds may not be feasible for all, we believe that a similar intrapreneur-in-residence programme such as the ones described by Lindegaard (2010) could be tailored to one's needs.

Summary

The role of the OI professional is to bring forth opportunities through partnership more effectively than an organization can do alone. Based on our personal experience, we believe there are at least seven soft skills that underlie this goal – intrapreneurial orientation, strategic influencing, top-notch communication skills, talent for relationship building and maintenance, being a quick study, tolerance for uncertainty, and passion and optimism.

Whether you are enhancing your company's innovation capabilities or interviewing candidates for a new OI group, one thing is certain – your ability to ultimately drive growth for your company will in part be influenced by the soft skill set your OI practitioners bring to the table. That is because OI success is about building and maintaining relationships and establishing trust to create mutually beneficial opportunities.

Chapter 13
Open Innovation with Customers: Co-creation at Threadless

FRANK PILLER

Challenges of identifying what customers want

Recent research studies confirm large failure rates in new product commercialization.[1] Newly launched products have shown notoriously high failure rates over the years, often reaching 50 per cent or more. The primary reason for these flops has been found to be inaccurate understanding of user needs. Many new product development projects are unsuccessful because of poor commercial prospects rather than due to technical problems. Research found that timely and reliable information on customer preferences and requirements is the most critical information for successful product development.[2] Conventionally, heavy investments in market research are seen as the only measure to access this information.

So the basic question remains: how can a company identify perfectly the customers' needs to forecast their future desires and design and produce the optimal assortment? One opportunity to handle these challenges is shown by Threadless (threadless.com). Besides reducing inventories, eliminating markdowns and increasing customer loyalty, it does a marvellous thing: producing exactly what its customers want – by co-creating with them in the product development process. How is this different to a conventional company? Most fashion companies also 'ask' their customers 'what they want' by various means of market research. But the clue to Threadless's approach is that, 1) it asks not just a sample, but almost every consumer of its products, 2) it tests every single product concept with its customers, and 3) the decision about its assortment composition is entirely based on the customer's feedback. In addition, all of its designs are co-created by its community, not by in-house designers.

Co-creation at Threadless

Threadless follows an innovative business model that allows it to create a high variety of products without risk and without heavy investments in market research to access customer preferences before production starts. Its business model has been called 'the most innovative start-up' by *Inc. Magazine* in 2008. Started in 2000 by designers Jake Nickell and Jacob DeHart, Threadless focuses on a hot fashion item: T-shirts with colourful graphics. This is a typical hit-or-miss product. Its success is defined by fast-changing trends, peer recognition, and finding the right distribution outlets for specific designs. Despite these challenges, none of Threadless's many product variants ever flopped. But the company does not have sophisticated market research, forecasting capabilities or a complicated flexible manufacturing system. Rather, all products sold by Threadless are created, inspected, improved, approved and selected by a user community before any larger investment is made in a new product. Together with fewer than 50 employees, the company's founders sell about 160,000–170,000 T-shirts per month with a 30 per cent profit margin on sales. Sales in 2009 hit almost US$30 million, with profits of roughly US$9 million.[3] Since 2006, annual growth continued at more than 150 per cent, with similar margins.

Threadless has 1.5 million followers on Twitter and more than 100,000 fans on Facebook.[4] This is achieved by transferring all essential productive tasks to its customers who, in turn, fulfil their part with great enthusiasm. Customers design their own T-shirts and help improve the ideas of their peers. They screen and evaluate potential designs, selecting only those that should go into production. Since customers (morally) commit themselves to purchase a favoured design before it goes into production, they take over market risk as well. Customers assume responsibility for advertising, supply models and photographers for catalogues, and solicit new customers.

Threadless is a textbook example of customer co-creation. The term 'co-creation' (also: co-design, user innovation, or OI with customers) denotes a product development approach where customers are actively involved and take part in the design of their own product. More specifically, co-creation has been defined as an active, creative and social process, based on collaboration between producers (retailers) and users to generate value for customers.[5] Customers are actively involved and take part in the design of their own product and their co-creation activities are performed in an act of company-to-customer interaction and cooperation.[6] The method breaks with the known practices of new product development. It utilizes the capabilities of customers and users for the innovation process. The main benefit of customer co-creation is to enlarge the base of information about needs, applications and solution technologies that resides in the domain of the customers and users of a product or service.[7]

So how is co-creation working at Threadless? The process starts when an idea for a new T-shirt design is posted on a dedicated website by a community member. All new designs are submitted entirely by the community, which includes hobbyists but also many professional graphic designers. The company exploits a large pool of talent and ideas to get new designs (much larger than it could afford if the design process had been internalized). Creators of submissions that are selected by other users get a US$2,000 reward, US$500 worth of free T-shirts, and their name is printed on the particular T-shirt's label. Today, Threadless has over 1 million registered users and receives approximately 300 submissions per day.

Next, reactions and evaluations of other consumers towards the posted idea are encouraged in the form of internet forums (comments) and opinion polls. Users evaluate each week all new designs on a scale from zero ('I don't like this design') to five ('I love this design'). On average, each design is scored by 2,500 people, and about 90–100 users also write an explicit comment on each design. A good score corresponds to a value above 3.0. In addition, customers not only express their marked preference for specific designs, but can also opt-in to purchase the design directly once it has been chosen by the collective. For this, they check a box 'I'd buy it' next to the scale – providing an informal commitment to later purchase the product concept if it is selected. From the designs receiving the top votes and largest commitment of users to purchase, Threadless is producing about six new products each week, awarding about 600 winners each year. New designs regularly sell out fast, but are reproduced only if a large enough number of additional customers commit to purchase a reprint first. This process of getting the market's exact feedback first before committing any resources in final product development, manufacturing and sales has been called 'collective customer commitment'. It exploits the commitment of users to screen, evaluate and score new designs as a powerful mechanism to reduce new product flops.

It is important to note that in the end management keeps the final word. First, the Threadless team reviews each short-listed design to make sure that no user cheated by analyzing IP addresses and IP chains for voters and the respective scores given. But more fundamental, Threadless' team also has its own say in the selection process. The company learnt that the collective input of its customers has to be combined with the company's internal market knowledge to succeed with the commercialization of the selected products. At Threadless, the winning designs are chosen from among the top-scoring designs, but they are not necessarily the absolute top-scoring designs. Important factors are the originality of the design (is it somehow timeless, not too similar to other recent winners), legal issues (any copyright-related issues), and assortment policy (will the design contribute to a wide variety of styles). For this decision process, however, the community again provides important input: their long list of comments on each design provides helpful information if a design is plagiarism, but also if it could be modified to look better.

Over time, Threadless has refined the customer co-creation process. For example, to keep the competition interesting and encourage users to participate continuously, the number of designs at any given time has to be limited so that users don't get confused. Usually, each design gets seven days to be scored. But if a new design has received a low arbitrary score (made up of multiple variables including the number of 'I'd buy it' requests and the design's average score) within the first 24 hours of its positing, it will be dropped from the running. This happens to about one third of the submissions. The early user feedback has proven to be a very strong indicator of the success of a design in the competition and enables the company to increase the usability and experience for users who vote.

Threadless has inspired a number of similar companies. While some have just cloned the idea (eg, projectnvohk.com, look-zippy.com, buutvrij.com, lafraise.com – in total there have been more than 30 exact clones of the Threadless idea in the T-shirt market), companies like RYZwear, myfab.com and dreamheels.com have transferred the idea into another market segments (shoes, sneakers and furniture). The latter companies start the entire process when the voting and commitment process has been finished.

When customer co-creation makes sense

The kind of co-creation employed by Threadless makes especial sense in markets where customer demand is very heterogeneous, a common situation today. Here, information about the demand for (new) products is distributed in an extremely diverse way. If the knowledge of manufacturers about the needs of an emerging market is scarce and costly to achieve via conventional market research, user contributions become a valuable source of innovation. The possibility of open contributions encourages self-screening by potential contributors.

When discussing the specifics of customer co-creation, it is important to note that not everyone wants to participate in product development activities. Not all customers are highly motivated co-creators. Customers can decide about the degree of their involvement: at Threadless, most new designs are indeed submitted by young professional designers, ie users with typical lead user or trendsetting characteristics. They contribute not only because the monetary incentive of US$2,000 is higher than the average honorarium paid for a commissioned design by a conventional clothing company (about US$300 to US$500); their main motivation is to get greater exposure in the professional design scene, a rather closed market that is difficult to enter for newcomers. The openness of Threadless's community makes it easy for designers to present their work and to get immediate feedback.

But Threadless also allows pure hobbyists to submit a design as the screening activities of its community enable this openness at no risk and with no costs. Indeed, one of its most successful contributors is a gifted teenager without any formal design education – and with little chance of getting a contract with a traditional company. The majority of Threadless's users, however, just screen the proposals and contribute to the elicitation of demand by polling for the designs they like most. For these customers, browsing through the ideas is often a novel experience and a welcome change from traditional shopping activities. They discover new potential products, exchange comments, and feel empowered by their authority to make a favourite idea happen. Some users want a bit more of engagement: they comment on the submissions and propose amendments or additions.

While everyone who submits a design has the same chance of winning the contest, the expert knowledge of the designers gives them a clear advantage. From an economic point of view, having expert knowledge provides a cost advantage to the contributor. Another participant with less domain knowledge may be able to submit an equal contribution in the end, but at a much higher burden (development cost). However, there are many examples at Threadless where an outsider has submitted some highly creative and innovative designs. In these cases, often the intrinsic motivation of these hobbyists has counterbalanced their lack of experience. It may be exactly this openness to utilizing expert knowledge on the one hand but also allowing contributions from 'untrained' (and hence, unbiased) outsiders on the other, that explains the success of the Threadless model.

Implementing co-creation

There are several benefits for manufacturers in implementing customer co-creation. By creating an open line for their customers, manufacturers get access to ideas for new products or even complete designs. Supporting customers in organizing themselves as a group and expressing commitment for a specific design turns market research expenditure into sales. Once this commitment is explicit, manufacturers can exploit this collective demand and serve the market very efficiently without the conventional costs of identifying this segment and the risk of developing and producing an unappealing offering.

However, we do not claim that customer co-creation is always beneficial. Conventional product development and customer co-creation have to be seen as supplementary – not as substitutes. Successful innovation management is like any other management task: making decisions about trade-offs and choosing what to do and what not to do. There will be contingency factors in favour of a manufacturer-dominated innovation process without any customer participation. But there is no doubt that customer integration matters in the new product development process. A number of conditions tell whether customer co-creation makes sense:

1 Companies have to face uncertainty of demand. Especially in volatile markets influenced by fast-moving trends, integrating the customer in a different, much closer way makes sense.

2 The product has to be modular in a way that it can be split into components that are predefined (and which in the best case could be prefabricated to reduce lead times), and others where customer

co-creation can take place. This split reduces the complexity of the entire process and allows the external contributors to focus on just one aspect of the co-development. Splitting the product in such an 'internal' and 'external' way should start at the level of uncertainty about market demand. The components that are rather certain and bear a low planning risk (like the basic T-shirt and size distribution in the example of Threadless) will become predefined. Those components with larger demand uncertainty will become customer co-created.

3 Consumers have to be interested and motivated in co-creation of the product. This demands a specific level of involvement for the product. Establishing the motivators of potential contributors is crucial for success.

4 Finally, the company has to be able to create a community of contributors or to connect with an existing one. This often is the most challenging task. It took Threadless more than five years to get its community up and running. An important condition for success is the full disclosure of the entire process from initial consumer comments to final product commercialization. Co-creation, like OI, demands an open, transparent development process contrary to the conventional practice of keeping innovation private and secret. Being able to make this mental shift is perhaps the most important condition for implementation.

Threadless has been able to make this cultural shift. But even further, it has tapped into a fundamental economic shift, a movement away from passive consumerism. Eventually, Threadless-like communities could form around industries as diverse as semiconductors, auto parts and toys. 'Threadless is one of the first firms to systematically mine a community for designs, but everything is moving in this direction', MIT Professor Eric von Hippel has been quoted in an interview (*Inc. Magazine*, August 2008). This may or may not come to pass, but the lesson of Threadless is more basic. Its success demonstrates what happens when a company allows what its customers want it to be. Threadless succeeds by asking more than any modern fashion company has ever asked of its customers – to design the products, to serve as the sales force, to become the employees. Its founders have pioneered a new kind of innovation. It doesn't require huge research budgets or creative brilliance – just a willingness to keep looking outward.

Chapter 14
Introducing Open Innovation at Intuit

JAN BOSCH AND PETRA M BOSCH-SIJTSEMA

Setting the context

A chieving growth, in revenue, number of customers or market share, is the central goal for any organization. A growing organization feels healthy to its employees and creates opportunities for them, achieves better results for its stakeholders and can serve its customers better. Traditionally, organizations achieve growth organically or inorganically. The latter achieves growth through the acquisition of companies whose revenue can be added to its own, whereas the former is concerned with internal innovation as a basis for serving existing customers better and for acquiring new customers.

Due to its importance, innovation has been studied extensively by the research community as well as by consulting organizations and companies themselves. The purpose of this chapter is not to provide a conclusive overview of that research, but rather to discuss one particular domain that has received significant and increasing attention over the last decade: Open Innovation. Initially popularized by Chesbrough (2003) in research and P&G's AG Lafley's new direction for the company, OI operates in the space between internal innovation efforts and the acquisition of external companies – it seeks to find promising collaborations with other organizations that can drive growth for both partners against a significantly lower R&D investment than the amount each company would have had to invest by itself to achieve the same outcome. In fact, due to the constantly increasing demands for speed, in many cases it would be impossible to achieve the same outcome as the opportunity would have closed by the time the organization by itself could have acted on it.

OI thus may bring not only speed and R&D efficiency, but also skills, risk mitigation, access to new markets and the ability to pursue more radical, disruptive innovations. However, there is a reason that OI has not yet become the new 'normal' of innovation: at the meeting point between two organizations, priorities differ, trust may be lacking, perceptions of risk and ROI differ and the time horizon for the effort may differ. Simply put, managing an effective innovation partnership is a skill that few organizations exhibit to the optimal degree.

In this chapter we discuss the introduction of OI at Intuit, a US Fortune 1000 company that provides financial solutions to consumers and small businesses as well as those who serve them, ie accountants, financial institutions and healthcare providers. Although OI is a journey in progress at Intuit, there are relevant experiences and insights to share.

The contribution of this chapter is twofold. First, we present the unique innovation culture that had been developed and established at Intuit before the start of the OI initiative. This, we believe, is a critical success factor for the introduction of OI. Second, we present a staged model for introducing OI at Intuit that we consider to be a generic model that can be applied at other companies as well.

The remainder of the chapter is organized as follows. In the next section, we introduce Intuit and the organic and internal innovation culture that has been established over the last five years. In the third section we present the four-stage model of introducing OI at Intuit as well as the experiences that we have gained at each stage. The final section focuses on generalizing our four-stage model and presents its broader applicability across a range of companies.

Internal innovation culture at Intuit

Intuit is Fortune 1000 software product and services company that primarily serves consumers, small businesses, accountants, financial institutions and healthcare providers with finance and accounting-related solutions. Intuit is organized in 10 business units that address different customer segments or provide solutions in specific domains.

Intuit serves more than 40 million customers with tax software, personal financial management, online banking, small business accounting, payroll, payments and customer management solutions as well as solutions for accountants and healthcare providers. Finally, it increasingly serves emerging markets in addition to the United States, Canada and the UK through its global business division.

Originating as a company that sold its software on CDs in retail stores, over recent years the company has made a rapid shift towards connected services that are already generating more than 60 per cent of its revenue. Next to offering web-based solutions, mobile solutions are becoming increasingly important in capturing customers and are starting to generate relevant revenue.

In the mid-2000s, the company decided it needed to accelerate its organic growth and started a number of initiatives addressing its internal innovation muscle. Over time, these initiatives formed the foundation of a strong innovation system where each part reinforces the others. The elements are unstructured time, idea jams, Brainstorm tool, Intuit Labs and horizon planning. We'll describe each of the elements below.

The first element is unstructured time: employees in product development can use 10 per cent of their work time on projects of their own choosing. These projects can be concerned with education and training, or fixing an annoying problem in one's work environment, but many decide to spend their time on innovation. Unstructured time can be used as half a day every week or it can be accumulated over time, giving people multiple days in a row to work on a project of choice. Unstructured time allows for a pool of resources available across the organization that can be applied in a self-selected, self-directed and self-managed fashion.

Every business unit at Intuit periodically organizes idea jams. During an idea jam, interested employees come together for a day to brainstorm ideas, develop them into concepts to be presented and, sometimes, to receive feedback in the process. Typically, the idea jam has a specific focus that is set by senior management as a means to drive ideation and concept development in a strategically important area.

The third element of Intuit's internal innovation culture is the Brainstorm tool (**http://www.intuitbrainstorm.com/**). The tool, developed internally, offers a social network, web 2.0 style approach to ideas management, team formation, a means of providing feedback on ideas entered by others, etc. From a user's perspective, Brainstorm can be used to enter an idea, receive feedback and ratings on the idea, recruit team members who are willing to contribute to the idea and jointly evolve the idea into a concept that can be tested. The tool is incredibly valuable in connecting people who normally would not meet each other because of geographic location or differences in role and background.

Intuit Labs (**https://www.intuitlabs.com/**) is an externally facing website where Intuit presents its innovative demos and prototypes. It is clearly differentiated from Intuit's main web properties, but it offers a place where customers can provide feedback on a large variety of ideas and solutions developed by Intuit employees.

Finally, the company introduced the notion of horizon planning, requiring each business unit to allocate its resources towards horizon 1, horizon 2 and horizon 3 offerings. Horizon 1 represents the mature, high revenue, but often slower growing offerings; horizon 2 consists of the newer, rapidly growing offerings that have proven themselves in the market. Horizon 3 offerings are funded market experiments where customer interest, scale and the business model are tested to determine which ones have the potential to grow into horizon 2 businesses and which are not viable. As each business unit is expected to divide its R&D investment over all three horizons, there is a constant need by the business units to fund new horizon 3 initiatives.

The elements of Intuit's internal innovation model build a synergistic system where bottom-up, employee-driven innovation harnesses the creativity of R&D staff, employees have time to explore their ideas, can find others to form teams with, build prototypes, get feedback from customers and, if the results are compelling, have a good chance of getting their initiatives funded as a horizon 3 initiative. This innovation model provides an excellent foundation for introducing OI at Intuit.

Introducing OI at Intuit

OI is concerned with complementing a company's internal innovation processes with collaborative innovation efforts with outside partners. Although this is conceptually something that is easy to understand, actually executing it is particularly difficult. There are several reasons that complicate adoption of OI. At Intuit, the following problems were the most prominent:

- *Outside partner fatigue:* Virtually every employee at Intuit is constantly bombarded with messages about all kinds of material and offers from outside companies. Over time, people tend to develop an attitude that just 'tunes out' all external communication and the interaction with the outside world is relegated to a very small number of people who aim to provide a bridge between the outside world and the company. This team, however, is consistently overworked and under high pressure to deliver results, leading to a situation where the least risky, rather than the highest return projects are the ones that get the time of day.

- *'Not invented here':* Although this is a cliché, it is so one for a reason – there is a basic human tendency to discredit innovation found elsewhere. In a world where knowledge is so widely spread and so many people have relevant solutions, no company can afford to ignore outside innovation. However, companies are made up of people who make decisions based on their belief system and hence often see a gap between their behaviour in use and espoused behaviour. Espoused behaviour is made up of the words we use to convey what we do or what we would like others to think we do, while the behaviour in use is related to actual behaviour and tends to be tacit structures (see Argyris and Schön, 1974).

- *The gap:* Once the aforementioned problems have been addressed, the next challenge is a gap between the specific innovations that teams in the organization are looking for and the innovations offered by outside partners. In addition to that, teams tend to be constrained in their thinking about new innovations by the available technology and what can reasonably be built by the team, rather than starting from an unconstrained, customer-oriented vision and identifying the technology that would be needed to deliver on that vision. This causes a situation where even if there is a reasonable match between internal needs and available external innovations, the opportunity is still not capitalized. The focus at this point is concerned with development teams clearly expressing their needed innovations in a fashion understandable by outside innovators and at a time that still allows for external innovations to be brought in.

- *Having to think about it:* Once the above has been achieved, the final challenge is to institutionalize the approach rather than view it as a special activity separate from daily operations. Instead, OI needs to be part of the mindset and the operating mechanisms in the organization. Ingraining even successful and positively perceived initiatives as part of the operating mechanisms of the organization is a large challenge in and of itself and requires continuous attention and effort to achieve.

Staged model for introducing OI

These challenges build on each other. One has to solve the earlier ones before embarking on the subsequent ones. In response to that realization, the adoption of OI at Intuit is performed in a staged approach where each next stage is initiated when most of the earlier challenge has been dealt with. This has translated itself into a four-phase transition model where each phase has a number of activities and initiatives associated with it:

Phase 1: Creating awareness.

Phase 2: Undirected OI.

Phase 3: Directed OI.

Phase 4: Institutionalizing OI.

In the remainder of this section we describe each phase and the activities that we initiated in each stage in more detail. Finally, we provide a summary and discuss how we organized activities from different phases in the same time periods as mechanism to build phases on top of each other rather than as mutually exclusive.

Phase 1: Creating awareness

The first step in the transition model is to establish a baseline in terms of the current state of collaborative innovation with outside partners. At Intuit, the baseline was established as a study where the innovation leaders from each business unit and selected senior product managers were interviewed using a semi-structured interview technique. Most of the questions were qualitative, but a significant subset asked the interviewee to quantify the extent of OI in Intuit or the interviewee's business unit. In the study we focused on eight categories of potential OI partners, defined by a central team, and interviewees were asked how effective their business unit was in OI with different partners, compared to an ideal state (see Figure 14.1). The average effectiveness across all categories was slightly below 30 per cent. The one significant outlier

FIGURE 14.1 Summary of Intuit's OI baseline

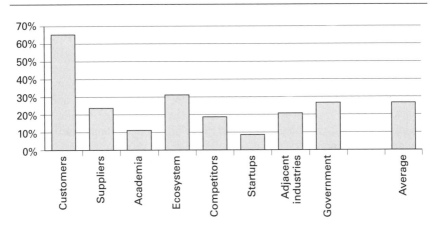

is the 'customers' category. The reason for this is that Intuit has a long history of customer-driven innovation and works closely with customers while prioritizing, developing and evolving new products or new functionalities for existing products.

Based on the study, we decided to focus our OI initiatives on four categories: start-ups, suppliers, academia and crowdsourcing. The latter is mostly focused on the ecosystem and parts of Intuit's customer base.

The transition Phase 1 of creating awareness had two purposes. First, the study helped decide where to focus the initiatives to accelerate the company's OI capability. An important second reason, however, was to address the 'outside partner fatigue' problem and to stress to key decision makers and influencers across the company that significant opportunity to drive growth and to reduce R&D expenditure and risk existed through more effective collaborative innovation with the outside.

Once the baseline was in place, the next step was to define a metric that tracked whether Intuit is getting better at OI. The metric currently used is the number of products with a significant external innovative component.

Phase 2: Undirected OI

Once the initial awareness of the potential of OI had been established, Phase 2 was about seeking to capitalize on these opportunities. The best way to achieve this, in our experiences, is through event-based initiatives. Events are separate from the day-to-day operations and do not require a change in daily behaviour, instead reserving some time for a special project by the people attending the event.

We organized several events at Intuit, each addressing one of the focus areas. For start-ups, Intuit periodically organizes Entrepreneur Days. For strategic suppliers, there is a yearly innovation contest organized as part of the strategic supplier summit. For academia, Intuit's main effort is being a sponsor of MIT Media Lab, and during its sponsor weeks there is a significant contingent of Intuit innovators who visit. We decided to leave crowdsourcing initiatives for the next phase.

An important common characteristic of these events is that the onus for proposing concrete collaboration projects with Intuit is on the external party, rather than on Intuit. For each of the events, Intuit innovators and senior decision makers evaluate the proposals, or in the case of Media Lab the research projects, and decide which of these are sufficiently aligned with the strategy to proceed with.

The OI events again have two goals. The first is the direct and obvious intent of exploring business partnerships that are mutually beneficial. The second is to strengthen and reinforce the perception and understanding of the company's innovators of the potential of externally developed technologies and business solutions. This contributes in the transition from a 'Not invented here' attitude to a 'Proudly found elsewhere' culture.

Similar to activities from Phase 1 persisting as the company evolves, the activities from Phase 2 persist as the company enters the third phase. Intuit has continued to organize the aforementioned events even after it started to move to the next phase.

Phase 3: Directed OI

The third phase is concerned with two main goals. First, the aim is to move from events to a continuous model of interaction with outside innovators. Second, innovators start to express their needs for business solutions and technologies.

Once needs are expressed, the interaction model with outside innovators needs to change. For Intuit, in Phase 3 the category of crowdsourcing and the use of online web 2.0-style tools became important. This led to the introduction of **www.intuitcollaboratory.com** as the main site for interaction between inside and outside innovators. Although the site allows for outside innovators and Intuit's customers to submit ideas and collaboration proposals, the main purpose is to publish technology and business solution needs identified by the business units and to engage with the outside innovation crowd to seek to meet these needs.

The transition to directed OI is the hardest as it requires changing the standard processes around development. In closed innovation, most innovators start from the technology assets available and then explore how these can be combined into new products. The new approach is to start from an ideal solution for a customer for a specific problem, identify the technology assets required to address that need and then, for those assets not available inside the company, to find external innovators to partner with to address the need.

Intuit is currently in the transition to Phase 3. We published an early version of the Intuit collaboratory website for a small audience to test it with our target innovators. The feedback has been processed, which, at the time of writing, has resulted in the launch of a new version of the website. One thing we learnt early on is that challenges, ie time-limited contests on a specific topic, are an important element of a crowdsourcing website. For the first contests we managed to reach small, highly specialized communities that provided critical expertise for the business units putting up the challenge.

The transition to directed OI closes the gap that often exists when external innovators propose collaborations. The more precisely the internal innovator is able to specify a need, the more likely it is that external innovators can provide a matching solution.

Phase 4: Institutionalizing OI

The final phase, which is still in the future for Intuit, is to institutionalize OI. This would mean that collaborative innovation with external partners in a variety of forms has become part of the normal operating mechanisms and processes in the organization.

Institutionalizing is critical for firmly grounding the new principles and ways of working in the organization without having to be concerned with a retreat to the old ways of doing things. Several mechanisms exist for securing institutionalization. An OI dashboard that tracks metrics indicating the health of OI is an important mechanism for providing visibility. Also, an important forcing function is provided by project initiation and resource allocation processes that explicitly demand exploration of open-source or commercial components and collaborative innovation before deciding on internal R&D investments. Increasing the permeability of the interface between the organization and the outside world by relying less on secrecy and IP protection and more on collaboration on identified business opportunities is the third factor in driving institutionalization.

Reflection and generalization

In this chapter we have discussed the internal and OI model applied by Intuit as an example of how companies apply OI in practice. We discussed the unique internal innovation culture that had been developed and established at Intuit before the start of the OI initiative. The internal innovation culture is perceived as a critical success factor for the transition towards OI. Within the case study we identified a number of challenges that companies face once they want to change their innovation strategy. These challenges can be dealt with through the four-phase transition model developed by Intuit as a generic model for introducing OI. The transition model presented in the chapter focuses in the early phases on enriching a company's knowledge base

(Chesbrough, 2003; Enkel *et al*, 2009) through integration with suppliers, customers and external knowledge sources. However, in the later phases the transition model develops into a co-creation innovation strategy in which complementary partners establish long-term relations in which knowledge is shared and new ideas are brought to the market by several parties (see Enkel *et al*, 2009).

OI is a young research field and insights and lessons learnt from experiences from companies can help develop more generic models of how to implement and execute OI strategies.

Acknowledgements

We would like to express our gratitude to Intuit for its support in this work.

Chapter 15

Problem description in Open Problem Solving:

How to overcome cognitive and psychological roadblocks

KLAUS-PETER SPEIDEL

The person who understands and fixes the problem is not necessarily or even usually the person who first characterizes it. Somebody finds the problem and somebody else understands it. (Linus Torvalds, Linux Founder)

Open Innovation vs Open Problem Solving

Open Problem Solving (OPS) is one of the practices of Open Innovation (OI). But this is misleading. Efficient problem solving isn't necessarily an innovation practice. While you need to solve a series of conceptual, technical and communication problems in the innovation process, problem solving doesn't imply innovating. Some problems are solved in innovative ways, but most aren't. Not being innovative doesn't make a solution less valuable. 'Going open' is useful in solving all kinds of problems. The aim of this chapter is to show how companies can efficiently integrate OPS into their Research & Development (R&D) processes.

From 'define and try' to 'describe and search'

A typical roadblock for problem solving is lack of information. There are two ways to obtain information: producing it or finding it. That you lack a piece of information doesn't imply that it doesn't exist and has to be produced. In most cases, a lack of information is in fact a lack of access. In many cases we've assimilated this reality. Nobody near a computer with internet access would go from house to house to get a close approximation of how many inhabitants their city has. But for the problems we are talking about, it is more difficult to obtain solution information. However, the fact that it's harder to find doesn't mean that nobody has the relevant solution information and that it's best for the problem-owner to go into a resource-consuming information-production mode to solve it, for example by conducting experiments in the lab. Given the likely existence of the solution somewhere, this would be grossly inefficient. And yet it often happens.

In the last 10 years, many methods to help find potential solution-owners and problem-solvers have been developed. There are listings (innocentive, ninesigma), solver- and expert-identification technologies (expernova), or mixed approaches that combine advanced solver- and expert-identification technologies with listings and community-building like hypios. With these services it becomes very attractive to move from Define and Try (DAT) to Describe and Search (DAS).

It's important to understand that we are not talking about replacing all internal (or closed) problem solving by external (or open) problem solving, but about making it part of the standard procedures for all complex R&D challenges to search for existing solutions (inside and outside) before going into solving mode yourself.

The DAS process

There are four stages in the process of OPS, shown in Table 15.1. Stage 2 is what makes the process efficient. As the table shows, stage 2, when solution-search is running, doesn't consume much of the problem-owners' time: their time becomes available for other projects and problems. In the DAS paradigm, engineers and researchers will work on different projects or sub-problems of a project while outside solvers work on solutions. The time being consumed for solving is the solution provider's time. In this phase, problem-owners will usually have to answer some solver questions, but can also work on adapting and implementing solutions that have been found earlier on or develop solutions for problems for which a solution search didn't yield results.

The new rationale for solution search

There are multiple reasons why DAT was so influential in problem solving. Trying to find relevant information was much more difficult before the internet existed and until very recently, training in finding information was not an essential part of high-school education. Quite the opposite: from our first day of school up to our last days in university, we've learnt that copying neighbours' results is morally inferior. Even though copying, in the form of citation and reference, becomes part of researchers' everyday practice in university, we are all initially and strongly conditioned against using someone else's solution.

TABLE 15.1 The four stages in the OPS process

Stage	Allocation of Problem-owner's Time (%)
1. Problem description	5
2. Answering solver questions during solution submission phase	5–10
3. Solution evaluation and selection	10–30
4. Solution adaptation and implementation	30–60

This conditioning, where solving it yourself is considered far more worthy than finding it elsewhere, is one of the factors that limit the adoption of the DAS paradigm. 'Proudly found elsewhere' is much more than a slogan. It introduces a new value system.

Before the age of IT, obtaining solution information could be so difficult that first trying to do it yourself was often the most rational choice. This has changed fundamentally. The possibility of finding relevant solution information first became available to the wider public through technological solutions like search engines, then through social solutions like forums and Q&A services. In the field of high-level corporate R&D, solution search used to be way more difficult because the number of potential solvers is much lower. But with the rise of the social web, the increased online presence of users and development of advanced semantic technologies for expert- and solver-identification, it has now become possible to target high-level researchers very precisely.

Every new solver joining a problem-solving community online and every advance in technologies for intelligent crowdsourcing decreases the rationale for DAT. In any forward-thinking organization tools and processes for OPS should be available for everyone and their use should be richly incentivized.

Psychological roadblocks in OPS

While the voices for adoption of OI grow more numerous, the mindsets have largely remained the same. The long domination of the DAT paradigm has brought about many bad habits that are deeply entrenched in the culture of problem solving and may lead to irrational rejection of the DAS paradigm.

At each stage, multiple stakeholders are implicated, and thus one person or function in an organization adopting the new paradigm is insufficient if others, mainly the organization's engineers and researchers, are opposed to the initiative. OI and problem-solving leaders need to anticipate and disarm potential resistance through adapted communication and processes.

Stakeholders will rarely formulate the reasons for their opposition as explicitly as I do here. But many of the seemingly rational reasons ('Nobody from outside our organization will be able to understand the problem', 'The problem is confidential', 'Nobody who doesn't have our expertise will be able to solve this', 'We already know everyone who could be relevant for solving this', 'We'll have legal problems', etc) may be linked to one or more of the roadblocks discussed below.

Roadblock 1: Copying is perceived as cheating

Blockbuster Communication: Foster a 'Proudly found elsewhere' culture. Make sure it is perceived as an achievement to find a solution. Explain that outside solutions will become part of the internal problem-solving process, that they won't be perfect and will need to be intelligently adapted and implemented by your researchers and engineers.

Blockbuster Process: Implicate the internal problem-owners in formulating, choosing, adapting and implementing solutions to 'their' problems.

Roadblock 2: It's pleasant to figure it out yourself

People who like to solve problems will usually want to find the answer to a puzzle themselves. There's a specific pleasure related to figuring something out: the pleasure of achieving a breakthrough yourself.

Blockbuster Communication: Appeal to shared rationality: why should you do it if someone else has already done it? Explain that problem description is an important and complex task in itself that shouldn't be taken lightly.

Blockbuster Process: If they insist, give owners more time to figure out the solution themselves, with a clear deadline. Obtain agreement for them describing and posting the problem within a second time limit if no solution has been found before the deadline. When posting a problem online, make sure that problem-owners still work on challenging problems while you wait for solutions. Give problem-owners a similar kind of recognition for successfully adapting and implementing solutions and for finding solutions themselves.

Roadblock 3: It's frustrating if someone else figured it out and you haven't

It may be perceived as humiliating that someone else figured it out and not you. The frustration may be even bigger if you have the feeling that you could have done it ('If only I had had more time, I would have found a solution').

Blockbuster Communication: Make it clear that you believe in the problem-solving capacity of your team, and explain that you want problem solving to be as efficient as possible, which is why you also look outside. Furthermore, there will always be problems for which you won't find solutions outside, and for anyone in the company solving them this will be even more impressive.

Blockbuster Process: Make adaptation and implementation rewarding experiences and value them.

Roadblock 4: People own problems

Researchers and engineers can have a strong sense of ownership with certain problems, especially if the problems are part of a larger project they are working on. They may thus be reluctant to share the problem with someone else.

Blockbuster Communication: Explain that you look for an outside solution because you perceive the problem they are working on as critical. Make it clear that outside solutions are a tool that internal problem-owners can use.

Blockbuster Process: Never link looking for an outside solution to disenfranchisement. Don't make researchers or engineers work on other problems that they are less interested in instead of the problem they 'own'. Let them manage and implement solutions.

Roadblock 5: Fear of being replaced by solvers from outside

When you tell people someone else will be working on 'their' problem, they may be afraid that this means outsourcing their tasks to others and thus replacing them.

Blockbuster Communication: Present the possibility to appeal to outside problem-solvers as a way to support your researchers and engineers. Encourage them to use this possibility. Don't use 'going open' with a problem as a menace. While a menace may have positive short-term effects by stimulating them, it will make employees suspicious of outside solutions and will ultimately lead to rejection and sabotage.

Blockbuster Process: Give your researchers and engineers the chance to appropriate the tool and processes for OPS. Organize groups for problem description and let employees manage the process themselves.

Describing a problem for others to solve

This should be done as openly as possible, as precisely as necessary. When I began writing this chapter, I surveyed different methods for problem solving and one thing struck me: while there is sometimes some collective brainstorming involved, none of the methods includes a phase where you run a search for existing solutions. In other words, they all conceive of problem solving as a pretty isolated business. The methods are all designed for people who try to solve their problems themselves. Defining a complex problem for yourself may itself be a complex problem. Describing it to others isn't necessarily more complex, but definitely different. If the people who have defined and formulated a problem are also those who work on solving it, they can always go back and reframe the problem when they realize their solution approach wasn't the right one. In OI and crowdsourcing, where the problem-owners and the problem-solvers aren't identical, this is different. For external problem-solvers the problem description is all they have about the problem; they cannot go back to any fact of the matter and review it, finding a new problem description themselves.

As opposed to a Google search, queries for open problem solving address human problem-solvers who need to appreciate and understand your query. In principle there are two kinds of solvers you can find through open problem solving approaches: experts you don't know yet and solvers from other sectors who might have analogue solutions. The rules below will help you to reach both. They thus maximize the chance that you get unexpected solutions that work. Rules 1 to 3 will help you make your description as open as possible, Rules 4 to 6 will help you to make it as precise as necessary.

Rule 1: Say what you want and not how

Frame a problem in terms of function and not in terms of solution approach. *Aim:* making sure that potential solvers think about your problem and not about how you think about it.

Missing this point yields terrible results. Unfortunately we don't always realize that our problem description can be biased by a preconception of the solution (or what we think the solution will look like). Having someone who's not part of our team read it and discussing the description is always a good test.

As Moshe F Rubinstein underlines, 'a common error in approaching problems is to move too quickly into a problem solving mode'. In many cases you will already be in solving mode when you pose the problem. Say you are running a mill where mice are getting smarter and your old mice-traps stop working. So you need a better way to trap mice. Or do you? Maybe not. Isn't it more likely that you just want to keep the mice out of your mill (or certain rooms of it)? Trapping mice is only one way to achieve this result.

Making this kind of error in problem definition is worse if you want others to help you solve your problem. Unless you provide them with the broader context (see below), solvers won't be able to take a step back in the problem-solving process. Your preconception of the solution will be all they have. If you run a solution search early, you are less likely to get stuck with a rigid conception of the problem than if you quickly move into problem-solving mode.

One famous example of a limiting preconception is part of the story of the Longitude Prize, one of the first cases of what is now called 'problem broadcasting in OI'. At the beginning of the 18th century, English mariners still didn't have any reliable method to determine longitude while at sea (function). For many years, different experts, among them Isaac Newton, had been trying to find an astronomical solution (approach). As research and grants didn't yield any results, in 1714 the English parliament decided to organize a large public prize competition. John Harrison, a self-taught clockmaker, came up with the best solution. He built a series of chronometers, very precise clocks that were set on London time upon departure of a ship. Comparing London time and local time allowed you to determine longitude. Had the scientists working on the problem been less rigid with their solution approach, a precise chronometer might have been developed earlier. It took the committee a long time before they accepted Harrison's solution because they were still waiting for the results of another approach based on lunar tables.

Interestingly enough, I recently experienced a very similar case, with a company looking for a method to synchronize two precise clocks. In fact, what they really wanted was a method to localize divers under water (without relying on GPS). By defining their problem in terms of the solution approach, which they expected to succeed, and not function, they limited the scope of possible approaches enormously. But they were lucky: when they saw the problem online, several external solvers guessed what they were trying to achieve with the clock synchronization and told them that they were asking the wrong question. But this can only happen with exceptionally smart solvers, and many expert-solvers who might have been able to help them locate people probably didn't even read the description.

Limitations

What you can do. Not every company has the same degree of flexibility. You may need a solution to be of a certain kind because that's just what you can produce (or use). If you are a watchmaker, you may need your solution to be a watch. If you are in chemistry you have certain production facilities and a mechanical solution may not be workable for you (see Rule 4). The degree of flexibility will generally be higher if your products are assembled, eg security solutions, and if you can decide to buy and put together the most suitable elements independently of your own production facilities.

Note: in some cases, it may be sensible to envision your business differently. If you happen to build cars and your research consistently shows that people want to share cars, you can either try to oppose that trend or start to develop car-sharing yourself and thus redefine yourself as a mobility company rather than a car manufacturer (see Mu by Peugeot).

What you want to hide. This is an issue in itself, which I can only mention here. In some cases, talking about 'solution approach' instead of what they need their solution to do is a way for companies to try to hide what they are working on. Some solution seekers are afraid they'll give away too much information by posting their real problem. This may be perceived as a problem even where companies are anonymous, like on hypios, and where solutions are confidential. It will help you to determine if non-disclosure of your problem is really an issue if you apply the rule Kevin McFarthing coined at Reckitt Benckiser and ask yourself the following: 'Will it surprise my competitors that I am posing the problem?' If the reply is no, post it.

Example

> *Problem:* There are too many foxes that bite people and transmit rabies.
>
> *Closed description:* Company X is looking for more efficient ways to kill foxes.
>
> *Opening description:* Company X is looking for a way to keep foxes from transmitting the rabies.
>
> *Potential solutions:* Killing foxes, trapping foxes and checking them, finding ways to prevent foxes from getting close to people, feeding them meat with vaccine, etc.

Rule 2: Describe context

Aim: sometimes the real problem lies in what you think is part of the context. To make sure solvers can see and solve the right problem, you need to describe the context of your problem as precisely as possible. Your preconception will influence what elements of context seem relevant to you. Make sure that you don't only provide elements that seem relevant to you – the more context you provide for your problem, the more elements solvers will be able to consider to solve your problem. If you only describe the very precise problem you believe you are facing, the effect is very similar to defining a problem with a specific solution approach in mind (see Rule 1).

Let me take the hotel key problem as an example. There are regularly people who don't give back their keys when they leave their hotel. The keys then get lost and the hotel needs to have someone make new keys very frequently, which is a resource-consuming task. How would you describe the problem? One way that comes to mind is: 'We need to find a way to make sure that people give back their keys when they leave the hotel.' Someone trying to solve this problem came up with the idea of attaching big key-fobs to the keys, thus making them heavy and uncomfortable to carry. This leads guests to leave their keys at the reception. While this solution has the advantage of being very low-tech, it will only work in hotels with 24/7 receptions, and some hotels won't find it elegant enough. Another solution is more procedural: some hotels will keep your passport and only give it back when you leave the keys. But this is often perceived as intrusive. Furthermore, you could forget your passport and keep the keys. It's only by thinking of the whole context that you can discover that the real problem is having to make new keys each time keys are lost. A completely different solution emerges: replacing keys by keycards. This way, it doesn't matter if people forget to give back their keys, because cards are cheap and can be easily replaced and reprogrammed.

Limitations

Your specialization. There may be elements of context that you can't modify (see Rule 4). If the division posing the problem designs keys, the solution may need to be linked to a traditional key.

Context out of your control. If you replace keys by cards you also need to change all the locks. This is a big investment that may or may not be part of the problem-owner's authorization. Similarly, a traditional car manufacturer can do a lot to make cars more comfortable, but they can't get rid of traffic jams.

Example

Closed description: Company X is looking for a method to make sure people give back their keys before they leave the hotel.

Opening description: Company X loses a lot of money from making new keys because people don't give back their keys when they leave the hotel.

Possible solutions: Redesign the check-in and check-out process, replace keys and locks with some other system, etc.

Remark

Sometimes a new solution will open the way for others. For example, in many hotels with key cards, the cards have two functions: they open the door and they control the electricity in the rooms. You can't switch on the lights unless you insert the card into a slot in your room. When you leave the room you take your key card out of the slot and lights and electronic devices are switched off. Electricity savings thus pay back the investment you make to change the locks.

Rule 3: Define concepts

Aim: making sure that the many possible solvers can understand what you are looking for. One of the most appealing aspects of OPS is that you may get solutions from people whom you wouldn't have asked.

'Specialist' language or jargon will limit the number of potential solvers to the number of experts in your sector. You want it to be dry? Say it must be dry; don't say the molecules must be linked. While the equivalence may be clear for a chemist within context, it's not necessarily clear for other solvers. If you hope to find an elegant and surprising solution from different people, don't describe your problem as if you were talking to the people you see every day.

If you need to use difficult concepts that are specific to your domain, explain them or provide a link with an explanation. This is not about getting amateur solutions. The same expression is often used for different concepts in different sectors and misunderstandings among scientists from different specialisms are common.

Limitations

Domain specificity. Let's face it: some problems are really too specific to be solved by anyone who hasn't had training in your domain. OPS will then be an efficient way to find expert solvers.

Example

> *Closed description:* Company X is looking for a method to determine state of cure online.

> *Opening description:* Company X is looking for a reliable method to find out if the surface is dry.

Rule 4: Say what you won't be able to do

Aim: making sure that the solutions you get can be implemented by your organization.

If you are a company making glue, the set of tools you use will not allow you to implement all kinds of solutions. Specify that you can implement chemical solutions, but not mechanical solutions if this is the case.

Limitations

Being too quick in excluding approaches. One of the most important features of OPS is the possibility of finding unexpected solutions. If your limitation is linked to internal organization, because you only get to treat part of the problem while other divisions treat the rest, it may be useful to figure on what points they can be flexible on or to get round a table and describe the problem together.

Rule 5: Say what you know

Aim: making sure solvers don't lose time working on problem approaches that you are aware of and have already rejected. By listing approaches to solving your problem you are familiar with and briefly explaining why you didn't find them useful, you'll increase the chances of getting a new and useful solution.

Limitations

Through a modification of problem context, solutions that you excluded first may become useful (see Rule 2).

Rule 6: Set the values

Aim: making sure that your and the solver's understanding of all expressions are aligned. While I encourage you to use ordinary language, it sometimes has the disadvantage of being imprecise when taken out of context. Check your meaning for words like 'cheap', 'fast', 'light', 'easy' and describe what you mean. If you can't provide objective values, use terms that allow for reconstruction of your needs.

Example

> *Imprecise description:* Company X is looking for a light tool.

> *Better description:* Company X is looking for a tool that can be carried for several hours by a man who is already carrying a 10 kg rucksack.

Suggestion: Tell a story

Aim: increasing solver engagement, describing context. The solvers you address in OPS are not working for your organization, and the best solvers will usually have a large choice of problems they could be working on. Telling a story is a good way to get them interested. For example, you can describe the situation where the problem occurs and what happens in such a situation. If your problem happens to be part of a bigger context that's noteworthy, talk about it. Even if we only bring a stone, we like to see the edifice we are contributing to.

Telling a story can be also be a good way to tell solvers about problem context. We tend to censor less when we tell a story that contains the problem than when we try to describe a problem in itself. Storytelling is therefore a good way to trick yourself into providing more context than you think is necessary.

Chapter 16
Building the Culture for Open Innovation and Crowdsourcing

CATHRYN HRUDICKA, GWEN ISHMAEL AND BORIS PLUSKOWSKI

A ll sorts of organizations have successfully employed Open Innovation and crowdsourcing. What they have in common is not their size (Threadless and Lego), industry (Millennium Pharmaceuticals and Dell), or their legacy (MEDL Mobile and Pepsi). What runs through all of them is a culture that supports and encourages looking to the outside for ideas and opportunities. While there is no one 'right' culture, there are things that have undoubtedly helped make these organizations' efforts successful, listed below.

Positive culture traits

1. Commitment from the top down

OI and crowdsourcing efforts have explicit support from executives, which raises visibility, promotes buy-in and helps remove roadblocks. For example, AG Lafley, CEO of P&G, publically announced in that the company would source 50 per cent of its innovation externally. Today, Connect & Develop, the company's innovation strategy, is one of the most productive OI practices in the world.

2. Deliberate design

It's common for successful companies to have formal mandates and strategies that direct their innovation efforts. Whether it's partnering with entities outside the organization or working with internal contributors, it's not just a happy coincidence that successful efforts are the results. For example, the John Lewis Partnership has a written constitution outlining its principles, governance system and rules, which serves as guidelines for current innovation activities and keeps the company from being distracted by short-term trends. BBC's One In Ten initiative is another example – where employees are given the mandate to spend one day in 10 working on innovative ideas, which are then pitched at monthly show-and-tells judged by a panel of peers who can approve the idea's eventual implementation.

3. Focus on value

It's one thing to launch an OI or crowdsourcing initiative; it's another to keep it going. Longevity comes from being able to tie results to recognized and measured value created for the company. Whether the goal is increased IP, new product launches, gaining efficiencies, or creating cutting-edge design, OI and crowdsourcing activities and outcomes are linked back to objectives either as direct or indirect contributors.

4. Right resourcing

Serious efforts are made to put the right people in the right places. Successful companies recognize that the skills that allow someone to lead internal innovation don't always transfer. Instead, external and crowd-driven innovations are spearheaded by people whose forte is in managing relationships inside and outside the organization – 'bridge builders' who are able to keep the initiative going when difficult issues arise.

5. Failure = learning

Since innovation has inherent risks, it almost goes without saying that successful organizations are willing to fail, and in many cases they plan to fail. This doesn't mean that failures are glossed over; rather, they are treated as learning opportunities. 3M is one such company, in that it continues to operate by a principle set forward by long-time CEO William McKnight:

> As our business grows, it becomes increasingly necessary to delegate responsibility and to encourage men and women to exercise their initiative. This requires considerable tolerance. ... Mistakes will be made. But if a person is essentially right, the mistakes he or she makes are not as serious in the long run as the mistakes management will make if it undertakes to tell those in authority exactly how they must do their jobs. (McKnight, website)

After a failure, these companies conduct debriefings, identify what went wrong, discuss what was learnt and how to correct it, and then move forward.

6. Raising the bar

Successful companies realize innovation shelf-life is short, and continually seek to evolve and improve their OI and crowdsourcing initiatives. P&G recently launched Connect & Develop 2.0; other organizations are embracing the concept of partnering beyond that of traditional ties with external universities and R&D labs – reaching out instead to consumers, outside experts and even competitors.

7. Spirit of collaboration

Successful companies accept the premise that not all the smart people work for them. Many also acknowledge that not all the innovative people work in marketing or R&D. Therefore, the spirit of collaboration that is fostered with outside partners is also evident internally. Ideas and perspectives are openly shared between departments and divisions, and innovation teams are comprised of individuals from all parts of the organization.

8. IP perspective

Legal departments and leaders in successful organizations value intellectual property in a different way. The traditional practices of 'protecting and confining' give way to active searches to identify licensing and leveraging partners. These companies look for new ways to gain value from IP. If IP has been sitting on the shelf, they seek out others who might want to buy it for their own use. Or they may look for viable partners who have complementary abilities or knowledge and can help monetize the IP.

9. Formalized communication

Communication isn't left to chance in these companies. Partners are brought in for periodic reviews of how efforts are progressing, and successes are shared throughout the organization. Efforts are made to keep a high level of momentum going in order to maintain high levels of innovation awareness and an energizing stakeholder base.

10. Trust

In a successful company, participants in the innovation programme are imbued with a sense of trust in the organization. Trust that allows them to take risks without fear, trust in the organization's ability to both value and act on submitted ideas and suggestions, and trust in their interactions with their peers.

Common cultural blocks

These 10 cultural traits are all positive, but it is worth remembering that there are negative cultural behaviours that can easily kill a programme. Innovation, after all, for any size company, can be a scary thing. Innovation is all about change – and specifically enforcing and embracing it on a regular basis. Through a well-balanced programme, norms are challenged, 'newness' abounds, failure is commonplace, and the organizational processes originally put in place to encourage standardization and efficiencies are stressed. These kind of stresses frequently engender fear in individuals and the organization as a whole, and it's up to the savvy business leader to provide a safe environment where people are no longer scared to step out from the illusion of safety of doing 'business as usual'. Common cultural blocks include the following.

1. Punishing risk takers and failure

Traditional companies are typically not set up to celebrate failure, but rather to remove the associated risk with trying new things. Innovation requires an atmosphere where experimentation is encouraged, as mentioned earlier in the chapter, yet that atmosphere is impossible to instil in organizations that have been known for terminating 'risky' employees or marginalizing 'renegades' to undesirable parts of the business where they can 'do less harm'.

2. Knowledge hoarding, silo behaviour and non-collaborative environments

Innovation relies on the free flow of information and knowledge – both within the business and with the outside world. However, many traditional corporate hierarchies disincentivize sharing by having measuring and reward mechanisms that only value the performance of a single business unit/group in isolation.

Organizations with a high turnover of staff will frequently exhibit non-collaborative attitudes among their employees as people try to maintain their unique value to the company in the hope of avoiding the corporate chopping block. However, the successful innovative company values not just knowledge sources, but also the habit of sharing and the actions of 'connectors' – who are able to find and marshal knowledge and information from diverse sources to drive the creation and execution of innovative ideas.

3. Lack of transparency

One of the common mistakes that companies make when they undertake a collaborative process such as innovation is neglecting the 'social contract' they enter into with participants, both internal and external to the organization. The contract, while not a physical document, is just as powerful.

That contract basically says, 'If you ask me for my ideas and my opinions, I want to know that you are listening, that you value that input, and that you're acting on the input you're getting.' In order to be able to communicate that value, you have to embrace a large degree of transparency with your audience. A company that lacks in transparency will typically have useless ideas (because the right information defining the problem to be solved was not properly shared), and a sharp decrease in participation rates as people react to the lack of communicated progress on collected input, by having less motivation to take part in future innovation efforts.

A lack of transparency with the outside world can also be reinforced by overzealous legal departments, which will attempt to neuter external partnership opportunities by insisting on having numerous onerous legal contracts in place prior to beginning under the guise of needing to protect the company from potential IP losses.

4. 'Not invented here' syndrome

One negative trait specific to crowdsourcing and OI efforts is that of 'not invented here', ie an aversion to searching for, or considering as viable, any outside input into the innovation process. External ideas and solutions will typically be dismissed out of hand with little or no serious consideration. This is usually a factor with internal incentive programmes and Key Performance Indicator scorecards that will typically measure individual internal contributions to an innovation programme – for example, the number of patents an employee has originated. Strong leadership and a change in metrics are required to change ingrained attitudes to a culture of embracing an 'innovation everywhere' approach.

Initiating an OI project

So how do we ensure that we're using the best methods to foster an open, innovative culture? What are some specific steps managers can take? How do we make course corrections and overcome some of these common cultural blocks, especially if we're working in a large organization with a history of entrenched silos?

An organization interested in initiating an OI project might first start with a cultural assessment of the overall organization, to help uncover strengths and weaknesses or areas to improve. Often, outside innovation consultants or executive coaches are brought in for this purpose, because they can frequently see blind spots that are not apparent to the company leadership, and they can create a 'safe' environment for employees at different levels to reveal truths about what it's like to work at the organization. Some organizations have been successful in hiring their own internal coaches or developing an innovation leadership position to develop and implement a cultural assessment.

Usually, it is advisable to do a 360-degree assessment (various models are available online, or from a wide range of consulting and coaching firms) that at least samples employees across the organization, in different departments, at different levels, or in different roles. The goal is to obtain as honest a picture of the organization's current culture as possible.

The next major step is to become aware of behaviours within the organization that hamper OI – or any innovation – and the development of a more transparent, open corporate culture. Then, a strategy must be formulated and an action plan made with steps the organization can take to change limiting behaviour. This should include a timetable with a framework of accountability delegated throughout the organization to specific managers, starting at the top. Cultural changes should always be mapped to the organization's overall business goals, mission and long-term vision. The strategy and plan must include steps to not only develop and foster a more open culture but also how to sustain it in the future.

If, following the cultural assessment, it is determined by the leadership that the organization as a whole is not yet ready to move into OI, top management or other OI champions within the organization might consider starting a small 'skunk works' OI project that would involve lower risk to the organization as a whole – but it is crucial to give the skunk works team adequate time and resources to obtain some real results, especially if outside collaboration and crowdsourcing (limited or not) are involved. Skunk works teams are relatively well known in the tech world (at Hewlett-Packard and Google, for example), but are less known in traditionally more 'siloed' industries, such as healthcare.

In recent years, especially following the proliferation of social media and social networking within organizations, large organizations such as Sutter Health, Kaiser, the Mayo Clinic and others have embarked on what could be called 'skunk works' or small-team innovation projects, often involving the use of social media and social networking tools, as well as collaboration processes between departments. (Examples are not limited to the consumer products, tech or healthcare industries, by any means, and these principles can be applied flexibly in organizations in other industries as well.)

Steps to take

Here are some steps organizational leaders – or other OI advocates with specific departments – can take.

Start a small skunk works OI project and include a variety of personality types to bring different perspectives and solutions to the problems being addressed. Include some of your organization's 'positive deviants' or change instigators who are passionate about the pilot innovation project at hand, and give them enough range to contribute, without micromanagement. When reaching outside of your own organization, define clearly what roles and personality types you need from the other organizations to make a top-notch OI team, which would also mean including people who are skilled at creative thinking and whole-brain innovation processes, not just those who might be skilled in day-to-day, tactical management areas.

Learn to influence more effectively above, below and across the organization, which can be achieved through coaching, mentoring and training. Once an OI skunk works project has achieved a defined level of success, it then becomes a pilot project that has been watched by the entire initiating organization for the OI project and, certainly, by all key constituents. The main task of the team then is to influence the leadership 'above them', managers across departments, and staff 'below them' in rank, so that the results can be applied throughout the organization(s), or at least, in the most appropriate departments.

An 'influence programme' can be designed, and it requires an effective strategy. Some components would include:

- Learning the principles of influence, and training key team members to apply them effectively (guidance is available from several key sources, including one mentioned below*).
- Setting goals for the influence programme.
- Assessing the situation at each point, in addition to overall progress.
- Finding a hook* to use to successfully influence others.
- Structuring the influence approach.
- Planning for the worst outcome, as well as the best, including back-up measures.
- Rehearsing the influence campaign with other team members or allies.
- Creating and mapping out each individual's influence campaign, as well as the entire OI team's approach.

(*A hat-tip to Andrew Neitlich, Executive Coach, business owner and author of the book, *Elegant Leadership* (2001) for these steps, with some modifications.)

Set up a system of 'OI advocates' within the team or larger organization and a regular reporting method to foster communication. Unfortunately, since many innovation projects have had a high failure rate, it seems even more crucial to sustain and continue to develop effective innovation processes, both inside an organization and in an OI context. To do that, OI teams and the leadership of each involved organization should establish a regular, open reporting system, timetables and accountability for follow-up, and assign 'monitors', 'OI advocates' or 'OI champions' who not only keep track of the project(s) and monitor results on an ongoing basis, but also do regular 'innovation check-ups' to make sure the results of the initial project are being used and implemented correctly, in line with their stated purpose and values.

Survey all OI constituents and potential crowd to crowdsource – decide if a limited crowd is needed. When using any social media, social networking and community-building strategy or process, an organization or team must be clear about the reasons for these tools being used, and where constituents really are in using social tools – for instance, they may or may not be using the more commonly used social networks such Twitter, Facebook and LinkedIn. Indeed, they may or may not be using the web, and they may be using mobiles more than a computer.

It is imperative to map any social or crowdsourcing strategy to business goals, including both short- and long-term; and to clearly define the segments of constituents that would yield the most useful results for crowdsourcing, particularly for an OI project. Surveying an organization's constituency can involve online, e-mail and traditional mail surveys, telephone and in-person interviews, with carefully selected questions that will yield the responses needed to move the OI project forward. For instance, a 'limited crowd' may, in some cases, yield more useful responses for an OI project than a general crowd or the organization's audience as a whole.

Use processes that involve emotional responses and right-brain as well as left-brain (or whole-brain) engagement to foster and sustain organizational or team creativity, plus team collaboration processes. Also, identify personality types on the skunk works (or larger) team and use specific processes to draw out more introverted personality types. There are a number of techniques and processes that can be used effectively to reap the benefit of everyone's most creative thinking and best decision-making capabilities, including obtaining the input of more 'difficult' personalities, and also the quieter, more introverted members of the team, who often have the most creative and unique ideas.

Just as it has been shown that consumers buy products and services based on appeal to their emotions, even more than their intellect or logical decision-making process, it has also been demonstrated that creativity can be accessed and enhanced more effectively when a team is moved emotionally, at least at key points in the innovation process. Innovation teams, including those engaged in an OI project, have used many creative thinking processes that go way beyond brainstorming, which may include storytelling, guided imagery, creative writing (for example some Disney Imagineering techniques), team collage, photography and video walking exercises (to enhance perspective and promote team cohesion), drawing, painting, building with clay, movement, theatrical improvisation, team music, creative thinking and perception exercises and others that do not require specific expertise in an art form. These not only engender deeper, more unique creative thinking, they're also fun and engaging for the team members and connect them more directly to their passion for the innovation project, as well as promoting better interaction and communication with fellow team members.

There are also more 'left-brain' or scientific processes, such as TRIZ; and decision-making techniques, such as the deBono Six Hat process, which can be applied at key points in the overall innovation process. (At Creative Sage™ we have developed unique processes to meet the goals of specific innovation projects at crucial points in the overall process.) What is most important is to know when to use which technique or process to gain the optimal results, and that is why it is often vital for an organization to either bring in a skilled outside facilitator, or to hire specifically trained innovation staff who can facilitate these processes and fully understand their uses.

Plan collaboration strategies and methods to set up internal and external collaboration systems, platforms and project management tracking, using social media, innovation and collaboration tools and software. Above all, remember that it's more about the people and processes than the tools!

There are many excellent collaboration and innovation tools and platforms available today, including both proprietary and common social network platforms, which can be used for both internal and external innovation and collaboration. But sometimes a simple tool can be better than a more complicated one, depending on the training and adoption timeline, and the resources available to your OI team. People make the mistake of focusing too much on the technology; it is far wiser to concentrate more on who the OI team members are, what skill sets, perspectives and personality types are needed, and what processes will be used to engender optimum results, utilizing the resources at hand.

Keep in touch with your crowdsourcing 'crowd', reward them with incentives and continue to build community among them. Your 'crowd' can be 'repurposed' to become your organization's key influencers and evangelists when the new innovation products (or services) come to market!

Chapter 17
Overcoming Resistance to OI

TODD BOONE

'Open innovation' has become a mainstream term in the media and in general business discussions. But the term and the underlying logic behind it are not yet so widely adopted that everyone immediately understands it. Therefore, when we think of overcoming internal resistance to OI it is important to take a step back because for many people it is about overcoming the unknown. Consequently, it is important to understand the backdrop of why our organization adopted OI in the first place because it is core to how we drove organizational acceptance – people need to understand the upside to why they are being asked to change before success can be realized.

Status quo to modularity

Consider our market, which is rugged handheld computers for enterprise-focused applications. Over the last few years this has become highly commoditized with little differentiation (and consequently constrained profit) opportunities for us and partners alike. We are not the largest player in our space, which means that continued competition based on price as a primary differentiator would be of little value in the long term. And, much of the technology attributes (such as ruggedness) that used to differentiate have become standard within our market. As a result, we started to explore new differentiation strategies.

First, we focused on the modularity of our devices. Modularity gives us production efficiencies, but perhaps more important, it delivers post-production flexibility that enables customers to change technology options throughout the lifecycle of their mobile computing deployment. Though interesting, modularity didn't go far enough. Why? In most cases, we were still pushing our device against competitors purely on the basis of specifications.

Modularity gave us certain advantages, but it was not the game-changer we were looking for. So we started thinking about the incorporation of OI and crowdsourcing philosophies in the business. Just think about the change that this entails.

Breaking out of the comfort zone: modularity to OI

What's the traditional corporate philosophy towards information? Secrecy at all costs. Protect the intellectual property. We know best. All of these point to one essential tenet of OI – you must give up control. If you are not prepared to relinquish some control, you are destined to fail. This is tough for professionals who are used to solving things and used to being 'right'. At first blush, they feel this is akin to a slap in the face that indicates a lack of confidence in their ability to create a solution on their own. In short, it diminishes their perceived value.

Our interpretation of OI is our corporate strategy called 'Open Source Mobility', or OSM. This changes our business model – the way customers solve problems and make purchases as well as the way partners offer solutions. In the words of John Conoley, our CEO:

> Our open business model is designed specifically to better meet customer expectations by leveraging the collective ingenuity of Psion, its resellers, partners, developers and customers, globally. By adopting this approach, we create valuable opportunities to substantially increase, and accelerate, research and development resources to better meet customers' specific requirements.

To do this, we combined three critical elements:

1 our uniquely modular computing platform;
2 an open, collaborative online community; and
3 highly customizable products, services and programs.

This combination delivers hugely powerful and transformational results:

- the best lifetime total cost of ownership for customers;
- unique choice and flexibility for customers;
- unique differentiation opportunities for our partners;
- a collective approach to our business – an open model.

What does this really mean? Well, it is about OI adapted to our business. The combination of an open business model and a modular product platform means that the company can explore how to use and develop its IP with other companies, globally. Our expectation is that other companies will create unique-to-market products by building entirely new products and services on top of our modular platform. So, we have created processes and tools that open us to both partners and customers in a way that, 1) enables customers to express their need (the online community), and 2) enables partners to develop unique business opportunities that expand their addressable markets and drive more profitable growth.

So, sounds good on paper, right? But, given that the underlying threads on this are 'openness' and 'collaboration', how do we shift the organization to do this in a way that is externally focused yet still empowering the employees to feel that they are contributing in a valuable (even revolutionary) way? We knew we needed to change the way our business operates, the way we communicate and the way we interface with our partners and customers.

How to get there

Here are five examples of key things we've done and will continue to do to break people out of their silos and comfort zones:

1. Restructure to change

This was a first and critical step for Psion in terms of changing the mindset of the organization. We changed from a regionally-based model to a functionally-based model to eliminate unnecessary overlapping functions within regions and to ensure consistency throughout the organization. A regionally-based organization structure leaves too much room for different execution methodologies within the company. To ensure a successful shift to OSM, we needed to make sure that the level of centralized control, and hence consistency, were higher.

To illustrate, consider the following. Each region was led by a managing director who (depending on the size of the region) typically had human resources, marketing, operations, finance and sales functions reporting into him or her and a significant amount of autonomy in terms of how he or she approached the business. Given that we had about 12 such organizations globally, it was a large problem to execute any comprehensive change and do so consistently.

Consequently, each function (marketing, ops, HR, etc.) was aligned into a single, globally-focused business unit represented within the executive of the company with direct accountability to the CEO. Not surprisingly, this change was not fully supported by all (particularly those who saw their job scope become narrower) and so required very strong leadership to drive into the organization.

But this simple step (on paper anyway!) was a key variable in terms of giving Psion the 'footing' to start making changes that supported the philosophy of OI. It shifted the control of information away from the regions and back to the centralized corporate management, which in turn enabled the gradual opening of the information protocols necessary to support OI.

2. Living the values

This is critical and starts from the top. OI requires an 'open' business – by that I mean open to new ideas, willing to take calculated risks, comfortable if not all ideas are internal and the courage to act in new ways. This starts with the CEO, but includes the entire executive suite; frankly, if key leaders are not on board, this permeates into their organization in a negative way. However, if the leaders live the values, it makes it much easier for their respective teams to also get on board and embrace the change to OI as well as the constant opportunity for change that OI represents.

The entire executive team was involved in formulating the OSM strategy, and all of them were also responsible for ensuring adoption within their functional areas. Everyone was told (with several reinforcement messages) that nobody would be fired or get in trouble for sharing too much information. Rather, it was the opposite and the message was clear: if you were not prepared to get on board with the change in philosophy, you were welcome to leave.

To make sure that the values were understood, our CEO created a set that was and still is communicated often in a variety of formats. Inherently, many of them have a direct relationship with the theory of OI and they support openness and change in a way that enables people to understand the organization's expectations of them:

- Openness
  - we are easy to do business with;
  - we are courageous and transparent in our way of working;
  - we create choice for our customers.
- Trust
  - we all play a role in the success of our business and brand;
  - we work as a team with partners and not as a competitor;
  - our decisions will earn us trust from our partners and customers.
- Collective ingenuity
  - we are inventive, clever and resourceful in solving problems;
  - we nurture ingenuity from all quarters of the world;
  - we never stop listening to and learning from our customers and partners.

An interesting offshoot of these values is the expectations placed on the executive team. John Conoley, our CEO, relates:

> By choosing to live our corporate life openly and by adopting a set of clear values that support it, the executive team is held to a set of behaviours much more rigidly than I have ever seen before. In fact, the values are frequently consulted or cited in decision making. The executive team is not perfect and mistakes will be made, but the 'openness' holds us to account in a whole

different way. To not uphold the values would undermine the whole transformation project.

So it is an interesting dichotomy that you have to create rigour and structure to enable the company to open up.

3. Provide tools

A key enabler of OSM is a new open, online community called Ingenuity Working. This tool was implemented as one way to begin the transformation of the company by starting a very open dialogue between Psion and developers, partners and customers. In step with our corporate values highlighted above, we stated the following goals for Ingenuity Working:

- Live Psion values, our highs and our lows in full view, to become more trusted than any comparable company or competitor.
- Leverage Psion's significant IP portfolio with a wide range of vendors and component suppliers.
- Accelerate a fuller, and uniquely open, dialogue with global customers and resellers. It will enable them to cater to the explosion of micro-niches in the market, which recognizes that customers all have different and individual needs.

What you see on Ingenuity Working is extremely candid and open information that allows outside parties to get a much quicker read on what Psion is truly about. We don't edit the bad stuff out. Upset customers or partners get a response and the information is public for all to see. It was this very aspect that had employees most concerned: 'What if a customer complains' or, 'What if a competitor gets on and sees the complaint?' Further, we populated the community with significant amounts of technical information that had previously been considered too sensitive to share publicly.

Based on the perceived risks, people were initially intimidated by the community. But what became clear to many over time was that the tool was in fact our eyes and ears with our market. From our side, the volume of new information available to both partners and customers on the community added to the perception that we were truly being open. Employees saw that if we listened and helped within the community, customers and partners were pleased with the outcome. What may have started as a negative issue often became praise for how the problem was solved and the situation was handled. These elements started to lend credibility to the notion that tangible benefits could come from inviting our customers and partners in more closely with us.

One such benefit is trust: trust that we'll do what we say for both our partners and our customers. If you are considering partnering on a development initiative or conducting a purchase, wouldn't you rather do it with someone you trust? So, as we expand our network of partners and customers, this seemingly innocuous tool does some very powerful things:

- Builds more trust with those who already know us and builds it more quickly with those who don't.

- Allows us, our partners and our customers to talk across regions, languages and organizational boundaries – express needs, solutions and potential solutions.

- Delivers a platform upon which collaboration can occur between diverse parties – a defining requirement and need for OI to succeed.

4. Bring people with you

You need to provide opportunities for people to get on board. As with any fundamental shift, it will take time for people to fully digest the change that OI represents and its implications on the business and their specific role. To do this successfully, you need more than an e-mail or single presentation. Rather, it typically requires a variety of communication tools (e-mails, presentations, signage) and interaction to make sure that people really do 'get it'. It is easy to mistake a lack of understanding and the resulting lack of activity as a lack of support. It can be amazing how the activity level and perceived support increases once people truly do 'get it'.

Let's look at a concrete example. Initially, some factions of our service organization were intimidated by the new types of information we were sharing as well as the perceived ability for customers to get 'free' support. By opening up a much greater proportion of our technical knowledge to our online community, the feeling seemed to be that their influence and contribution would be diminished. However, they quickly learnt some key things:

- With more information available, some customers and partners were solving their own issues.

- Taking this a step further, some customers were helping others and partners were also contributing to the discussion and resolution even if it wasn't their direct customer.

- Finally, partners, typically perceived to be competing against each other, were helping each other out.

These dynamics created a complete shift in the mentality of the service organization. They realized that sharing more information actually made their job easier based on the learning and collaboration that was happening outside of the organization. In effect, the service model had naturally evolved based on the contributions and needs of the market itself.

A final element to bringing people with us was to communicate this very intent. We took up a rallying cry entitled, 'You make the difference' that looked to focus them on the fact that they as individuals had to contribute to the change. We were also quite upfront that if people were indifferent to the change, then they might want to consider exiting the business. There is no room for passengers that don't believe in the destination.

5. Push people as you bring them

Best intentions aside, people often need a little push to drive them from understanding OI to embracing it and modifying their activities to support it. What we did at Psion was to have a set of workshops that focused on, a) what are you going to do to support OSM, followed four months later by b) what have you now done to support OSM? Functional heads were required to present in front of each other at off-site venues to ensure a suitable level of peer pressure on them. It is hard to show up and say, 'We have no plans and haven't done anything' in such a public forum, so it did help drive both inter-group dialogue and actions. We also held a series of regional workshops to ensure global inclusion within the process and make sure that we were not leaving out key individuals.

In closing

Psion is still completing our transition to an OI business model. Having started the process in mid-2009, it is clear that there is no 'light-switch' approach by which an organization could just turn OI 'on'. The structure, tools, processes and products all need to be in alignment, and that takes time.

That said, our resolve remains strong. John Conoley said, 'We decided to embrace open innovation at Psion to be faster and competitively unpredictable. The real question may be, do we know what we are doing? The answer is no, but we are creating conditions, not outcomes.' And this is key – we are creating the environment for OI to flourish as a key contributor to Psion's business.

To date, all indicators are positive. Initial feedback from customers, partners, investors and analysts has all been extremely positive as they can see that the transition to OI will bring more value to customers and subsequently to us and our partners. So, we are staying the course and looking forward to this shift enabling us to substantially advance our business.

Chapter 18
Managing Legal and IP Issues

DENYS RESNICK

O pen Innovation creates such an intoxicating 'buzz' that it is enticing every imaginable sector, ranging from business and manufacturing to education and the government. The promise of accelerating ideation and new product development is alluring, especially to business leaders who envision improved profitability from opportunities to expand product portfolios, reduce overhead and improve time to market. OI looks great from 10,000 feet.

Now down to reality: before the collaborating parties can enjoy the benefits of OI, they will need to hurdle the legal issues associated with intellectual property. IP is the cup of strong, black coffee that follows the intoxicating buzz of OI.

For every article revelling in the promise of OI there is a sober tale of lost opportunity, unyielding potential partners and never-ending negotiations. Many scholarly articles and law journals address the legal details of IP and confidentiality, prescribing protective measures that will circumvent failures between collaborating partners. This advice tends to focus on activities related to the 'deal' that the parties forge when, in fact, there are critical IP considerations before the innovation seeker has any contact with external parties. A more comprehensive approach is to create a strategy for managing IP in OI.

Defining IP and confidentiality in the context of an OI strategy

As IP and confidentiality are key legal terms with regards to OI, it is worthwhile to understand them in the framework of an OI strategy.

IP

IP is the way that our legal system confers tangible value to something that is intangible, like an idea or concept. A patent is the attempt to define the essence of the inventor's creativity such that the intangible nugget of intellect can be protected and attributed to the inventor. Needless to say, the hazy nature of ideas makes them challenging to protect, and defining where they begin and end is more art than science.

While IP is often embodied in a patent, IP can also be in the intangible form of trade secrets. A trade secret can be almost anything, such as a product formula (an example is the recipe for Coke), a client list, a pricing strategy and even test data. Some companies define IP more broadly as intellectual assets, further blurring the boundaries for what must be protected vs what can be shared.

Confidentiality

Confidentiality is generally defined and protected by a confidentiality agreement (CDA) or non-disclosure agreement (NDA) in order to create a 'safe' space in which two parties can exchange information with the confidence that they are protected from losing control of their trade secrets. The agreement defines the scope of information that is covered by the agreement and the purpose of the exchange, and ensures that the recipient of the information will not share it with a third party or use it for purposes outside the scope of the agreement. Parties generally attempt to limit the scope of the agreement specifically to what will be most valuable to advance the dialog.

Given the imprecise nature of IP, one can understand why a Fortune 500 company might establish blanket policies prohibiting employees from engaging in any dialogue with external parties without first establishing confidentiality protection. For the inventor, an unprotected discussion could result in a large corporation 'stealing' his or her life's work without fair compensation. However, NDAs create their own challenges. The value of the NDA is determined by its content scope, and the parties' ability to enforce it. Many companies have learnt that an abundance of NDAs are nearly impossible to manage, and that the time spent creating the document can be a drag on the OI process, rather than a valuable protection.

Managing vs protecting IP

Often practitioners distinguish between 'open innovation' and 'innovation', suggesting that 'innovation' is the collaborative activity that occurs between parties within an organization (internal innovation), and that 'open innovation' is when that collaboration extends beyond the organization's boundaries to engage with external parties (external innovation). However, 'openness' is a key success factor in any innovation, internal or external, that includes collaboration with at least one other entity, whether that entity is a person, business unit or company. Embracing openness allows the innovation approach to shift from protecting one's IP to managing it.

Protecting IP communicates that your interests are at risk of being threatened and that pre-emptive action is required. A common example of a protective approach is a blanket prerequisite that the innovation seeker owns all IP created by any collaboration. While protective approaches may be prudent from a legal perspective, they often create barriers to the collaborative environment of OI.

Managing IP embraces the more nuanced perspective that the processes, documents and relationships in a collaborative environment should maximize value for all parties. The corporate entity is likely to measure 'value' according to its commercial interests and opportunities in its key markets. A university, by contrast, may place a higher priority on recognition or thought leadership in a specific scientific discipline, but not necessarily in a specific field of application. A private entrepreneur may define value as intellectual independence, financial security or expertise in a defined technology arena with no aspirations to scale or manufacture. When the collaborating parties are open to different definitions of value, it becomes more obvious that one can't assume there is a universal optimal IP approach that applies to every collaboration. Instead, managing IP presupposes that multiple business, market, technology and individual interests contribute to shaping the IP approach that maximizes outcome for each party in an OI collaboration.

Creating an OI IP strategy

Corporate OI initiatives begin with visionaries and entrepreneurs. In a top-down initiative, the CEO issues a goal to allocate a given percentage of R&D funds to collaborative external innovation projects. Internal entrepreneurs can launch a bottom-up OI initiative by seizing an opportunity to collaborate with an external partner when they realize that their company does not possess a competency in the specific area of need. In both cases, an external collaboration jump-starts the company's innovation activity and often precedes any OI process. The CEO creates a momentum and the internal entrepreneur must forge a path through the organization's existing channels, using his or her persuasive skills and internal network to champion projects through to completion.

The collaboration inevitably encounters challenges as it works its way through standard process channels in R&D, marketing and business units. The group often unfairly perceived as an obstacle in OI is legal, whose champions are often excluded from the process until the final stages. Seasoned champions learn the hard way that delaying legal's contribution to the innovation collaboration actually increases the likelihood that IP issues will impede the collaboration, which may ultimately result in a lost opportunity.

Creating an OI IP strategy is a way to proactively nurture external collaboration and increase the probability of reaping the benefits that are most enticing to visionaries. It builds on the understanding that the collaborative nature of OI projects is different from other supplier or purchase arrangements, creating unique assumptions, decision points, investment structures and benefits. The standardized 'one size fits all' or fixed IP policies that drive most corporate legal interactions with external parties rarely embrace the 'openness' and customization that will nurture projects to the point of value creation. Companies frequently recognize the need for an IP strategy specific to OI only after an opportunity is lost, IP or confidentiality has been compromised, or relations become strained between legal and the innovation champions. Although these events are painful and give rise to the stories of failure in innovation lore, they create the critical impetus to proactively create an OI IP strategy.

In the remainder of this chapter, I will outline the key features of an OI IP strategy and the issues that contribute to decision making. The purpose of creating a strategy is to establish precedent and boundary markers to address events within a specified range of activity and to provide the flexibility to manage activities or events that are outside the company's boundaries. Whereas traditional IP policy closes the door to 'out of bound' activities, OI IP strategy guides practitioners in customized problem solving.

Building 'inclusiveness' into the OI IP strategy

Embracing 'openness' starts with creating an IP strategy that is 'inclusive'. To build a coherent and realistic IP strategy with cross-discipline ownership, all OI stakeholders – R&D, marketing, business units, engineering and of course legal – benefit from being engaged from the inception of the strategy through to its implementation. These stakeholders are prime candidates for an OI steering committee, which can act as a board of advisers to guide the organization through implementation challenges. This OI steering committee can also play a leadership role in building the company's organizational structure, processes, metrics and best practices, fully integrating the OI IP strategy into the company's support structure.

In the absence of an OI strategy, R&D project owners often delay engaging with legal until the technology has been evaluated against performance criteria. The logic is that until R&D establishes an interest in the technology, there is no need to introduce legal into the process. The project owner's unstated assumption is that the evaluation process is sequential and single faceted: If R&D determines that the technology is desirable, then legal will handle the contract.

The reality of the matter often defies common logic. In fact, evaluation of OI opportunities is multi-faceted and multi-functional. A cross-functional evaluation team should assess the viability of the opportunity concurrently along three criteria planes: technology performance, relationship fit and commercial opportunity. This approach recognizes that OI is a unique and valuable collaboration opportunity, and not necessarily an acquisition of 'off-the-shelf' technology. If there is potential to jointly create IP, then the solution provider is likely to be a long-term partner in the development process. Therefore, the viability of the solution provider as a partner is not simply a question of the technology's performance, as assessed by the R&D team, or of IP value, as assessed by legal. The innovation seeker must assess the fit and value of the partnership, and understand that the solution provider will be going through the same exercise.

In the absence of an integrated, cross-functional OI IP strategy, innovation seekers jeopardize their prospects for a successful collaboration by engaging in a sequential evaluation process. The unfortunate but common scenario is that the innovation seeker and solution provider technology teams invest time and resources to assess the technology fit and performance. Both teams are highly vested in the relationship, having exchanged samples, information and testing data over the course of several months. They believe they 'have a deal', even though IP may have only been addressed superficially. When that 'deal' falls apart in the hands of legal, they blame legal for standing in the way of innovation.

The benefit of creating a cross-functional OI IP strategy steering committee is that all stakeholders proactively bring forward their assumptions and goals to streamline the recurring OI process. The committee's responsibility is to establish guidelines for commonly accepted best practices that integrate legal's recommendations for handling IP, patents, confidentiality and contracts, with the often competing goals of R&D and the business units. A balanced OI IP strategy can address this compromise with a tiered approach, which establishes broad best practices to guide new practitioners and funnels more challenging, higher-value issues requiring experienced judgement to OI experts or the steering committee. For example, a stated best practice may be to engage with solution providers in early, exploratory non-confidential discussions to minimize the issuance of NDAs. When the solution provider refuses to engage in discussions without a lawyer present, or without an NDA, what should a project owner do? This barrier can potentially be overcome by agreeing to either condition, but an R&D project owner may not be the best individual to assess these options. An OI IP strategy will outline action paths to guide the project owner through common obstacles, either by empowering him or her to make decisions within specified ranges, or to tap into designated OI practice leaders who may be outside his or her personal network.

The ideal OI IP strategy committee member is an enthusiastic, 'out-of-the-box' thinker, who is an internal OI advocate. Within his or her area of expertise, he or she should be able to recognize opportunities as well as barriers, and to leverage the company's resources to maximize real OI benefits. Finding the balance between cheerleaders and naysayers will give the committee the credibility that it needs to create an effective and reasonable OI IP strategy.

Weaving together the threads of IP, confidentiality and timing

The standard legal questions of 'Who will own what?' and, 'What can I share with whom?' are easily addressed in fixed IP policies. The answer in an OI collaboration is, 'It depends.' An OI IP strategy gives OI practitioners a guidebook for managing IP and confidentiality throughout the OI process to achieve a successful outcome. Since IP and confidentiality are managed differently at different stages, timing is the thread that weaves them together into a strategy.

The flexible OI IP strategy establishes a structure that parallels the OI process and defines an acceptable course of action based on a given scenario. It helps the project owner determine when the situation is 'outside the boundaries' and requires special consideration or creative problem solving.

Figure 18.1 illustrates how IP and confidentiality are managed differently based on timing throughout the OI process.

Moving through the stages of OI

All innovation initiatives, internal and external, progress through four distinct phases before progressing to joint development. These four phases are: preparation, discovery, evaluation and agreement. By understanding the objectives, events and desired outcomes of each phase, we can create a comprehensive IP strategy that complements the activities within each phase and facilitates progress to the next step.

1. Preparation

IP management in OI often focuses on the activities that occur when the innovation seeker and external parties engage directly. In contrast, an OI IP strategy anticipates the issues and decisions that will contribute positively to future engagement between the seeker and external parties. The preparation phase, though often neglected, is critical in laying the groundwork for maximizing outcome throughout the OI process.

The innovation seeker's objective in the preparation phase is to select a need that has high strategic value, in an area in which he or she is free to engage in the solution space. This need must be pre-qualified specifically for the OI arena in order to create a higher likelihood of success. During preparation, the organization is making a commitment to a specified outcome (eg follow through, financial investment) against a set of established criteria, while also minimizing the risk of surprise IP restrictions once the project is under way.

FIGURE 18.1 IP and confidentiality management in OI project phases

PHASE	OBJECTIVE	TASK	CONFIDENTIALITY	INTELLECTUAL PROPERTY
PREPARATION	Select strategic Need with freedom to operate	Select and defining the Need	With whom in this space do we have NDA's? What is the competitive sensitivity?	What is the prior art?
		Defining the Evaluation Process	What information can we reveal pre- and post-NDA?	Do we need to consider IP contamination in selecting project team members? What are our IP ownership vs access needs?
		Selecting the OI tool	Should we reach out to known or unknown collaborators? Do we need to maintain external anonymity?	Should we seek an internal solution or reach out externally?
DISCOVERY	Identify high-quality potential solutions without IP risk	Articulating the Need	What information do we reveal in the Need Statement? How specifically should we describe our criteria?	What kind of information do we want to receive from potential collaborators?

PHASE	OBJECTIVE	TASK	CONFIDENTIALITY	INTELLECTUAL PROPERTY
EVALUATION	Vet and select solutions to meet Need without IP risk	Creating the Evaluation Process	Will we engage directly with potential partners or through an intermediary?	What information will we reveal pre- and post-NDA?
			Who will evaluate potential partners?	
		Implementing the Evaluation Process	To whom and at what point do we establish confidentiality?	Are expectations aligned regarding performance, business, and IP goals?
			What kind of information do we need to establish interest in a potential partner?	
AGREEMENT	Define collaboration terms including IP and confidentiality	Defining the Work Plan	What confidentiality terms are necessary prior to, during, and post-collaboration?	What legal framework best protects and promotes our collaboration?
			How will we exchange and share information?	
		Negotiating ownership and access to IP	How is access to the collaboration protected?	How is access and ownership of existing and new IP managed?
			Who can share what type of information pre-, during, and post-collaboration?	

As business units and departments select and define a strategic need, the existing legal landscape should be evaluated to qualify the need for an OI pursuit. Research into prior art and adjacent intellectual property will help the team assess the competitive environment in the target IP space, the freedom to operate without infringing on existing IP, and the opportunity to create new IP. For example, the innovation seeker may learn that the IP is well established for a desired technology in an application completely outside the company's industry. Therefore, a steadfast goal of 'owning IP' may not be as valuable as exclusive licensing of the IP in a defined field, or creating IP related to the application of the technology. The seeker's expectations about IP ownership vs IP access impact how he or she conducts the OI search, engages with solution providers, and frames the terms of agreement.

By proactively defining the evaluation process during the preparation phase, the project owner has the opportunity to control the nature of the information that will be exposed and submitted throughout the OI search. If the innovation seeker does not want to tip-off competitors to its strategic pursuit, he or she must consider whether the need can be shared in 'camouflaged' language, through an intermediary, or anonymously. Can enough information be shared to attract high-quality responses? Perhaps there can be a preliminary round of vetting in a non-confidential exchange, saving the exchange of more sensitive data for selected solution providers under NDA. If the topic is very sensitive, it may be worthwhile to have an intermediary create a firewall to manage the exchange of non-confidential information or create anonymity for the seeker.

In addition to controlling the nature of the information, the innovation seeker should plan who on his or her side will be exposed to the solution provider information. While an R&D expert may be most knowledgeable about the desired technology, that person is also the most vulnerable to IP contamination and the greatest threat to IP leakage. Predetermining what information can be shared in a non-confidential environment vs what can be shared under NDA is an important training exercise for the project team, giving the members the tools to engage most confidently and effectively throughout the OI process.

The preparation phase outlines the IP strategy for each specific OI pursuit. This roadmap guides the team and stakeholders through subsequent phases when the strategy is implemented. Most IP strategy decisions arising throughout the project should have been addressed during the preparation phase.

2. Discovery

The goal of the discovery phase is to identify a variety of high-quality potential solutions and partners that could provide the missing expertise, insight, technology and capabilities to address the defined seed. The innovation seeker compiles a portfolio of potential solutions that contributes value through their approach (eg alternative paths, sustainability, cost savings, breakthrough) to funnel into the evaluation phase.

The challenge during discovery is how to maximize the quantity of high-quality information by tapping into the greatest breadth and variety of resources, without compromising IP. Finding this balance between confidentiality and openness can be achieved by carefully selecting the appropriate OI vehicle. For example, internal networks and external ecosystems of preferred suppliers, academic partners and consortia connect the innovation seeker to known partners, allowing the seeker to closely manage who receives information. To extend the outreach beyond known or obvious networks, seekers can evaluate a broad variety of options that range from highly open networks, like internet-based crowdsourcing to highly-managed global OI searches through OI intermediaries. OI service providers can even conduct global searches on the seeker's behalf, allowing the seeker to remain anonymous until an NDA is established with selected partners.

This OI vehicle will impact how information is revealed and received during the discovery phase. For example, many companies seek ideas by stating their needs as broad, general statements on their websites. A packaged food company states its desire to find packaging technologies that preserve high-moisture foods, extend shelf-life and eliminate microbial growth. A respondent may submit non-confidential or protected information describing the unique benefits of their innovation, its application and its state of commercialization, in 500 characters or less. The innovation seeker has minimized the IP risk by not sharing any information on application and performance criteria, but the quality of the response is also likely to be lower value. Seekers can select a highly interactive forum by posting a need on an open chat forum on which seekers and solution providers dialogue directly. The openness of this environment presents the opposite challenge, since it is more difficult to control how and to whom information is revealed. An intermediary can offer a compromise between confidentiality and openness since they can communicate high-value information about the need, like performance criteria, to solution providers, while camouflaging the seeker's identity or application goals. An intermediary can also dialogue with the solution provider on behalf of the seeker, providing an additional IP firewall.

Rigid IP policies that inhibit the discovery phase greatly diminish a company's potential OI success because they narrow the scope and the value of potential solutions and providers. Often, an IP strategy gives seekers the confidence and the tools to create the high-quality funnel they need to select a viable partner during the evaluation phase.

3. Evaluation

The innovation seeker's goal during the evaluation phase is to assess the funnel of potential solutions and partners against pre-established criteria, in order to identify a single or several vetted potential solutions. The selected solutions and partners represent the best path to address the stated need, and the parties have stated a mutual interest in forming a defined type of collaboration.

In the absence of an OI IP strategy, the evaluation phase may be the first time the project team contemplates reaching out to the legal department, perhaps seeking guidance on what information can be shared and received in a non-confidential exchange without compromising IP. Traditionally, legal's response might be that an NDA must be executed before the seeker and provider can interface. However, companies are embracing the value of pre-NDA vetting as they recognize the challenge of managing and enforcing hundreds or even thousands of NDAs. Within an OI IP strategy, the evaluation phase represents a narrowing of the funnel, creating a framework for non-confidential vetting of potential solutions and partners, and selecting a chosen few to pass to a confidential environment.

The value of an inclusive, cross-functional project team that assesses potential solutions across diverse criteria (including solution capability and technology performance, the 'fit' of the proposed relationship, commercial viability and legal implications) was discussed earlier in this chapter. The evaluation process can include teleconferences, exchange of materials, samples and test data, and on-site visits. Ideally, the early exchanges should be non-confidential, allowing some partners and solutions to rise in preference while others are eliminated. The most desirable and viable short-listed options can then progress to confidential exchanges with the execution of a confidentiality agreement. The filtering that occurs in the evaluation phase should result in the selection of a minimal number of potential partners and solutions with whom to negotiate collaboration agreements.

4. Agreement

The agreement phase is the point when the innovation seeker and solution provider make a mutual commitment to engage together in a collaboration or mutual exchange. This commitment may result in a series of collaboration agreements that begin with proof-of-concept, in a single joint development agreement that leads to commercialization, or in a single event that transfers IP or access to IP from the provider to the seeker. In all cases, the goal of the agreement phase is to define the relationship between the innovation seeker and solution provider such that the agreement outlines the shared obligations and mutual rewards that will engage both parties enthusiastically in the collaboration.

The agreement phase is traditionally when the legal team is most highly engaged. Without an OI IP strategy and a cross-functional project team, project responsibility may shift abruptly to legal, significantly altering the nature and tone of the engagement between the seeker and provider. An effective OI IP strategy integrates confidentiality and IP expectations into all previous phases so that the agreement phase is a confirmation and documentation of the mutual understanding established earlier.

During the agreement phase, the contracts are defined by the work plan and goals, and are negotiated and executed. These agreements are varied, and are likely to outline the confidentiality terms and how IP will be owned, managed and accessed by the parties. These agreements can include material transfer agreements (MTAs) and exploratory research agreements (ERAs) in early stage collaboration, and joint development agreements (JDAs), joint equity agreements and licensing agreements in the co-development stage. The negotiations to establish IP ownership and/or access, and commercial terms like licensing and commercial supply, do not need to be contentious if the focus is on maximizing value for each party, as was discussed earlier in this chapter.

Bringing it all together

A flexible IP strategy to advance one's OI goals

To realize the benefits and opportunities of OI, both innovation seekers and solution providers must find a balance between their competing and shared interests. An IP strategy gives seeker companies the framework to evaluate the IP and confidentiality issues in each phase of the OI process. By anticipating the legal issues during the preparation phase, the project team can more effectively communicate their need during discovery, target the best opportunities during evaluation, and drive to a balanced and successful outcome during agreement.

When innovation seekers adopt a flexible and inclusive IP strategy, they approach each OI collaboration as a unique event, and assess how to maximize outcome and minimize risk in the context of the specific situation. Both innovation seekers and solution providers value the IP strategy process because, ultimately, it seeks to maximize value for both parties.

Chapter 19
Fast, Open and Global
The future of innovation

STEFAN LINDEGAARD

The field of innovation has been in a significant state of flux over the past decade as corporations have tried to systematize their innovation efforts to bring about greater predictability, and Open Innovation has developed as a new phenomenon with enormous potential but equally large challenges. Predicting the future of any field that is undergoing massive changes is, of course, risky. But I have a clear vision that the future for this increasingly important discipline will be built on three key elements: fast, open and global.

Few would argue that OI is where the field is headed. This paradigm shift is inevitable for many companies and industries. It is just a question of which company gets there first and executes the best to reap the benefits of being the preferred partner of choice within their industry. But while OI is one of the key elements of the future, it cannot stand by itself. In a global economy where competition is super heated and rapid change the norm, OI must be global in its reach and be supported by an ability to move fast.

The case for OI is made admirably elsewhere in this book, so I won't dwell on that aspect further. Instead, I will discuss why I believe OI cannot stand by itself and why fast and global are the other two key elements of the future of innovation.

Fast as in fail fast and fail often

Companies will no longer have the luxury of spending the time they have in the past to develop new products and services. Development cycles are already shrinking, and once a product or service is in the market, the time it has to enjoy a competitive advantage is also growing shorter and shorter. As the speed of change accelerates and the lifecycles of products and services decrease, companies need to work hard on bringing their offerings to market faster and cheaper.

This increased speed to market inherently involves greater risk of failure since it will allow little time for extensive testing of concepts. This, in turn, means companies, from the leaders on down, will need to become much more comfortable with failure than they have been in the past and embrace the concept of learning through failure, because in the rapid-fire innovation environment of the future, failures are almost certain to be much more prevalent. Both of these notions present great challenges since currently, in most companies, the corporate culture does not tolerate failure and in fact punishes it severely in some cases. As a result few if any productive systems are in place to learn through failure. Sure, plenty of lip service may be paid to activities like debriefings or post mortems, but for the most part, if something fails, everyone is primarily focused on sweeping it under the rug and hoping it will quickly be forgotten.

So the challenge is how do we move from that type of culture to one where failure is of course not desired, but is acceptable and where learning through failure, what I have termed 'smartfailing', becomes the norm? How do we engender an understanding that quite frequently success is an outgrowth of past failure? And ultimately, how do we create a culture where failures are actually valued for the learning that can be extracted from them, what I call 'fail capital'?

When I wrote about this subject on my blog, it drew more comments than almost any other topic I've raised over the past few years. Some people objected to even using the words 'fail' or 'failure' because of their highly negative connotations in most corporate environments. For me, this pushback just further illustrated how averse people can be to acknowledging that failures occur, never mind to discussing them openly to mine such situations for new learning.

Some people were concerned I was talking about planning to fail, which, of course, is not the case. But since it is highly likely that the rate of failure will increase as companies move faster and faster with their innovation efforts, having a plan in place to learn from the inevitable failures is advisable. Paradoxically, having a culture that accepts failure as part of the innovation process and that has tools and techniques in place to assure that valuable lessons are mined from each failure, should reduce the rate of failure and help the organization move faster and faster.

Here's how Randy Voss, Senior Manager, Global Strategy and Business Development, Whirlpool Corporation, summed it up on my blog:

> I would say that fast really needs to be faster. Whatever speed a firm is comfortable at, ratchet things up until you become uncomfortable. Failing fast with a purpose will yield the type of results that will generate real learning. Quickly translate that learning into the next round of ideation and keep repeating until you find the marketable item.

Global as in innovation happens anywhere

Global companies continue to move their R&D and innovation activities away from their corporate headquarters into a growing number of global innovation hubs. Some typical examples of this strategy come from IBM and Xerox.

IBM's Global Rail Innovation Centre in Beijing, China, is billed as a worldwide rail innovation centre that brings together rail companies, universities, government leaders and a wide range of rail experts to advance the next generation rail systems in countries throughout the world.

Xerox recently opened an innovation hub in Chennai, India, that will focus on OI. According to Xerox CTO Sophie Vanderbroek, this new centre differs from the company's other research centres in that instead of hiring lots of researchers, the in-house employees they hire will serve as 'connectors' who link the centre with outside partners in industry, universities and government.

'Every person we hire will partner with at least 50 or more people,' Vanderbroek says. She continues:

> Every person will be working on at least five projects and with each project there will be at least 10 people and hence, it has a big magnifying effect. There will be a large number of innovators working … For instance, IIT Madras' computer science department is partnering the innovation hub on how we can leverage cloud computing technologies to improve the way services are delivered for small businesses. (Singh, 2010)

As with any innovation strategy, establishing such a hub requires having a clear innovation mandate and strategy. There will be false starts and lots of learning along the way. It is inevitable that some of these hubs will be more effectively operated and more productive than others. As the number of such hubs established by the IBMs of the world multiplies, smaller organizations, ranging from start-ups to mid-size companies, will have to figure out how they're going to become involved with these centres. They will also need a clear innovation mandate and strategy to help them make the right choices about which hubs are right for them to connect with.

The other interesting addition to innovation globalization is the emerging trend of 'reverse innovation', a term coined by Vijay Govindarajan of the Tuck School of Business to describe the phenomenon in which Western-based companies innovate in emerging countries and bring this innovation back to the Western world. In other words, it is no longer just a one-way game. Companies such as GE, Microsoft, Procter & Gamble and Nokia are testing the reverse innovation waters. In an oft-cited example of this process, GE Healthcare's ultra-portable Mac 400 electrocardiogram machine was developed for markets in India and China and sells for only US$1,000. After further improvements were made to the breakthrough technology, a more advanced model, the Mac 800, was introduced into the United States, where it is finding new applications such as for use by EMTs at accident sites. The price is approximately 80 per cent lower than similar products available in the US market.

In the consumer goods world, Procter & Gamble developed Vicks Honey Cough cold remedy for the Mexican market and then found it also had a market in Europe and the United States. Similarly, Nestlé took its Maggi brand of low-cost, low-fat dried noodles for rural India and Pakistan and began selling them as a healthy and budget-friendly alternative in Australia and New Zealand (see 'Reverse innovation: definitions and examples', **http://www.casestudyinc.com/reverse-innovation-definition-and-examples**).

At the same time, companies in the developing world are introducing their own products into the developed world. For example, Tata Motors, a multinational company headquartered in Mumbai, India, is India's largest company in the automobile and commercial vehicle sectors. It plans to sell an upgraded version of the Tata Nano, which has been billed as the world's cheapest car, in Western markets under the name Tata Europe.

Clearly, whether products are developed by Western companies in the developing world and then come West or whether they are developed by companies native to emerging markets like India and China, these generally lower-priced goods are going to disrupt price structures that Western companies have enjoyed so far. Managing the local teams involved in reverse innovation also presents challenges. Professor Govindarajan (2010) makes the case for giving these local teams large amounts of autonomy, which may prove to be a difficult dynamic for some Western managers who are used to operating more in a command and control environment. This new model will also be problematical for companies that suffer from 'not invented here' thinking; certainly for some, relinquishing the notion that 'the developed world makes and the developing world takes' may prove difficult.

Throwing another interesting twist into the mix, cash-rich private and state-owned Chinese technology companies are going in large numbers to Silicon Valley in the United States in search of bargains (Boudreau, 2010). In addition to looking for start-ups to buy, they are opening offices and hiring talent, which means that eventually they will be developing new products and services in California for use in markets worldwide.

We live in a world in which customers don't care where ideas came from; they only care about quality, value and price. With both the developed world and the emerging world concentrating on innovation, the speed of innovation should accelerate to an even faster pace than today. Change has already become a familiar friend to most organizations, but the intensity it is likely to become greater in the future, leaving some even more uncomfortable and reluctant to give up the status quo than they are today. Yet the reality is that as innovation adapts to the fast, open and global model, companies have begun a creative destruction involving their organizational setups, technologies and business models. Corporate innovation people will become the facilitators and integrators of this disruption and change, helping to usher in a new innovation mindset that highlights a holistic approach and skills in networking and communication.

The future of innovation brings uncertainty, but it definitely also brings lots of opportunities. The big question you need to ask is this: are you ready for a future of innovation that is fast, open and global?

Chapter 20
The Power of Open Collaboration in Connecting People

PEKKA POHJAKALLIO AND PIA ERKINHEIMO

Around two thirds of the planet's population (more than 5 billion people) use mobile phones, making mobile the most popular global technology ever.

Nokia is the world's largest manufacturer of mobile devices. Founded in 1865 as a paper manufacturer, the company developed diverse businesses such as electricity generation, rubber boots and electrical cables before making a 'big bet' on GSM technology in the 1990s, refocusing the company to take advantage of the growth in personal communication devices.

At Nokia, our objective is to bring new connections, contacts and knowledge to billions of disparate individuals across the globe. Our business operates in a complex ecosystem, where partnership and collaboration to drive innovation are not simply desirable but essential. Since the early days of the mobile industry, manufacturers and network operators have worked hand in glove to develop successful consumer propositions and offer user services that add value to their lives.

The business environment in which we operate is extremely complex and constantly evolving. Devices that were traditionally fixed are becoming mobile. Consumers expect to be connected to information and entertainment from a diverse range of sources, everywhere, all of the time, and increasingly on any device. No business can now expect to have the range and scope to fulfil this alone. In this complex world, partnerships and open collaboration are more important to Nokia's commitment to innovation than ever before. It is therefore important to understand the parameters within which innovation takes place at Nokia.

Arki – inspired by everyday life

Arki is a Finnish term meaning 'everyday life'. It describes the things people do all the time, and how they overcome day-to-day issues and problems.

Some may see Arki as the boring minutiae of life, but at Nokia, Arki provides us with the inspiration to develop products and services based on the real needs and desires of people.

To achieve this we need to have a real, deep and extensive understanding of people's needs, desires and behaviours. People are the single most important inspiration for our innovation: particularly how they live their lives and how they resolve their everyday (Arki) issues.

People driving innovation

Technology is an enabler but innovation is not achieved in a research laboratory. For any new product or service to be successful there must be a real human need or desire being satisfied.

Consider the example of text messaging. This technology was created to enable network engineers to contact each other over the GSM network. It was effectively a two-way paging capability, built into a mobile phone. The service was not created to have any practical use for the consumer. The technology is not especially compelling: you can only send 160 characters of data; the message is expensive to send; and it is hard to type on a phone keypad.

Yet as we know, text messaging developed into one of the single most important ways by which people communicate today. What happened? There was a real human need, an Arki, to be contactable without being disturbed; and this was solved by SMS. Human need drove the success: the innovation happened almost by accident.

Innovation at Nokia

Our objective is to make sure that innovation does not happen by accident, but by design. Most people struggle to visualize what is missing from their lives or to describe the 'next big thing'. Traditional market research has its role when verifying ideas, but when new products and services are being created, we aim to look deeper.

For Nokia, the cornerstone of innovation is a deeper understanding of trends; knowledge of needs and behaviours; immersion with people to observe their individual Arki; and data analysis of information we receive from people's use of our products and services.

Bringing cameras to mobile phones

Each of these cornerstones has an impact on innovation development in Nokia. An example that encompasses all four is the integration of digital photography into mobile phones.

In the early 1990s we noticed the development of a trend in photography: the move from traditional photography to digital. Previously, we went on holiday loaded with reels of film. We got our pictures developed when we came home and then bored our friends and neighbours with slide shows or albums of our holiday. Digital photography changed this. Suddenly we could take as many pictures as we had memory for and share them quickly and easily.

This led to a change in behaviour. People began to snap pictures wherever they were. Photography became a snapshot of a moment or a feeling we were experiencing. This made the mobile phone and the digital camera perfect partners: a way to instantly share our moments from the device we always have in our pocket.

We started making it easy to connect a digital camera to a mobile phone, but immersion and observation of people made it clear that this was clumsy. People wanted an integrated device. In 2001 the Nokia 7650 camera phone was launched with a VGA camera. VGA digital camera technology had been available for at least five years; it was Arki that drove the integrated solution and the technology simply served as an enabler.

It is important to understand this focus on Arki, because it is central to what drives our open collaboration projects, partnerships and cooperations. We work hard to create the environment where Arki-inspired innovation can take place openly with other companies, universities and individuals.

A case in point is our relationship with Carl Zeiss, a company with more than 120 years' experience of photographic innovation. In 1902, Carl Zeiss Tessar lenses created the first portable cameras, enabling photography to become mobile for the first time. Carl Zeiss recognized the Arki of people at the time to capture the moment wherever they were.

Exactly 100 years later, Carl Zeiss and Nokia joined forces with a commitment to fulfil the same Arki in the 21st century, creating lenses for mobile phones that delivered a quality usually only found in SLR cameras. This partnership has created better mobile phone camera lenses, improved the pictures people get from mobile phones and helped to accelerate the development of mobile phone cameras to match the quality of a digital camera. Today, with Carl Zeiss' critical help, Nokia is the biggest manufacturer of digital cameras in the world.

This partnership demonstrates exactly what Nokia looks for in innovation collaboration – long-term open partnerships with organizations that have the same commitment to developing people-centric innovation as we do.

Sharing the moment

In a similar vein, in 2001 Nokia collaborated with a partner called Satama Interactive. Together, we set up big screens and let people send pictures and comments to them from their phones. This activity had two outcomes: it showed people how much fun they could have sharing their images, but we also used this as an early form of crowdsourcing, using data analysis from the project to understand what people were prepared to share in a public arena.

If we had simply asked people, 'Would you be prepared to share your photos and thoughts on a public screen?' I suspect that the answer would have been a resounding 'no'. Yet one of the major lessons from the activity was that people were excited by the opportunity to share their images and messages publicly. It was fun and personal.

The results from this project, along with the emerging trend of social networking, led to the faster development of one-click sharing of images taken on a mobile phone with social networking sites – making it as easy as possible for people to capture and share the moment. Today more than 30 billion pieces of content are shared every month on Facebook alone, billions of which are photographs taken on mobile phones and uploaded instantly over the mobile networks. This has developed from scratch in only half a generation – less than 15 years. A combination of people-inspired innovation, partnerships with like-minded companies and observation of the behaviour of crowds, has enabled us to retain a leadership position in camera phones by innovating to help solve people's Arki.

OI driving new opportunities

Our collaboration is not only driven by partnerships with established companies. Such an approach would limit our ability to develop and grow in an environment where companies can emerge to dominate a market in a short space of time.

Recognizing this can be challenging, yet it is essential in creating the right environment where ideas and innovation can come from anywhere and anyone. It is impossible for any single company to expect to have all of the answers. This is why we are increasingly participating in OI projects, enabling developers and communities to find solutions to Arki for anyone or anywhere. To this end, in February 2010 Nokia and Intel established MeeGo, an open development project hosted by the Linux Foundation. MeeGo combines Intel's Moblin and Nokia's Maemo projects into one Linux-based, open source software platform. MeeGo will run on the next generation of computing devices such as televisions, handheld and in-car devices, and netbooks. The software is available for anyone free-of-charge and without additional licences or contracts beyond the standard open source licences of the components.

MeeGo is creating an open ecosystem where people can develop relevant services and applications for new devices, from the car to the kitchen and from the living room to the handheld portable. Future devices will come in all shapes and sizes and perform all kinds of functions, but all of them will need to enable people across the world to remain simply and elegantly connected to entertainment, information and communications. By creating an open environment, we aim to help developers recognize the particular Arki of a diverse range of user groups and create their own solutions, facilitating new people-inspired innovation and still remaining at the centre of connecting people across the globe.

Global innovation

While global human behaviours such as the desire to share, the thirst for knowledge and the hunger for information are all identifiable, the Arki of life for a farmer in sub-Saharan Africa obviously varies significantly from that of a student in the United States.

As a global company this is not something Nokia can ignore. And there is no short cut to understanding the Arki in different cities, countries and continents. It is not possible to create relevant and meaningful products and services for sub-Saharan Africa from a research centre in Silicon Valley. As our business has evolved beyond hardware into mobile services and applications, we have placed increasing significance on the importance of sharing our ideas with local populations. Nowhere is this truer than in emerging markets such as India, where 10 million new mobile phone subscribers are added every month.

Ovi Life Tools

In 2007 we recognized the need to develop new service opportunities in emerging markets, where they did not currently exist. This could not be done from Finland, so Nokia set up a team in India to do it, led by Jawahar Kanjilal, a Nokia employee and Indian national who grew up in a small city 120 miles from Mumbai. The brief was a blank sheet of paper – strange as it might seem for a large company, we empowered Kanjilal to build his own team and develop services that addressed the Arki of the local population.

Kanjilal created what was effectively a widespread crowdsourcing project, not using the internet but by directly engaging with the rural people of India. The objective was to understand which kind of services would help people to improve their lives. Kanjilal led a team that ran detailed observations of what people's needs were in a part of the world where the internet, as most in the Western world understand it, does not exist. We talked to, listened to and observed people first hand, to get a better understanding of people in the region and to build meaningful services for mobile phone users in developing markets.

In 2009, a message-based service that delivers information across three main categories of agriculture, entertainment and education was launched, called Ovi Life Tools. In agriculture, Ovi Life Tools offers local knowledge to help farmers run more successful businesses. Users get up-to-date information on which crops to plant, which fertilizers and pesticides are relevant at a given time, agricultural market price information and weather forecasts – all via their mobile phone. This information was previously unavailable and helps take the guesswork out of farming for the best commercial gain.

Education services include 'English learning assistance'. This provides daily language lessons, based on the needs of the user. Exam preparation coaching and instant exam results via a mobile remove the need to wait for results and provide easy ways for students to learn on a daily basis, remaining engaged with the subject even when they are alone with five minutes to spare.

The Ovi Life Tools Entertainment service delivers pop music information, quizzes, ringtones and sports information. One of the most popular services is horoscopes. Our team on the ground noticed how important horoscopes were to people – they showed a real passion for this information. By integrating horoscopes into Life Tools, we are truly tapping into the Arki of the local population.

Ovi Life Tools is a real-world example of the benefits of mass observation and applying relevant technology to solve human issues and enhance people's lives.

Innovation and collaboration, driven by people

By placing people at the centre of our innovation, we strive to deliver products and services that people want and are relevant to their Arki, even before they are aware they need them. We have commented, not entirely in jest, that all our people really need to be anthropologists to contribute to the future of Nokia. The future is linked to a deeper and richer understanding of people's behaviour and their needs, based on their own, very particular situation. To achieve this we will continue to create open ecosystems that people can engage with easily and effectively, encourage people to participate fully and enable them to create their own solutions to local Arki issues.

We are also developing more alliances and partnerships to inspire future innovation. Nokia aspires to be the best company in the world to partner with and we strive to find more ways to add to the wide number of partners we collaborate with, large or small, especially those who share the philosophy of people-centred innovation like our own. However, such a transformation is not without its challenges; it requires a change of mindset for many who have been used to a working environment where 'not invented here' is a derogatory term.

Our maxim remains that innovation is not something that can be limited to within the four walls of the company, or separated from people, taking place only in isolated research and development laboratories or science parks. Quite the opposite – innovation today, more than ever, is democratized and driven by people, working together in increasingly open and transparent ways, so that the knowledge and insight this provides can be the catalyst for moving the company forward.

Chapter 21
Common Mistakes and Stress Points

ANDREW GAULE

S etbacks are an inevitable part of any innovation process. Indeed, some are a necessity, since they provide the learning opportunities that ensure only the fittest ideas survive. Yet, from our experience advising leading organizations, we know that when innovation activities hit certain 'stress points' they can come to a grinding halt.

An idea that initially looks cost-effective may turn out to be prohibitively expensive to develop. A technology that performs well at first may fail during its transition into commercial production. A business may wither because the organization that gave birth to it lacks the skills base to keep it alive. These are the kinds of problems that executives imagine will stop them from bringing innovations to market. However, there are other stress points which, while less easy to distinguish, are more likely to destroy value – for example, the misalignment of an idea with the organization's overall strategic purpose.

Our research suggests there are, in fact, five broad categories of innovation stress points that correspond to various phases of research, new product and new venture development; these are shown in Figure 21.1.

Defining your innovation strategy

When is an innovation worth pursuing? For most people the answer is simple: whenever one perceives an opportunity to generate value. This is a well-meaning view, but it is also one that can lead to tremendous waste. If organizations fail to determine and solicit the types of ideas that will serve their overall strategies, staff can end up innovating in different directions. Their definitions of 'value' may differ, from short-term commercial benefits to long-term fundamental knowledge. They may find that what seemed ingenious in the laboratory proves unscalable on the production line. Ultimately, they may divert significant resources away from the organization's most sustainable sources of value – the ones that differentiate it from its competitors.

FIGURE 21.1 Five broad categories of innovation stress points

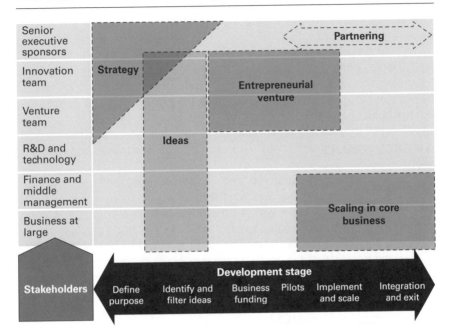

Innovation should, therefore, begin with a clear definition of *purpose*. This represents the first of the '5 Ps' that we use to describe the key elements of the ideal corporate innovation process – one that is aligned with corporate goals and effective in the delivery of measurable results. (For more on the 5 Ps, see Chapter 7.) If you operate in the private sector, your most basic purpose may be to build shareholder value, while in the public sector it may be to improve productivity. Any statement of purpose must set innovation priorities based on the organization's long-term objectives, and circumscribe the areas in which you would like your staff to innovate. The consequences of misalignment of purpose can be serious. (Further discussion on strategic context can be found in Chapter 7.)

Identifying and selecting innovations

A healthy innovation process generates many more ideas than can possibly be developed by one organization. So how do you decide where to put your resources?

Many organizations fail to be sufficiently methodical or holistic in their analysis of ideas, often because they simply are not aware of helpful tools and techniques. Typically, they will invest in an idea because it performs well against a few criteria, only to abandon it later realizing that, say, it cannot be scaled, that it requires a prohibitive level of investment, or because the organization does not have the right environment to encourage the form of innovation concerned.

To overcome this tendency, we use a tool called the 'new business traffic light' (Gaule, 2006). This encourages venture teams to ask questions such as: 'How does this idea support our strategy?' and, 'Does it distract or does it help us get to where we want to go?' It enables the innovation leader to act more like the head of a venture capitalist (VC) fund, investing in ideas that promise knowledge if they fail as well as value if they succeed. A failure, in this context, is an opportunity to learn about the health of a particular business model or sector.

VCs are especially keen to see leadership capabilities in a new entrepreneurial venture. They would rather back a great team with a mediocre idea than a mediocre team with a great idea. Yet, in a corporate setting, inventors will often be permitted to carry their idea forward regardless of their suitability for running a business. The need to reward the innovator while serving the interests of the organization as a whole is just one of the stress points you are likely to encounter at this stage of the innovation process.

Where is the demand?

An idea's point of origin can often have an unhelpful bearing on its research and development. For example, if it is conceived by a technologist then the way it is pitched internally and externally may end up being 'too academic' – that is, with too much emphasis placed on the technological advances that have been made and not enough on the ultimate market potential.

Imagine, for example, that your organization manufactures advanced healthcare technologies, and that one of your scientists has devised a new type of wound dressing with the potential to speed up patient recovery times. The dressing is much more expensive than traditional alternatives on a unit-per-unit basis, but could ultimately save the hospital money by freeing up resources. To generate value from this proposition, the scientists need to persuade those with most influence over the procurement process that this product will benefit them directly. That is, they need to persuade health practitioners that they can heal their patients faster, and thereby give them more bed space. It is not enough to make either the health economics case or the 'academic' case in isolation.

A renewable energy venture may have a very good environmental case, but who is going to pay for it? Equally, it is important to be mindful of how potential customers handle procurement. The average hospital's tendering process may not be sophisticated enough to recognize that by paying more for products in the short term, it will save money in the long term. To generate value from technology it is often necessary to revisit cost structures or reconsider the proposition altogether.

To assess the idea and define the resulting proposition, robust systems of communication are needed at various levels of the organization. There must be a rich and prolonged conversation between innovators, prospective customers and marketing teams. And there must be a system in place for ensuring the best ideas are brought to the attention of senior executives and the 'queen bee' (see Chapter 7).

To encourage the transmission of good ideas from individuals to the core of the organization, it is essential to ensure that those individuals can circumvent the stress points that usually quash creativity. Leading organizations make this easy, not by creating a suggestions box or some glorified online equivalent, but by dedicating a team of individuals to spotting and promoting radical ideas that do not meet the usual criteria on which internal initiatives are generally judged. Procter & Gamble's 'Connect and Develop' programme, for example, actively looks for ideas both inside and outside the company. It gives innovators funding to develop those ideas within the organization and with external partners.

Hard and soft obstacles

Sometimes it can be helpful for an idea to hit problems at this stage of the innovation process. If it fails to meet certain 'hard' thresholds, there is no clearer sign that it should be rejected. For example, when looking for third-horizon innovations (ie those that will build new capabilities within the organization), an idea may be rejected on the grounds that it only represents incremental change. Alternatively, it may be insufficiently scalable to merit the investment it will take to commercialize.

However, the identification of a winner or loser is not often so clear cut. An idea may be here, for example, because it has been withdrawn from a later stage of development and needs to be reassessed. There are many instances of products and services developed into fully-fledged ventures only for their consumer relevance to be questioned in the run-up to commercialization. In such instances, the executive team is generally astonished by the failure of the venture, even though their lack of attention was a contributing factor.

A lack of real-world commercial thinking can be prevented if, from the early stages of an idea's consideration, it is discussed with potential customers, funders and even external partners. A VC fund approach to internal investment in ideas can also help to encourage rigorous analysis of ideas and to install performance measures that act as a 'stop-loss' should an idea prove untenable later on. Similarly, a poor economic model can be fixed provided an idea is given clear and appropriate performance metrics at both the business and personal level. These metrics may need to be entirely separate from those of the core business, since the idea being considered may require its own extrapreneurial® (see page 63) profit centre to function successfully. The venture may even need its own premises to avoid any 'cultural contamination' from the core and to sustain its entrepreneurial dynamism. Either way, the metrics should be embedded into personal and team performance contracts, with performance and alignment monitored continuously.

In addition, there are numerous ways to ensure an idea is considered from every possible angle before it is permitted to continue its journey down the innovation pipeline. The customer focus group is an old favourite that remains useful but, in recent years, others have developed more sophisticated tools such as the 'Business Cube', a checklist of nine success factors that executives should consider repeatedly during the development on an idea. Bringing new ideas to market faster and at a lower cost is the overriding imperative for innovative organizations. It makes sense to trial solutions with customers and involve those customers in the innovation process early, rather than spend huge amounts of money initially on market research and analysis.

It is important to note that even if an idea meets every hard criterion required, there may still be soft issues to deal with – resistance to a 'gamechanging' idea from the core business, for example, where people are fearful of what is to come next. An open perspective can help to identify false positives (ideas that should not have been progressed with such vigour) and equally false negatives (ideas that were rejected initially that have value potential). However, implementation can be an issue in an organization that has difficulty dealing with new business models (for example, moving from products into services), entering new markets or operating in new parts of a value chain.

Turning promising ideas into commercial realities

When people think of innovation stress points they typically think of this phase – the attempted conversion of an idea into a commercial reality. This is where they expect to encounter the greatest number of stress points. Indeed, an innovation is never more at risk than at the moment it is introduced to those parts of the business that will be essential to its development. If the units in question feel they have no vested interest in the innovation's success then their reaction is likely to be: 'Great, but not on my patch.'

Sure, they understand the idea and appreciate how it might generate value for the organization, but they have got enough problems of their own already. Such a situation typically arises because job definitions are unclear, or because directors are insufficiently clear in their assignment of responsibility to managers and other staff. The confusion of accountability then leads to the withholding of resources from the venture in question and, more seriously, the lack of 'ownership' of a critical component. From our research, and a recent survey of H-I Network members, this emerged as one of the most problematic stress points of all.

Rigorous stakeholder management is needed to overcome such issues, as well as a comprehensive engagement plan, driven by the executive team.

Again, the importance of communication must be stressed: for an innovation strategy to be successful, it needs to be reiterated frequently at all levels of the organization and translated into aligned individual goals and objectives. There are stakeholder analysis and project portfolio analysis tools available that can help to ease the process, but ultimately it comes down to a healthy culture at the level of the venture team – the social interaction between 'scout bees' and the 'queen bee'. You can reinforce the positive behaviours with the simplest things, such as a social event, to celebrate successful cooperation.

One of the most common stress points encountered in this phase is a lack of funding. If an idea requires more resources than originally predicted, and if those resources are not found quickly, a valuable opportunity may be stalled or missed as innovators and extrapreneurs® disengage, and the momentum can be irretrievably lost.

An idea comes under even greater stress when it requires a higher proportion of development funds than competing ideas, or a greater overall sum than initially proposed. There are many ways to raise the necessary cash, assuming the idea cannot simply be given priority over others. For example, it could be supported by an existing business unit within the organization, or by an external partner. It could even be turned into a spin-out company in its own right. Or would the organization benefit more by concentrating resources on alternative ideas? A portfolio mentality is essential. If you define clearly, in advance, the conditions under which an idea should be abandoned, it becomes easier to cut your losses as the need arises. The failure of an idea can also generate a surprising amount of value in the form of organizational learning.

Another reason why an idea can have its resources choked is that it fails to meet the criteria on which previous ventures were judged. An organization may be unwilling to give a venture a discrete funding structure, or be unable to do so, because of investment constraints. As a consequence venture teams are often built and incentivized as 'projects as usual' when they should be given a structure that is most appropriate to their needs – one that supports entrepreneurial dynamism and flexibility. Together, these issues point to a lack of start-up experience in an organization. The mitigation strategy here must include training the innovation team in VC-style techniques and, where necessary, bringing in market specialists from outside the organization to help adjust the venture's course appropriately.

Such action was taken by Unilever, for example, in the development of Alleggra®, its soy-based egg substitute. Initially, Unilever planned to build a food service business around the innovation, supplying dry-mix products to large kitchens. However, when Stephen Manley, an experienced food entrepreneur, joined the team as non-executive chairman, he brought an external perspective to the strategy. He suggested that Alleggra would generate much more value if it were marketed as a food ingredient to manufacturers of baked goods, such as a cakes and quiches. Thanks to this redirection of the venture, and Manley's work in selecting the most appropriate executive team to drive it forward, Alleggra is now a global brand. The crucial thing to note here is that Unilever could not have developed Manley's expertise and perspective internally.

Even when adequate funds and structures are in place, it is still common to find that R&D takes too long, and this can have implications that are similar to those of funding problems. A project's first-mover initiative may be lost or the innovation may lose its alignment with market trends and needs.

The remedy to this situation can be to work on the venture's entrepreneurial culture while taking practical steps to ensure progress is more rapid going forward. For example, review project processes and recalibrate staff incentives so that, rather than trying to eliminate technology risks altogether, the team shifts into a mode of acceptance and management. To this end, it may be helpful to install members of the R&D team from the core business in the venture to accelerate development and review the roles and responsibilities of the innovation team. Only once the underlying issues have been addressed can tighter deadlines be imposed.

Be open to external partnering

Just as the best ideas may come from outside an organization, so an external organization may be best placed to handle innovations at certain stages of their development. This is the essence of Open Innovation: generating more value from an idea by sharing it with a partner who can help bring it to market at greater speed. Equally, by engaging actively with external partners, such as venture capital firms, 'false negatives' may be more readily identified – ie ideas that you decided not to fund internally but that may have commercial potential elsewhere, and 'false positives' – ie ideas considered viable that looked less attractive to an external, dispassionate eye.

A common stress point related to partnering is a lack of strategic alliance capability. If an organization's overall innovation strategy does not allow for external partnerships, then the chances are it will not have resources dedicated to soliciting help from outside. Alternatively, its existing joint venture and partnership structures may not be flexible enough to respond to the short-term needs of a venture in trouble. It therefore makes sense to build a strategic alliance capability and embed the processes that allow venture teams to regard partnering as another weapon in their armoury. These steps can be aided through internal workshops and through the arrangement of networking events such as the JOAs™ (Joint Opportunity Assemblies) run by H-I Network.

Leading organizations also make it easy for external innovators – especially smaller companies – to get in contact, suggest potential collaborations and forge strategic alliances or joint ventures. They have systems in place to reassure such partners that they will be treated fairly in terms of intellectual property rights.

Extracting value from every idea

Most organizations tend to measure the value of an innovation in terms of its impact on their bottom line. One of the most valuable aspects of an innovation process is the learning experience it provides. An innovation that fails may, in the right environment, generate more value in the long run than one that succeeds. Why? Because it should help to avoid numerous costly mistakes in the future.

The failure of one venture could generate market knowledge that helps another to succeed. The members of one venture could be transferred to another and help it become a huge success, thanks to their experience. As a whole, the venturing process will certainly provide insights into new or core markets and into new technologies or processes that will lower costs and/or improve performance in a core business. Such benefits can only be realized, however, if the organization's overall innovation strategy is clearly defined. It is this clarity that will ultimately build a 'platform' of knowledge that can be continually strengthened and built upon. The failure of a venture can also help to recalibrate the overall innovation strategy and make sure that it remains truly relevant to the needs of the market.

In our experience organizations tend to regard innovations as separate, distinct entities. They may analyse an idea very carefully in terms of discounted cash flow, net present value or other metrics. But they are less rigorous when it comes to deciding whether an idea is genuinely suited to their portfolio – that is, whether it will help to strengthen their innovation platform going forward. In such an environment failed innovations are regarded as little more than opportunity costs. Again, the 'new business traffic light' may help here.

Yet even with such tools in place, the return of employees to the core business can be a major stress point. First and foremost, it risks removing critical talent from a venture. Equally, if the same talented people are used to launch one new venture after another, a company may end up with a small cadre of start-up specialists who absorb a disproportionate amount of resources, not to mention incurring the resentment of other staff. Leading innovators have processes in place to absorb venture teams back into the core and to embed the lessons they have learnt. They also make a point of rotating staff who have an innovation remit. R&D staff at one leading corporate, for example, are given six-month secondments in the organization's venture funds and thereby get insights into how the venture capital market works, how start-ups work and what technologies the organization as a whole will be focusing on in the long term.

Another issue in the movement of staff, of course, is adjustment to different cultures. Those involved in a venture that fails will undoubtedly feel a sense of loss when they are moved back into the core. A major risk is that such people may leave an organization to start up on their own after a failed venture. Even if it succeeds – becoming a steady revenue stream for the organization – they can often miss the feeling of challenge, excitement and pace experienced in a start-up environment. Such problems can be mitigated by simply encouraging innovators to apply their learning to a new challenge: that of improving practices across the organization as a whole. They must be incentivized to embed all they have learnt in the core and be supported in this effort by the right systems and processes. Keeping innovators happy during the periods in between new ventures is challenging, but there are various management toolkits that can be used to aid the process; one-to-one coaching is also helpful at these times.

Conclusion

Many stress points can be avoided simply by defining a clear strategy for your innovation programme, based on the long-term needs of the organization as a whole. Many organizations find they have to define their strategy retrospectively, having allowed staff to pursue ideas in different directions for years. They may, therefore, have to be prepared to shed pet projects. However, once this process is complete staff will have clear boundaries within which to innovate, and the wastage of time and resources is dramatically reduced.

Concentrating forces this way ensures that an organization builds a 'platform' of knowledge going forward. Even when an innovations fails, it still helps to strengthen the platform by telling the organization something new about its technologies or markets. In this context, senior executives can take a 'portfolio' approach to innovation, backing internal ventures that meet their investment criteria with the same rigour that VCs apply to independent ventures. An overall 'statement of purpose' makes it easier to identify relevant ideas, easier to say no to those not playing to the organization's strengths, and easier to identify potential external partnerships that could realize the value of an innovation faster than going it alone.

Other types of stress points are less easy to pre-empt, but preparations can nevertheless be made to mitigate their effects. For example, political issues, such as the reaction of middle managers to a radical change of direction in a core business, can be avoided. The key to overcoming these softer issues is to improve communication across all levels of an organization and with external partners as necessary. A system of communication must enable the CEO to act as a 'queen bee', receiving information continually about new sources of value, sending out squadrons of workers to harvest that value and, if necessary, moving the whole hive. With such systems in place, stress points become valuable opportunities to learn about the markets in which an organization operates and to recalibrate their overall innovation strategy.

(For further examples and details, see *Innovation Stress Points – Identifying and overcoming the barriers to creating strategic value*, H-I Network, **www.h-i.com**.)

Chapter 22
Attracting Open Innovation Partners
Portals, publicity and people

KEVIN MCFATHING

Why is attraction important?

For the lucky ones among us who have a strong relationship with a partner, I'm sure we remember what initially drew us to him or her. He or she was attractive. Whether it was: looks, intelligence, humour, wealth or an extraordinary combination of all four, something drew us. It's unlikely we believed the attraction would develop into a lifelong partnership at that early stage, but one thing was very clear – attraction. It's the same with Open Innovation. The first step in any OI is finding somebody to whom you are attracted. So if you want more OI relationships, it's in your interest to become more attractive to potential partners.

A partner should be viewed as a person or company with whom you are engaged in joint activity, the result of which will be a benefit to both of you, and with whom you want to pursue the relationship beyond the current transaction. Some valuable projects may only require a one-time relationship. There's nothing wrong with that, but the same principle still holds: step one is to be attractive.

How attractive a partner are you?

There are many components to your attractiveness. Some must be accepted as 'basic facts': your annual sales, brands, product categories, number of countries with operations, etc. These should not be taken as read; rather the positive features should appear prominently in any communication you make about OI.

Beyond the basic facts, OI should involve an initial period of self-reflection on the attractiveness of your ways of working. Some questions you could ask are:

- Culture
  - Which elements of our culture influence our partnering?
  - Which ones are positive and which negative?
  - How open are we as a company in other areas of operation?
  - How long do we take to make a decision?
- Policy
  - Are our legal policies defensive and inflexible?
  - Does our policy on intellectual property mandate that we own all the IP?
- Organization
  - Do we have a complicated multi-layered structure?
  - Is it clear who is responsible for dealing with unsolicited enquiries?
  - Is it clear who is responsible for seeking new partnerships?

Why would people want to work with you?

What is your partnering USP? What is it about your company apart from the 'basic facts' that make you an attractive proposition? Companies that are well advanced with OI understand these parameters, and have a good sense of what makes them attractive.

A good example is Clorox. Despite being a US$6 billion enterprise, it is second or third in some of the categories in which it competes. This means that it has to 'try harder'. Reckitt Benckiser has entrepreneurship as a stated corporate value. It also has a reputation for direct, straight talking and fast decision making. This is recognized by external partners as a positive partnering attribute, because they prefer to know where they stand as soon as possible. Whirlpool has a reputation as a trustworthy, reputable Midwest US company and, like Clorox, always wants to 'do the right thing'.

Partnering in action

Once you understand your partnering strengths and weaknesses, action is the next step. The process of seeking out partners inherently involves making yourself attractive. The attitude of 'you should work with us because we're big' will only get you so far. You should first consider how you want to attract partners. Figure 22.1 shows one way to segment your partnering strategy.

When you know each other

Building and cultivating an existing relationship to create new value is the easiest partnering strategy. This assumes that your top OI priorities fit with

FIGURE 22.1 Partnering segmentation

You Don't Know Them	You Know Them
They Know you	They Don't Know You

your partner's competencies and priorities, and you can continue being happy with each other. It should be your first port of call, but you will need discipline and objectivity to be sure that your needs are being met.

As part of an ongoing relationship, you should be meeting regularly with your partner to review existing projects and future possibilities. You will enhance your attractiveness even further if you propose joint initiatives to work out how you can do more together. This will not only produce new options, it will also strengthen mutual trust and reinforce the foundation for future success. Companies such as P&G and Kraft provide the right context for this exploration by communicating strategic goals, consumer/customer needs and technical priorities. This focuses all the time and energy on what the company wants, not what the external partner thinks they want.

The best people to manage this are the existing relationship champions in each partner company, but don't forget to succession planning and introduce new people as you go along. Like a good marriage, you can become complacent about good business relationships. They need to be nurtured and each company should periodically review its attractiveness in the relationship to ensure there is still opportunity in the future.

Existing relationships still involve risk in innovation initiatives. Clorox's 'Win Balancing' principle aims to mitigate that risk for its key innovation partners. Win Balancing means there is money on the table whether or not the project succeeds. The key is for its partner to invest time and resource on large opportunities, knowing that if the risk doesn't come off, it will be compensated for its costs. This ensures that Clorox continues to be an attractive option, so its partners return for the next project.

Nestlé's 'Sharing is Winning' programme allocates IP ownership to the inventing party, and exploitation rights to the company taking it to market. This

TABLE 22.1 Building and cultivating an existing relationship

Welcome the approach, using a portal	Publicity to increase awareness
Cultivate and build existing relationships	Approach and engage (scouts)

is a very attractive proposition to suppliers and has led to products such as Purina Fit and Trim, in collaboration with Cargill.

When you know them but they don't know you

In this situation, you should have already identified your needs from your OI strategy. Using your technology scouting organization, you will have identified the best people to work with. The next step is to approach them.

Your approach will be a reflection of your corporate style, and will directly influence how attractive you appear to be. That's why the personal characteristics and style of your technology scouts are important criteria in their selection, as well as experience and ongoing training. Unilever takes this seriously, and consciously trains its scouts on seven 'soft' skills of relationship management, shown in Table 22.2.

Scouts should appear professional, of course, but also be engaging, clear and open. There is usually so much that your people can comfortably say about your company that they should not appear closed and secretive, particularly in the context of OI.

The technology scouts will have a number of legal obligations to fulfil in the process of subsequent partner engagement. These should not dominate the discussions. The focus should be on the substance of the opportunity, and both sides should realize they are still in 'sell' mode and that they still need to be attractive. It's important to remember that the technology scouts are the internal advocates for the external partner, and must ensure that the project and related activities are integrated well with the internal processes.

When you don't know them but they know you

In this case you are likely to receive a number of direct approaches. These may arise as a result of your own PR and marketing activity, where you actively invite approaches from people with whom you haven't worked previously. Even if you haven't invited such approaches, your first step is to decide what to do with them. Some companies, most notably Apple, actively state that

TABLE 22.2 Unilever's seven soft skills for OI

Intrapreneurial skills
Talent for relationship building
Strategic influencing
Quick study
Tolerance for uncertainty
Balanced optimism
Passion

they do not accept unsolicited approaches. If people insist on sending information to Apple, they sacrifice all rights and confidentiality.

If you want to see what people have to offer, and there really is little to lose, it is important to have an internet portal. There are several reasons:

1 You need a process to channel any unsolicited approaches to the right people. At its most basic level, you need to be efficient and legally protected, and it is better that these proposals are dealt with by experienced and trained people. Clorox actually uses an external agency, Evergreen IP, to screen proposals.

2 The portal gives you the chance to tell the world that you are 'open' and to give details of what you seek.

3 Some of the proposals may just be worth something.

Compared to working with existing partners and technology scouting, leaders in the OI field believe that portals deliver a low rate of 'hits' and should not be the only OI activity, but are still an essential part of the OI portfolio. The key point is to organize it efficiently, using good design and minimal resource.

Examples of OI portals in the consumer goods industry include Procter & Gamble's Connect and Develop, Reckitt Benckiser's RB-Idealink, General Mills' WIN (Worldwide Innovation Network) and Innovate with Kraft. Each portal has its own strengths and weaknesses, but the ideal features of a good portal are as follows:

● *Easy to find.* The link to the portal should be on the corporate home page, like General Mills, or on pages dedicated to innovation, for example with Reckitt Benckiser. It should be easy to get to with the minimum of clicks, in a logical sequence. A route from the 'Contact Us' page also works well. Shell's Gamechanger site can be reached in three logical clicks from the home page.

- *Easy to navigate.* The internet is such a fundamental tool in everyday business and personal lives that website navigation should be easy. This isn't always the case, and when you're trying to help potential innovation partners it's important to make your site easy and quick to get around. Medtronic's website is compact and clear with a summary flowchart explaining the process for an idea submission.

- *Senior message.* A message to potential partners from a senior company executive tells people that you are serious. Whether it's the CEO in the case of General Mills or the CTO in the case of P&G, the message is clear. Of course, you must ensure that you follow up in the same serious mode.

- *Engaging.* The tone and navigation of your portal will set the tone for any future relationship. Legal requirements are extremely important, but if you make these the overriding message you may appear hostile and distant. P&G's Connect & Develop site uses videos from technology entrepreneurs to build a people element into the early relationship, at the same time explaining some of P&G's key technology needs. Hershey employs an engaging video describing the importance of new ideas to its business. The key is to draw users in rather than push them away.

- *Sell the company.* The place to start is with the basic facts referred to earlier. These, together with the other reasons to partner, should convey a real sense of pride in the company. Most of the good OI portals talk about the importance of innovation and the role that external innovation plays in that innovation strategy. It is best couched in the strategic purpose of the company, as Medtronic does: 'We're committed to innovating for life by pushing the boundaries of medical technology and changing the way the world treats chronic disease.'

- *Describe the type of engagement you want.* When people know a little about you, but you don't know them, there is little point stating, 'Send us something that fits well with our business.' They really do need a little more help. Put yourself in the shoes of the other person, and think seriously about what would help him or her produce a better proposal. Despite the obvious and legitimate concerns about disclosure of sensitive or even confidential information, there is a lot you can say if you follow a few simple guidelines:

  - Don't surprise a competitor. Your competitors will know your business very well. There will be little you can specify in your technology needs that would surprise them and indicate a change in your strategy. So you should test each listing by asking whether your competitors would be truly surprised.

  - Ask yourself what's the worst that can happen. You should be realistic and focus on the upside, and balance that against the rare chance that your description can result in any negative consequences.

- Be specific. The more detail you give, the more you make things easier for both yourself and the idea submitter. Good examples are Reckitt Benckiser's RB-Idealink and Glaxo SmithKline's Consumer Healthcare portal.

● *Respond promptly.* Anecdotal feedback suggests that idea proposers who are rejected in a timely and professional manner will bring their next idea to the same company. You should therefore get back to people as soon as you can. The leading edge here is with Shell's Gamechanger initiative, which promises a response within 48 hours, although most companies aim to respond within three months. Both Kraft and Clorox enable inventors to communicate with their scientists so that propositions can be refined further, making them more likely to fit with what is required. I would advise against using a system where no response after a certain time means rejection. Keep it simple, give people a time by which you commit to respond, and tell them as soon as you can.

● *Legal compliance.* It is advisable to avoid a scheme that overloads the proposer with unrealistic and intimidating legal demands. You don't need a four-page agreement for an initial non-confidential submission. The longer the legal part, the less engaging and more distant your site will appear. Having said that, it is important to ensure that the submitter:

  - owns the idea/IP or has the owner's permission to present it;
  - makes the initial submission using non-confidential information;
  - is encouraged to seek IP protection before making his or her proposal;
  - realizes you are under no legal obligation to adopt the proposal;
  - understands you may be working on something similar, or have already evaluated it.

Managing the portal

Each company has its own approach to managing proposals sent to an OI portal. For example, P&G allocates each proposal to a specific technology entrepreneur who is responsible for managing the internal evaluation, the external response and any subsequent engagement. Other companies like Reckitt Benckiser take a 'triage' approach where applications go to a central team. They provide a rapid response to those ideas where lack of fit or low commercial potential are immediately apparent, and proposals with interest are then directed to people with relevant expertise and responsibility within the company. Given that idea portals deliver a low rate of 'hits', you should ensure that your process to screen and assess the applications is resource efficient.

The OI portal is the 'cover on the book', not the book itself, and is a key part of your OI communication. It should complement an overall OI strategy that needs a lot more to it than the portal for OI to succeed to its full potential. These elements are covered very well in other chapters.

When you don't know them and they don't know you

You may not feel the need to reach out for unsolicited proposals or for more people to help you solve your tough problems. This is an extension of the closed vs open innovation challenge, so if you intend to be open, why not be open with as many people as possible?

Most people with an interest in innovation have heard of P&G's Connect & Develop programme, because the publicity behind it has been outstanding. This is not just luck. It is helped by P&G being one of the world's largest consumer goods companies, but it has been complemented by a coordinated programme of articles in the business press, a landmark article in the *Harvard Business Review*, many external presentations at conferences, continual communication from the CEO to the investor community about the importance of Connect & Develop, and countless individual conversations with members of the Connect & Develop organization.

The first step is for your potential partner to know you exist, which is where publicity about your OI strategy comes in. You can't build a relationship with somebody you don't know. You should ensure that your attractive story gets to the right people, using your public relations, social media and other communications plans.

Like any communication programme, you must take a clear message, which is a prompt for action, to a targeted audience. This can be through, for example, trade organizations, specialist publications, conference presentations, your own website(s) and of course your own people who can evangelize the message. Once you have a portal, this should be the centrepiece of your communications. After all, you have put it in place for unsolicited proposals from people you may not know, so it should be their means of entry to your company.

Developing portals further

Once you have developed your portal to achieve the basic objectives, what else can you do? There are some interesting developments already occurring. Clorox Connects has learnt from developments in social media and gone beyond a basic idea submission portal. It engages the consumer in conversations in specific communities; allows inventors to join 'inventor forums' to talk directly to Clorox scientists; lets suppliers/partners talk directly to Clorox as well as to each other. Indeed there are conversations on the site that appear to have nothing to do with Clorox but contribute to making Clorox Connects an attractive site to visit. Portals like MyStarbucksIdea and Dell's Ideastorm use crowdsourcing principles to attract consumers with ideas, allowing them to contribute, vote and build on suggestions that Starbucks and Dell can implement.

The overall message from these examples is that your OI portal can be just whatever you want it to be. Like all websites, it must be kept up to date, particularly if you have technology postings in date order.

The large vs small dynamic

Most OI relationships have large companies working with small companies. The power equation is different, and each has a stereotypical view of the other. This is caricatured in Table 22.3.

There are many variations on this theme, but the overall message is that conflict can often arise, not necessarily through substantive disagreement on the project, but through different perceptions and misunderstandings. Being an attractive partner includes taking perception into account.

The importance of people and relationships

Strong corporate and personal relationships are crucial to successful OI partnerships. They will never be the sole reason, but when times are tough they may well be the glue that holds the partnership together. Openness and communication are crucial to avoid projects getting into difficulty through poor relationship management rather than technical challenges.

Of course, like any relationship, you'll have to live through rough patches. If you're both still attractive, the will to resolve difficulties and move to a productive outcome will be there on both sides. Strong personal relationships with your partner company's people aren't just important to the project, they add enjoyment, new friendships and valuable connections to your working life.

Finally, looking out for your partner's interests doesn't mean you've become soft and laissez-faire. You must still be a tough negotiator, ensure the interests of your company are paramount, and ultimately win in the marketplace.

Summary

OI relationships are analogous to those in our everyday lives. They start with an initial attraction. Our chance of catching somebody really attractive depends on how attractive we are to them. Companies should understand what makes them attractive, build the positive features and work on the negative, and ensure they keep working at their attractiveness to build their OI portfolio.

TABLE 22.3 Large vs small company – a caricature

Large company view of small company	Small company view of large company
Disorganized	Bureaucratic
Demanding	Takes too long to respond
Unrealistic valuation	Too much analysis
Top priority for them, not for us	Scary negotiation power
but ...	*but ...*
Fast, with tremendous technology and products to fill gaps in our portfolio	Tremendous assets (brand, channels, people, etc), with global reach and economies of scale

A segmentation approach to the attractiveness of OI relationships can be used. An important component of this is an OI portal. There are certain key features and guidelines for best practice. In all of these, the principle of attractiveness should be considered.

OI needs open processes and open minds, so openness should be at the heart of communication to ensure there are no misunderstandings and both partners in the relationship succeed. You never know, the attractiveness may still be there when the relationship has wrinkles and both partners need the support of walking sticks.

Acknowledgements

I would like to thank Andy Gilicinski (Clorox), Adrian Timms (Hershey), Steve Goers (Kraft), Chris Thoen (Procter & Gamble), Richard Ellis (Reckitt Benckiser), Gail Martino (Unilever) and Moises Norena (Whirlpool) for their valuable input.

Chapter 23
Multistep Dynamic Expert Sourcing:
A novel approach for open innovation platforms

ALBERT MEIGE AND BORIS GOLDEN

Open Innovation platforms (and especially problem-solving platforms) have received increasing attention over the last few years. There has been some mistrust of this trend because of a number of drawbacks such as a relatively low number of solvers (ie, a person or organization that has registered on the intermediary website and that wishes to try to provide solutions), confidentiality issues, intellectual property (IP) management problems, disappointing solutions, etc. We propose a novel approach, Multistep Dynamic Expert Sourcing (MDES). This approach solves most of the existing drawbacks and leverages all the potential of online OI.

Resources in the traditional ecosystem of a company appear to be insufficient for many industrial or business needs. OI is the paradigm according to which companies need to use external ideas, knowledge and technologies to advance their business (Chesbrough, 2003). In particular, OI allows accelerating innovation by using most relevant external expertise and maximizes cross-fertilization between industries and between disciplines.

In the context of OI there is an increasing need for intermediaries to facilitate the connection between companies and external resources. Various types of intermediaries exist. Traditional intermediaries, such as technology transfer offices, clusters, boundary agents, etc are not web-based and have been around for decades. More recently, various types of web-based intermediaries appeared: crowdsourcing platforms (eg, problem-solving platforms such as Ninesigma or Innocentive), technology brokers (such as yet2.com), etc.

A common feature of crowdsourcing platforms is that they are registration-based: you need to register on the platform to be part of the system and participate as a problem solver, which leads to various serious issues. A second common feature is a 'black box' solving process: interactions between the input (a problem) and the output (a solution) are reduced to their minimum, which leads to poor quality of solving.

The first section that follows is an overview of the main issues with traditional registration-based crowdsourcing platforms. The second section presents the novel approach and its benefits.

Where OI crowdsourcing platforms fail

The way OI crowdsourcing platforms work is rather simple, at least in principle: they help companies to match a problem or a need to an existing solution or to somebody able to solve the problem. Underlying requirements are a large pool of problems, a large pool of solvers, and a good matching algorithm or process. In addition, the lubricant for all that to work is trust, which here means careful management of confidentiality and IP. However, behind this simple idea a lot of theoretical and practical difficulties have emerged from a decade of experimentation.

Registration yields a weak number of solvers

As an intermediary, how can you constantly find new and interested solvers around the world (ie people ready to propose solutions to technological problems)? You need efficient incentives to attract them to your platform, to make them subscribe, to engage them in solving problems and to release IP. Registration has a direct negative impact on the number of solvers although it may be, in principle, a nice way to select supposedly motivated solvers.

Few experts register on crowdsourcing platforms

How many experts go and register on crowdsourcing platforms – 10,000? 100,000? Most famous platforms hardly reach 300,000 solvers, which is far less than the tens of millions of experts in the world. In addition, figures claimed by many companies are unclear: how can the claims of newcomers be checked? How many subscribers really want to engage in problem solving? These systems lead to a misleading competition to get the 'biggest' pool of solvers, disregarding truth[1] and quality.[2] The large majority of registered solvers do not participate: self-registration is not the right paradigm to address global expertise. Many studies show that only 1 per cent of subscribers are active on such platforms. The largest existing OI communities have only a few thousands active users.

Solvers are not experts: crowdsourcing means that anybody can be a solver. This is a fashionable and demagogic argument to attract a large quantity of random solvers on a platform (the large number of subscribers being an argument to attract client companies and supposedly launch the platform).

But among registered solvers, not all of them are experts. Some platforms actually use this as an advantage and claim that what matters are the solutions or the ideas brought by the solvers, and not their background. This is true to some extend (user-driven innovation, etc), but idealistic for highly critical problems (as seen on most platforms) requiring a strong expertise.

Matching algorithm and process fails to engage solvers in problem solving

To maximize the probability of solving a problem, a trade-off has to be found between strong targeting of the solvers and large broadcast: even assuming a large base of solvers, it is impossible to guarantee their engagement in problem solving. To engage solvers, one needs to contact them (for example by e-mail) to 'advertise' the problem. Given a certain problem, who should be contacted? All the solvers in all the fields? Solvers whose online profile shows a certain 'potential' for the problem? Common sense would assume that it is best to target solvers to most-efficiently engage them in the solving process. However, a paradox underlies OI platforms: the 'holy grail' of these platforms is to maximize cross-fertilization (between industries and between scientific fields). Indeed, studies have shown that submitted problems are regularly tackled and solved by solvers outside of the 'natural' field. The initial problem broadcast to experts should therefore not be too targeted. However, recurring fuzzy broadcasting of problems to solvers leads to decreasing interest as many irrelevant problems end up being sent. The trade-off is uneasy and fails in most situations.

The solver has no guarantee that his or her solution will not be 'stolen' by the customer company. Since no trustable mechanism is proposed to incite the customer company to reward a good solution (as it may use it for free if it does not look for the IP rights), solvers are very reluctant to propose a valuable solution when they have one.

Confidentiality and IP issues are poorly addressed

Confidentiality is the big issue on the customer side. Companies using OI platforms are mostly concerned about the confidentiality of the information they provide to the intermediary and to the rest of the world. Even if the name of the company remains anonymous, it may be easy for competitors to guess who is behind the problem, which is a serious issue. Putting a problem online and broadcasting it to *a priori* unknown solvers is too sensitive for many companies, and is a significant brake on the use of OI platforms. Online Non-Disclosure Agreements are not a satisfactory solution as anybody can sign them without real engagement or verification.

IP management is yet another extremely touchy aspect. Who owns the solution provided by a solver through the internet platform of an intermediary? The customer company, also called 'seeker', wants to own the IP to use the solution without any restriction and gain competitive advantages. As for the solvers, they may fear giving up their IP rights, but have to do so if they want to get paid.

In an ideal world, an OI platform would allow solvers to seamlessly transfer their solution IP to the seeker. In practice, such a feature does not work. Even with terms-of-use of the type 'As soon as any solution is submitted to X, its IP rights are also transferred to X.' This cannot work on a generic basis because, most of the time, the solver does not own the IP from the start. Indeed, the solution may already be patented by others or, worse, it may not be patented and because the solver (say a researcher in the public sector) has an employer, the IP belongs to this employer. Such IP management leads to unsatisfied customers, unsatisfied research centres and unsatisfied solvers.

Overall, OI crowdsourcing platforms, although still a very promising concept, have failed to provide fully satisfying services. The main issues have been to:

● attract and engage sufficient number of qualified experts in a sustainable way;
● properly match seeker problems with potential experts;
● develop incentives for customers and reward promising solutions;
● properly protect confidentiality and intellectual property.

A disruptive approach: Multistep Dynamic Expert Sourcing (MDES)

The French start-up PRESANS developed and implemented the MDES approach. It relies on a combination of a state-of-the-art web-mining technology and a secured multistep problem-solving process. In this approach experts do not register; instead the various digital tracks they leave on the web allow detecting them and inviting them on-demand to tackle most challenging technological problems. MDES has strong advantages for the platform, for the experts and for the client companies.

Figure 23.1 shows the MDES approach, which brings value to seekers by connecting their needs to worldwide scientific knowledge and intelligence. Seekers can be any department in a company with needs (a need is a 'pain' that can be addressed by scientific or technological expertise). The MDES philosophy includes three points:

1 expert sourcing;
2 dynamic (or on-demand); and
3 multistep.

Points 1) and 2) are covered in the next subsection and point 3) in the following. The main advantages are listed at the end of the present section.

FIGURE 23.1 The MDES approach

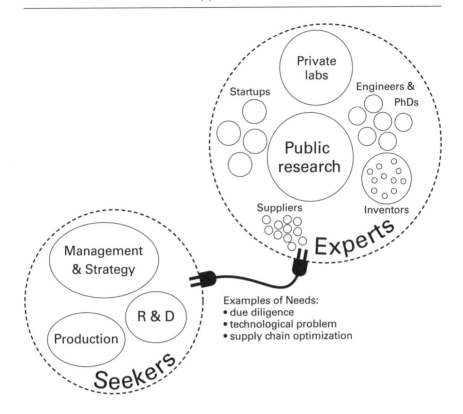

Expert sourcing and dynamic aspect

Expert sourcing rather than crowdsourcing: to solve highly critical and technological problems, a company needs experts, not random solvers. This is why MDES relies on highly skilled experts rather than solvers.

Dynamic (or on-demand) rather than subscription-based: as previously explained, most OI intermediaries or networks of experts rely on registration-based platforms: potential experts have to know about the platform and to register. This is not the right paradigm to address global expertise. Instead, we propose building a worldwide automatic network of experts that can be solicited on-demand and that allows automatic profiling of experts. This method enhances confidentiality since the visibility of the problems can be restricted to preselected experts.

Millions of experts exist in the world and most of them leave tracks on the web through scientific literature, patents, research centre corporate websites, blogs, forums, etc. Based on information retrieval and machine learning, an expert search engine (see Figure 23.2) allows these experts to be discovered and engaged in an automated manner:

- The expert search engine builds a fully structured map of expertise from unstructured data such as research centre websites, scientific literature, etc (steps 1 and 3).
- The textual description of the seeker's technological need is fed into the expert search engine that, in return, suggests an exhaustive list of most relevant experts in the world (step 3).
- The smart-broadcast software then automatically contacts and invites a number of the most relevant experts, using automatically generated personalized e-mails.
- Interested experts can then join the multistep problem solving process.

Note that the complex algorithm of the expert search engine is designed to improve automatic matching while maximizing cross-fertilization (see, for example, Lakhani, 2006).

Figure 23.2 shows the expert search engine technology, which crawls tens of millions of scientific sources (scientific literature, patents, research centre websites, etc). The engine indexes and structures the information into expert profiles. Sending a query (keywords or full-text description) from the search bar returns a list of potential most qualified experts.

Multistep problem solving process

Multistep rather than black box: the multistep approach allows engaging experts and satisfying seekers in a safe, secure and trustable environment. It ensures better performance for problem solving, less frustration among solvers and less disappointment among seekers.

Online problem solving is often thought of as a 'black-box process': the seeker gives the input, waits a few months and finally opens the box to discover the set of submitted solutions. This process, implemented by nearly all OI platforms, has various drawbacks, the main ones being:

- decline in motivation and risk-averse behaviour of solvers,
- inefficiency in reaching quality and relevant solutions,
- limited incentives for seekers to be fair and pay for all valuable solutions.

We propose instead a three-step 'grey-box' process for online problem solving. Based on our experience, we believe that this innovative process has a high potential to leverage expertise and intelligence through problem solving.

The three-step process serves to filter experts in order to select the two to five most relevant ones out of the initial automatically generated list. Each step is a gate where experts who have accepted the invitation to solve a problem are asked to provide additional information.

FIGURE 23.2 The expert search engine technology

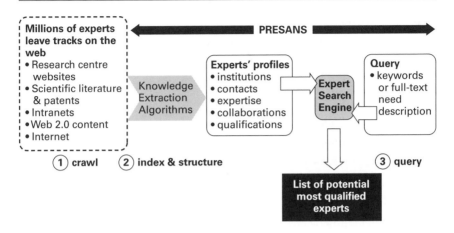

1. Abstract (typical length: half page)

In the first step, experts submit a short abstract in which they present their understanding of the problem, their approach and an outline of their solution. This submission is made through a web-based interface with mandatory fields, making it easy for experts to be exhaustive and for the reviewers to select promising propositions. Experts are then preselected by the seeker on the basis of their abstract.

2. Extended summary (typical length: three pages)

In the second step, each preselected expert is asked to submit an extended summary presenting the approach, the main lines of the solution, its main advantages and proofs of relevance. This more detailed submission provides a good overview of the solution without giving the keys to master it. At this point, the seeker chooses two to five submissions to be developed extensively, with financial compensation.

3. Full solutions (typical length: 10 to 50 pages)

In the third step, the remaining two to five experts write the complete solution as they would on a traditional problem-solving platform. The two to five experts all get paid for their full-length solution and the best one gets an extra financial reward.

Main advantages of MDES

Implementing the MDES approach with the right technological and methodological assets (ie a powerful expert search engine and a relevant methodology to enhance problem formulation) presents strong advantages for experts, seekers and OI intermediaries (problem-solving platforms):

- For the experts
  - get relevant problems without having to register;
  - ensure the protection of IP;
  - avoid irrelevant work and frustration;
  - get the guarantee of being paid for their work.
- For the seekers (the client companies)
  - have a better control of confidentiality;
  - get potential access to tens of millions of worldwide experts;
  - engage more and better experts;
  - get better solutions.
- For the intermediaries (the platforms)
  - decrease cost structures;
  - increase scalability;
  - build a reputation of quality and trust;
  - improve the solving rate and the solution quality.

Conclusion

In the first section, the main drawbacks of traditional problem-solving platforms were presented. These drawbacks are the difficulty of attracting and engaging sufficient numbers of qualified experts, efficiently matching seeker problems and potential experts, giving the seeker convincing incentives to reward all promising solutions, and managing confidentiality and ensuring a reliable transfer of IP.

In the second section, we presented the disruptive approach that we have developed and implemented. The Multistep Dynamic Expert Sourcing approach relies on both an innovative expert search engine technology and a three-step process for the actual problem-solving phase. The expert search engine ensures a relevant matching between experts and problems and avoids the necessity of getting experts to register on a platform. The multistep process reduces the risks of losing time, money and IP for all the parties.

We believe that this innovative and disruptive approach has a high potential to leverage expertise and intelligence through problem solving, and that it can contribute significantly to the success of online OI.

Chapter 24
The Acceleration of Innovation

CLINTON BONNER

Innovation has many forms. Not only are we discussing new products and services, but further efficiencies (cost- and resource-saving measures), unfamiliar paths to lucrative partnerships and novel ways to connect with and reward your masses. None of this is truly new, so what has changed? The short answer is the pace. We see new technologies, an emphasis on the democratization of the workforce, social listening and engaging the consumer and citizenry. There has been a cultural corporate change that has taken an otherwise forbidden word, failure, and illuminated the term, erasing uncertainties and emboldening the best and brightest to routinely attempt exceptionalism. All these have led to a hyper-paced innovation cycle that allows companies to innovate faster than ever before and on far less spend. That is the proper acceleration of innovation, and that is the focus of this chapter.

Bringing 'fail' into the fold

It begins and ends with your corporate culture. No matter if you are engaging your employees, citizens or consumers, the need to communicate that failure is not some forbidden fruit but rather a recognized aspect of innovation is essential. What I have described below will allow your initiatives to 'fail fast', meaning you fail more often, more quickly and on much less spend. When this happens, an interesting 'side effect' arises. You succeed. (For more on 'failing fast' see Chapter 19.)

What can be accelerated?

It is important to understand which aspects of innovation can actually be condensed and which ones you can affect through gradual and corporate cultural change. Often described as the FEI, or 'front end of innovation', these early processes that cultivate, illuminate, uplift and support new ideas should be your focus as this is exactly where you can have the biggest impact and accelerate innovation processes. I will highlight ways in which you can involve employees and partners traditionally much further down the innovation chain, harvesting their objections, rejections, opinions and expert advice to further accelerate the path from ideation to market-ready output.

Crowdsourcing, collaboration and co-creation

Corporations are looking to flatten processes internally while externally engaging in social discussions and initiatives with their consumers that offer end users new opportunities to help improve a product or service, or invent new products all together. Technically, 'crowdsourcing' is tapping a constantly evolving 'crowd' outside your company's four walls, but more and more often corporations are taking the same techniques that are the backbone of purposeful crowdsourcing projects and infusing these methods into the very way they innovate internally as well. The results are staggering, but how do we get to the point where our innovation processes (whether internal or social) are creating actionable outputs and not just random ideas that really add no value, and quite often drain resources? How do you avoid diminishing the role of experts within your organization while inviting in everyone to participate? Every organization and corporate culture will be unique, but there are best practices to ensure you are crowdsourcing actionable outputs. Below I share a few universal techniques almost every business can incorporate while looking to accelerate the way in which they innovate.

One actionable output vs 12,000 ideas

How to avoid the ultimate time sink and lift the needle from the haystack

How do you set up a corporate or consumer culture, backed by the proper technologies, to consistently draw out actionable and worthy ideas and not just a haystack of throwaway notions that will never see the light of day? Consider these suggestions as you progress in your quest to accelerate innovation:

1 Have in place the proper communications channels and technologies that facilitate ideation, iteration and collaboration. Small and agile companies may be able to manage this with very little new technology

and rely mostly on technique, whereas medium to large corporations need to have collaborative and/or crowdsourcing technologies woven into the fabric of their innovation processes. There are several quality software solutions, platforms and firms that specialize in bringing corporations up to speed on the best practices involving crowdsourcing and utilizing Open Innovation practices effectively.

2 Have a consistent reward system in place from the start. For larger corporations, the more robust software that supports innovation acceleration will have detailed and customizable reward structures in place. Each contribution will equate to some ranking system and particular types of contributions will garner more 'points'. But honestly, it's less about the 'flair' and more about the meaning of the 'points', the value to the individual. So whether you are a small company or a gigantic brand, first and foremost think about relevance to your audience. Understand what type of reward elicits action. If you're a huge corporation, perhaps a certain level of contribution or a 'winning' solution garners an individual the right to attend and present at a top-level event. Maybe you manage a technology brand and you know that getting the newest gadgets into the hands of your social evangelists is the ultimate reward for them as they will get to 'play' with the new technology and offer you candid feedback well before the public can touch the device. Recognize all contributions have value, be consistent, be fair yet reward excellence. Do not overlook this aspect as it is incredibly important to properly motivate your masses to contribute over and over again. For those interested in this specific subject, I highly recommend, *Game-based Marketing: Inspire customer loyalty through rewards, challenges, and contests* by Zicherman and Linder (2010).

3 For each ideation attempt, understand exactly what you are asking for. Even if your call to innovate is obtuse, your language and direction can be didactic. A good example of this would be a healthcare company asking for bold new mobile applications that deliver a hyper-relevant value to end consumers. You can clearly dictate to the crowd what the macro goals for this application must accomplish (focus on weight loss, being socially accessible and easy to share with a robust and public reward system built in), yet cast a wide net so as to not exclude some genius who might have otherwise been left out. Conversely, if your goal is to solve a specific identified challenge, then lay out concisely the problem, why you seek to overcome it (the benefits you expect to realize by overcoming this challenge), and exactly how you prefer the submission to be entered. Here the focus is much narrower, and that's a good thing.

4 Measure and vet submitted ideas against a multitude of criteria. Whether you are going for broad genius or fine-tuned hyper-specific solutions, a fantastic way to breed more actionable ideas is to share

with your crowd exactly the criteria the idea will be measured against. Instead of just asking for 'mobile applications with a focus on wellness', tell your crowds exactly how it will be judged. For something as broad as this mock 'call', you could expect criteria to range from, 'Is this application easy to share across Facebook, Twitter and other forms of social media?' and, 'What is the potential an end user would use this application more than once a month? Per week?' Conversely, if you were seeking a finite solution to a particular innovation challenge, your criteria might sound more like, 'Can this be produced under current international law regarding our manufacturing partnership agreements with our Chinese providers?' As you can tell, the criteria become much more focused, but again, so was the initial call for a solution. What good would a 'solution' be if it cannot be actually implemented? Plus, this is exactly where your internal experts, those with niche knowledge on particular subjects need to be iterating and participating with the initiative. Those with the exact knowledge to judge this criteria will 'self-select' to do so, while others who simply don't know the answer to this specific criteria question will stay away and contribute in other ways.

5   Keep it all under 'one roof'. By this I mean, have one branded place where all company and crowd 'calls' live and exist. You probably will keep this online construct password-protected so for the sake of ease; you don't want multiple forums making it difficult for the end user to interact with them. Furthermore, you want a construct where all of your contributors can come in and self-select which bits of work, projects, or challenges they wish to engage in. Why is this important? Two reasons. First, you want contributors to naturally gravitate towards 'work' they are passionate about. Sure the employee might today be on data entry, but she has a passion for mobile applications and you, allowing her to self-select what type of work she contributes to, will reap the rewards as your outputs will be stronger. Second, from a company perspective, this is a fantastic way to monitor who within your organization or consumer crowd is attracted to what type of work and where their skills lie.

6   Have a multitude of ways in which any individual can participate with an initiative. Look at your nearest Facebook wall for the reason why. Some people love to post (these would be your submitters of ideas), while others are more inclined to comment (these would be your iterators, those who like to add, help re-shape but perhaps don't typically brazenly innovate), while others still simply want to 'like' a notion (in your world these are your voters). Each contribution has real value, but once again allowing your crowds to decide how they will interact is most important. From there, you can begin to track who your most influential submitters are, which groups are your most accurate predictors of a new product or service, and so on. Understanding the

attributes of the individuals that make up your crowd allows you to shape initiatives more accurately so that they garner more and more collaboration and interaction. This delivers to you, the manager of these crowds, the ability to 'pluck' a group of individuals for specific future tasks. Let's say you have been monitoring your top predictors, and this particular group has an average accuracy rating of 89 per cent, meaning the products and services they felt strongly about were eventually brought to market. Clearly, this group has a keen collective eye for recognizing winners in your product pipeline. They should be rewarded with more similar work or at least be given a weighted vote or elevated position within this innovation construct.

7 Foster iteration: it is the 'meat' of any worthy crowdsourcing project. Most crowdsourcing constructs that sit under the umbrella of 'innovation initiatives' are nothing more than a voting contest and often that comes down to the popularity of the submitters and if they entered their idea early on in the process, giving the idea more time to accrue votes and therefore be elevated. Quality ideas often get buried because they don't receive enough 'votes' (perhaps they were entered later or maybe the submitter didn't have scores of friends he or she could reach out to solicit their vote), and that is just bad practice. Also, in ideation sessions that are purely voting mechanisms, there is no 'back and forth' dialogue, no modification to the original idea, no iteration and therefore no improvement. The point of crowdsourcing is not to generate thousands of mediocre ideas but to use the crowd's individual abilities to fine-tune the innovation, making it actionable and something the brand can actually bring to market and profit from.

Not everyone in your organization is going to have the breadth of knowledge it takes to properly vet an idea. But as you set your criteria checklist, it will help illuminate what types of expertise you need on this initiative to ensure that your outputs will be actionable. From there, I would suggest inviting in select members from various divisions of your organization (consumer insights, manufacturing, packaging) to form a panel of experts whose sole job is to absorb the raw ideas, offer non-biased feedback, objections and potential hurdles, and to essentially challenge the submitter to think about possible hang-ups and make the idea sharper and therefore more worthy. Keep in mind, this feedback, these objections offered to the submitter will be 'public' inside your construct, meaning that the 'answer' to the objection or hurdle may not come from the original submitter. Another contributor, who might have really liked the original idea, can read the needed modifications or suggestions and then collaborate with the original submitter to submit the re-worked idea, offering the original submitter an expert angle to overcome one particular objection that he or she alone would not have been able to formulate. That is where crowdsourcing becomes very powerful and also where you, the director of this acceleration, can greatly enhance the speed of innovation.

8 Take a long-view look at your project time-line. It is smart to invite in selected experts from various aspects of your project time-line. To properly condense the FEI you need to have the other factions of your innovation chain (those that would not typically be involved in the FEI) present and collaborating with these ideas as they are being born. Without their presence, you end up with buckets of 'fantastic' ideas only to find out that not one of them is actually marketable. You need discrimination in innovation. And only experts, with specific knowledge of your inner workings, can properly push back on an idea and challenge the submitter to make it better in hyper-specific ways that clear future hurdles and give the project a real green light and therefore an avenue to success. If these specific objections are being raised very early on in the innovation process, it allows the organization to properly eliminate scores of ideas that just won't make it to market, and therefore focus on the best initiatives that were able to overcome these early specific objections and hurdles.

The results

In a much shorter timeframe your organization can identify more potential winners and put precious resources behind these elevated ideas with more confidence than ever. If an initiative is a 'No', it is much more valuable to know this and to know why this is so on day seven as opposed to day 97. The contributor can go 'back to the drawing board' and tweak the idea or understand it will never come to market (at this corporation) and therefore his or her time is best spent on another project or idea. Employee morale remains much higher, productivity soars, and your company is attempting more innovation in parallel on far less spend. At this point, you have properly accelerated innovation.

Chapter 25
Envisioning the Future of Innovation

STEPHEN SHAPIRO

Many years ago I had a conversation with an executive from Chrysler. At the time, I worked for Andersen Consulting (now Accenture). I asked him who he felt his biggest competition would be in the future. He pointed at me and said, 'You,' referring to Accenture. Although he was half-joking, there was some truth in his statement. One of Accenture's core competencies is integration (its roots are in systems integration), and the role of car manufacturers (as well as many other companies) is less about manufacturing and more about integrating solutions from all of their suppliers.

Although I don't have a crystal ball, I believe that this brief conversation hints at where innovation is going. It's safe to say that the monolithic innovation models of the past are dead and that integrating solutions from external partners will become the norm.

Of course outsourcing isn't new. Although it has been used extensively for decades, we're only now beginning to see it being used in new ways. For example, there has been a move from the use of outsourcing for only transactional functions (such as manufacturing or payroll) to more creative endeavours (such as design and high-end problem solving). In fact, the use of outsourcing for innovation is rapidly becoming the norm.

One reason for this shift is that it's no longer good enough to be an expert in generic disciplines like electronics or chemistry. The focus now is on deep specializations like nanotechnology or bio-engineering. Although an organization can only specialize in one area, innovation typically involves bringing together solutions from multiple disciplines, not just one. It requires integrating a number of smaller specialized solutions into a strategic and marketable one. Because of this need for deep specialists, innovation can't be outsourced in the traditional way. It will become increasingly difficult to outsource a large chunk of your innovation efforts to just one organization. Instead, you will need to find dozens, if not hundreds or thousands, of outsourcing partners for a single product.

I predict that we will see a 'hyper-outsourcing model' in which internal innovation takes a backseat to external innovation, integration and commercialization. Being good at something internally will become less important than your ability to work with others and to integrate their solutions in a way that you can use to more effectively bring products and services to market.

How do you manage a hyper-outsourcing model? There are four key steps/ skills associated with hyper-outsourcing:

1 specifying well-defined challenges;
2 finding outsourcing partners/solutions;
3 integrating the resulting solutions; and
4 commercializing the final product.

The first step in hyper-outsourcing is to become masterful at defining challenges that can be outsourced.

Why Einstein was right

All companies have challenges. They might be technical challenges, such as how to create a particular chemical compound. They might be marketing challenges, such as how to best describe your product to increase market share. They might be human resource challenges, such as how to improve employee engagement. An organization's ability to change and innovate hinges on its ability to identify and solve these challenges. Challenges are sometimes referred to as problems, issues or opportunities, but at the end of the day they're all just various forms of challenges.

Where do you find these challenges? You can find them anywhere – your business strategy, known technology gaps, customers, employees, shareholders, consultants, vendors and competitors – the list goes on and on. Let's face it. Companies have no shortage of challenges. The 'meta-challenge' for all organizations is to find out which challenges, if solved and implemented, will create the greatest value. Given that organizations have limited resources and money, prioritization is critical.

My favourite quote is attributed to Albert Einstein: 'If I had an hour to save the world, I would spend 59 minutes defining the problem and one minute finding solutions.' Most companies spend all 60 minutes of their time finding solutions to problems that just don't matter. Therefore the first step is to identify, prioritize and frame challenges. One area where many companies fall short is in the definition of good challenges.

Defining good challenges

This 'challenge-driven' approach to innovation is quite different from an 'idea-driven' approach. With idea-driven innovation, concepts are not grounded in specific and identified needs. Instead, a wide variety of suggestions are solicited from a large number of people. Unfortunately, most suggestions are too broad, too vague, or insufficient for producing a positive return on investment. Many times the suggestions are solutions looking for a problem to solve.

One example that illustrates this nicely is a large retailer that holds a competition each year in which employees submit new product ideas. The winner gets a large cheque and the company implements the best idea. Is the programme a success? According to the individual responsible, 'It's a PR success but a commercial failure.' The competition generates a buzz in the media, but none of the products has generated a positive return. Contrast this with the retailer's more focused efforts in creating or improving particular product lines by identifying specific market opportunities. In nearly every case, these were commercial successes. Its idea-based programmes didn't generate good bottom-line results while its challenge-based initiatives did.

The other advantage to the challenge-driven approach is that you can assign owners, resources, evaluators, evaluation criteria and funding up-front. You know that the solution to a challenge will be relevant to the needs of the organization, so if a solution is found you know it will be valuable. Also, because of the nature of challenges, there are better tools to evaluate the amount of time spent on finding solutions. You can truly measure the ROI of each challenge and the overall challenge-based programme.

The difference between these approaches is analogous to two different fishing techniques. Idea-driven approaches are like a fisherman going randomly into the middle of the ocean and casting an extraordinarily expansive net. While using an untargeted approach like this might yield some fish (and it might not), that fisherman will also collect shoes, tyres, seaweed and other undesirable items. Contrast that with a professional fisherman who purposefully locates a school of fish and then deliberately selects the appropriate rod, reel, line, leader, bait and hook for catching exactly the type of prey he's looking for. As the old expression has it: 'If you want to catch fish, go where the fish are.' This is more akin to a challenge-driven approach. These fishing experts know exactly what they're after, so they can be purposeful in their approach, minimizing waste and maximizing their efforts. The key is asking better questions and constructing well-defined challenges.

When framing good challenges, you must adhere to the Goldilocks principle. Goldilocks enters the house of three bears. After sampling their porridge she's tired, so she decides to go to sleep. She finds the papa bear's bed too hard, the mama bear's bed too soft, and the baby bear's bed just right, and falls asleep. The same is true with challenges. They can't be too big (broad, abstract) or too small (specific). They must be 'just right'.

Dwayne Spradlin, CEO of InnoCentive, Inc., a leader in Open Innovation, provided the following viewpoint on the creation of good challenges when talking about drug discovery:

> The big problem is not the need for a new drug for a neglected disease. It is the elimination and/or minimization of the human suffering caused by the

disease. The right questions might include: How do we limit transmission? How can we produce cost-effective treatments that address the economics of low-income countries? How do we distribute treatments in the developing world? Even these questions require further decomposition until we get to well-formulated challenges (such as can we get five times more vaccine into the hands of those who need it in the context of real-world economic, cultural, and political constraints in sub-Saharan Africa).

Once you have a well-defined challenge that is granular enough (but not too granular), the next step is to find solutions.

Why Edison was wrong

Every challenge has multiple potential solutions. Solution-finding has traditionally been built on a paradigm of experimentation: keep on trying and failing until you find a solution that works. Innovators love to quote Thomas Edison, who supposedly said while inventing the light bulb: 'I have not failed 700 times. I have not failed once. I have succeeded in proving that those 700 ways will not work. When I have eliminated the ways that will not work, I will find the way that will work.'

This quote seems to 'validate' the iterative innovation process used in most R&D departments. There is a widely held belief that we learn as much from 'finding ways that don't work' as we do from our successes. However, call it what you want, the 700 attempts that didn't work were indeed failures. If Edison had found a solution to the light bulb challenge on the first try, would he have continued to seek out 700 ways that did not work? Did the 700 'failures' really add that much value? Can your organization afford to fail 700 times? Not in today's competitive environment.

Unfortunately, the reality is that failure is a necessary ingredient of innovation. We can never instantly know the solution to a problem until we test it out. But what if you could push the cost of failure into the market, where you only pay for value received instead of time invested? What if the failures happened in parallel rather than in series, speeding your time to market?

One way to do this is through OI – a key enabler to hyper-outsourcing. There are three ways in which solution-finding is typically outsourced:

- *Solution provider outsourcing:* Some challenges can be solved (and potentially implemented) by a third party who takes ownership of delivering the result. You might choose to work with a university to help find solutions or you might publish a request for proposal to find a solution provider. Regardless, in these situations you aren't buying a solution as much as you're selecting an outsourcing partner. This is the most common form of OI.

- *Solution outsourcing, single source:* In some situations your best option involves buying solutions, not solution providers. One common approach for solution outsourcing is tech-scouting. This involves searching existing solutions by scanning patent databases and other technology repositories. You can then license or purchase the technology for your own use.

- *Solution outsourcing, crowdsource:* Another potentially more powerful version of solution-finding is 'challenge-driven OI'. In a nutshell, you identify and formulate a challenge, then post the challenge to 'the world'. You allow a few weeks or months to find a workable solution. Platforms like InnoCentive allow you to post a challenge to 'the world'. Again, you buy solutions, not solution providers.

Alph Bingham, co-founder of InnoCentive, describes challenge-based OI as a 'massively parallel process where failures and successes happen at the same time'. You post a challenge and you get dozens (or hundreds) of people working to find solutions. Some solutions won't work, but all you need is one solution that does work, and with this form of OI you only pay for the solutions that work. Failures cost you nothing in time or money. With internal iterative development, you pay for the successes and the failures. Do you really learn enough from your failures to justify the extra cost and time involved? Probably not.

Integration and commercialization are key

If this outsourcing concept is taken to its extreme, the role of businesses will be more focused on integration and commercialization.

Integration and commercialization are difficult – and that's both good and bad news. While the rest of the world is focused on the trees (specific solutions to specific challenges), the innovation winners will become masterful at defining the forest (customer insight, strategy, architecture, sourcing, integration and commercialization). This is where value is created – and it's more difficult to replicate or to move offshore.

In today's economy we're in the forest business, not the tree business.

Recommended Reading

Chesbrough, HW (2005) *Open Innovation: The new imperative for creating and profiting from technology,* Harvard Business Press, Boston, MA

Chesbrough, HW (2006) *Open Business Models: How to thrive in the new innovation landscape,* Harvard Business Press, Boston, MA

Chesbrough, HW (2008) *Open Innovation: Researching a new paradigm,* Oxford University Press, Oxford

Foray, D (2006) *The Economics of Knowledge,* MIT Press, Cambridge, MA

Gaule, A (2006) *Open Innovation in Action: How to be strategic in the search for new sources of value,* H-I Network, London

Heim, M (2007) *Breaking the Musashi Code: Transcending competition through visionary strategy,* Visionary Partnership Press, Chagrin Falls, OH

Howe, J (2009) *Crowdsourcing: Why the power of the crowd is driving the future of business,* Crown Business Publishing, New York

Kelley, B (2010) *Stoking Your Innovation Bonfire,* John Wiley, Hoboken, NJ

Lindegaard, S (2010) *The Open Innovation Revolution: Essentials, roadblocks, and leadership skills,* John Wiley, Hoboken, NJ

Phillips, J (2008) *Make Us More Innovative: Critical factors for innovation success,* iUniverse.com

Pinchot, G (2000) *Intrapreneuring in Action: A handbook for business innovation,* Berrett-Koehler, San Francisco, CA

Rubinstein, M (1980) *Concepts of Problem Solving,* Prentice Hall, Saddle River, NJ

Sloane, P (2006) *The Leader's Guide to Lateral Thinking Skills,* Kogan Page, London

Sloane, P (2007) *The Innovative Leader,* Kogan Page, London

Slowinski, G (2005) *Reinventing Corporate Growth,* Alliance Management Group, Barstow, CA

Surowiecki, J (2005) *The Wisdom of Crowds, Why the many are smarter than the few and how collective wisdom shapes business, economies, societies and nations,* Anchor, Port Moody, BC

Tapscott, D and Williams, A (2008) *Wikinomics: How mass collaboration changes everything,* Portfolio Hardcover, New York

Von Hippel, E (2006) *Democratizing Innovation,* MIT Press, Cambridge, MA

Notes and References

Introduction
Peters, T and Waterman, R (1982) *In Search of Excellence*, Harper & Row, London

Chapter 1
Chesbrough, HW (2003) *Open Innovation: The new imperative for creating and profiting from technology*, Harvard Business Press, Boston, MA

Chapter 2
Amabile, T (1996) *Creativity in Context*, Westview Press, Boulder, CO
Christensen, C (1997) *The Innovator's Dilemma*, Harvard Business Press, Boston, MA
Howe, J (2009) *Crowdsourcing: Why the power of the crowd is driving the future of business*, revised edn, Crown Publishing, New York
Surowiecki, J (2005) *The Wisdom of Crowds. Why the many are smarter than the few and how collective wisdom shapes business, economies, societies and nations*, Anchor, Port Moody, BC
Von Hippel, E (2006) *Democratizing Innovation*, MIT Press, Cambridge, MA

Chapter 3
Chesbrough, HW (2003) *Open Innovation: The new imperative for creating and profiting from technology*, Harvard Business Press, Boston, MA

Chapter 4
Kelley, B (2010) *Stoking Your Innovation Bonfire*, John Wiley, Hoboken, NJ

Chapter 5
BCG (2007) *Measuring Innovation*, **www.bcg.com**

Chapter 7
Chesbrough, HW (2003) *Open Innovation: The new imperative for creating and profiting from technology*, Harvard Business Press, Boston, MA

Chapter 9
Ahonen, M, Antikainen, M and Makipaa, M (2007) *Supporting Collective Creativity with Open Innovation*, University of Tampere and VTT Technical Research Center of Finand

Badri Munir Sukoco and Wann-Yih Wu (2010) *The Personal and Social Motivation of Customers' Participation in Brand Community*, March, Airlangga University and National Cheng Kung University

Jones, Q, Moldovan, M and Rabin, D (2010) *The Life and Death of Online Communities*, March, ScienceDaily.com (retrieved 10 September 2010)

McKinsey & Company (2009) *And the winner is ...*, March, **www.mckinsey.com**

Nielsen, J (2006) *Participation Inequality: Encouraging more users to contribute*, 9 October, Jakob Nielsen's Alertbox (retrieved 15 September 2010)

Pajares, F (2002) *Overview of Social Cognitive Theory and of Self-efficacy*, Emory University (retrieved 12 September 2010)

Reinholt, M (2006) *No More Polarization, Please! Toward a more nuanced perspective on motivation in organizations*, Center for Strategic Management and Globalization, Copenhagen Business School

Chapter 12

Larcen, D, *Strategic Influencing. Help your projects succeed using the subtle art of listening* (**http://www.larcen.com/articles/leader_dev/strategicinfluencing.html**)

Lindegaard, S (2010) *The Open Innovation Revolution: Essentials, roadblocks, and leadership skills*, John Wiley, Hoboken, NJ

Pinchot, G (2000) *Intrapreneuring in Action: A handbook for business innovation*, Berrett-Koehler, San Francisco, CA

Slowinski, G (2005) *Reinventing Corporate Growth*, Alliance Management Group, Barstow, CA

Chapter 13

1 Balachandra and Friar (1997); Tollin (2002); Urban and Hauser (1993).
2 Henkel and von Hippel (2005). See also Adams *et al* (1998); Teas (1994).
3 Burkitt (2010).
4 Piller and Ihl (2010).
5 Franke and Piller (2003, 2004); Tseng *et al* (2003). A related method of customer co-creation is user-idea contests. Several studies investigate these in a consumer goods setting; for example, Ebner *et al* (2008).
6 A good review of research on customers as sources of innovation is provided by Von Hippel (2005). Sawhney *et al* (2003) show that these customers are often organized in communities by a manufacturer or intermediary.
7 Ogawa and Piller (2006). Elofson and Robinson (1998) describe a similar system called 'custom mass production': users first negotiate on a particular product design, find consensus about a solution that fits the wishes of all, and then auction the result to interested manufacturers.

Adams, ME, Day, GS and Dougherty, D (1998) Enhancing new product development performance: an organizational learning perspective, *Journal of Product Innovation Management*, 15, September: 403–22

Balachandra, R and Friar, JH (1997) Factors for success in R&D projects and new product introduction, *IEEE Transactions on Engineering Management*, 44 (3): 276–87

Burkitt, L (2010) Need to build a community? Learn from Threadless, *Forbes*, January, online at **http://bit.ly/8WYmdH** (retrieved 1 July 2010)

Ebner, W, Leimeister, M, Bretschneider, U and Krcmar, F (2008) Leveraging the wisdom of crowds: Designing an IT-supported idea competition, *Proceedings of the 41 Annual Hawaii International Conference on System Sciences*

Elofson, G and Robinson, WN (1998) Creating a custom mass-production channel on the internet, *Communications of the ACM,* 41, March: 56–62

Franke, N and Piller, F (2003) Key research issues in user interaction with configuration toolkits in a mass customization system, *International Journal of Technology Management,* 26 (5): 578–99

Franke, N and Piller, F (2004) Toolkits for user innovation and design: Exploring user interaction and value creation in the watch market, *Journal of Product Innovation Management,* 21 (6): 401–15

Henkel, J and Von Hippel, E (2005) Welfare implications of user innovation, *Journal of Technology Transfer,* 30, January: 73–88

Ogawa, S and Piller, F (2006) Reducing the risks of new product development, *MIT Sloan Management Review,* 47, Winter: 65–72

Sawhney, M, Prandelli, E and Verona, G (2003) The power of innomediation, *Sloan Management Review* 44, Winter: 77–82

Teas, RK (1994) Expectations as a comparison standard in measuring service quality: An assessment of a reassessment, *Journal of Marketing,* 58, January: 132–9

Tollin, K (2002) Customization as a business strategy: A barrier to customer integration in product development, *Total Quality Management,* 13, July: 427–39

Tseng, M, Kjellberg, T and Lu, S (2003) Design in the new e-commerce era, *Annals of the CIRP,* 52 (2): 509–19

Urban, G and Hauser, J (1993) *Design and Marketing of New Products,* 2nd edn, Prentice Hall, Englewood Cliffs, NJ

Von Hippel, E (2005) *Democratizing Innovation,* MIT Press, Cambridge, MA

Chapter 14

Argyris, M and Schön, D (1974) *Theory in Practice. Increasing professional effectiveness,* Jossey-Bass, San Francisco, CA

Chesbrough, HW (2003) *Open Innovation: The new imperative for creating and profiting from technology,* Harvard Business Press, Boston, MA

Enkel, E, Gassmann, O and Chesbrough, HW (2009) Open R&D and open innovation: Exploring the phenomenon, *R&D Management,* 39 (4): 311–16

Chapter 15

Rubinstein, M (1980) *Concepts of Problem Solving,* Prentice Hall, Englewood Cliffs, NJ

Chapter 16

McKnight, W, **http://solutions.3m.com/wps/portal/3M/en_WW/History/3M/ Company/McKnight-principles/**

Neitlich, A (2001) *Elegant Leadership*, Chatham Business Press, New York

Chapter 19

Boudreau, J (2010) Chinese companies are bargain hunting in Silicon Valley, 26 April, **http://donatdawn.com/content/?p=15549**

Govindarajan, V (2010) What is reverse innovation?, Vijay Govindarajan's blog, 15 October, **http://www.vijaygovindarajan.com.2009/10/what_is_reverse_innovation.htm**

Singh, S (2010) Xerox India hub to follow open innovation model, *The Economic Times*, 22 March, **http://economictimes.indiatimes.com/Interviews/Xerox-India-hub-to-follow-open-innovation-model/articleshow/5710009.cms**

Chapter 21

Gaule, A (2006) *Open Innovation in Action: How to be strategic in the search for new sources of value*, H-I Network, London

Chapter 23

1 Some claims of recent OI platforms can be easily refuted by the use of online website statistics analysers, showing that there can be a factor up to 30 between the reality and the claims.

2 The same remark applies for the pool of problems (especially regarding their formulation).

3 It supposes that the problem has been well-formulated, which requires a strong methodology and facilitation skills.

Chesbrough, HW (2003) *Open Innovation: The new imperative for creating and profiting from technology*, Harvard Business Press, Boston, MA

Lakhani, K (2006) *The Core and the Periphery in Distributed and Self-Organizing Innovation Systems*, Massachusetts Institute of Technology, Cambridge, MA

Chapter 24

Zicherman, G and Linder, J (2010) *Game-Based Marketing: Inspire customer loyalty through rewards, challenges, and contests*, John Wiley, Hoboken, NJ

Index

The sharpest minds
need the finest advice.
Kogan Page creates
success.

www.koganpage.com

You are reading one of the thousands of books
published by **Kogan Page**. As Europe's leading
independent business book publishers **Kogan Page**
has always sought to provide up-to-the-minute books
that offer practical guidance at affordable prices.

6828